UNION-FREE

UNION-FREE

Creating a Committed and Productive Workforce

Paul Mooney

The Liffey Press
Dublin

Published by
The Liffey Press Ltd
Ashbrook House, 10 Main Street
Raheny, Dublin 5, Ireland
www.theliffeypress.com

A catalogue record of this book is
available from the British Library.

ISBN 1-904148-71-9

Printed in the Republic of Ireland by ColourBooks Ltd.

TABLE OF CONTENTS

PREFACE

"The man who tells the truth should have one foot in the stirrup." — Turkish proverb

I first became interested in the non-union sector while studying at Trinity College. In the late 1980s, this was seen as a somewhat "exotic" topic, peripheral to the main thrust of the industrial relations system where the unionised "collective bargaining" model predominated. Over the next couple of years, the pattern began to change. Working as a management consultant, I came into contact with fledgling organisations that were committed to a direct relationship with employees. Some established clients were anxious to secure the "non-union" benefits of high flexibility and low conflict and wanted to know if this could be achieved in a unionised setting. I also encountered clients who were embroiled in recognition disputes, desperately fighting to keep unions outside of their business.

In ever-increasing numbers management teams began to explore the non-union model of working. The idea of a union-free organisation began to move from the fringes to the centre of the industrial relations stage. At management and IR conferences, HR and line executives came out of the closet and began to declare, "we're non-union and proud of it" — no longer afraid of public disapproval or a backlash from the media or trade unions. Managing a non-union organisation moved from being an "unspoken" strategy to a legitimate alternative mode of operation. At the time of writing, the non-union model has begun to replace the collective bargaining model and could soon dominate industrial relations practices in Ireland.

The goal of this book is to examine how a positive union-free employment relationship can be maintained. It details the development of the non-union sector and demonstrates how companies can successfully sustain this status (readers who are only interested in the "maintenance" question can skip the history lesson and move directly to the relevant chapters). To demonstrate the practical differences, I've reviewed HR practices at a number of large non-union companies and contrasted these against unionised companies of a similar size. I've also completed case studies on a number of companies which commenced operations on a non-union basis but subsequently unionised, in an effort to determine what lessons can be learned. In the later sections an attempt is made to explore the impact on employees of relinquishing union membership and to address some of the wider questions on the longer-term impact on the Irish industrial relations system which this throws up.

Much of the research for this book was conducted some time ago but it is my firm belief that the case study examples and points made by human resources practitioners and others are absolutely up-to-date and relevant to the 2005 marketplace. Indeed, the defining issue is not whether the ideas expressed are new or old but whether they are right or wrong, and I will leave that to the reader to decide.

Some people will see the book as a "union-bashers' bible". That is certainly not the intent. Several times I have recommended to non-union companies that they concede recognition because the organisation conditions or depth of management talent were not in place to run a non-union operation. Personally, I will not work with organisations that simply use their non-union status to exploit employees (as some companies do). However, I sincerely believe that, given a caring organisational culture, the sophisticated non-union model of working is entirely legitimate and has its place in the industrial relations landscape. While by its very nature this topic is contentious, an open debate on the development of the non-union sector in Ireland is long overdue.

A final possible objection is that the book puts forward a "unitary perspective", that is, organisations should be cohesive and harmonious with shared goals, values and interests between those contributing capital and those providing labour. Other perspectives, particularly the pluralist and Marxist views of organisations, are not fully explored. This criticism is justified to the extent that these alternative perspectives have been comprehensively dealt with by others and I have no wish (or the talent) to duplicate them. Where relevant, opposing perspectives are introduced to bring balance to the arguments made, however, my former work as a human resource director and latterly as a management consultant has inevitably led to a pro-company bias. The views put forward should therefore be seen as a partisan account — and challenged accordingly.

ACKNOWLEDGEMENTS

N o work is the fruit of individual effort. I am hugely indebted to the HR directors and the client companies who have allowed me to witness "best practice" at first hand. In terms of "who is learning from whom", sometimes the consultants should pay the clients (hopefully this idea will not catch on!). None of the companies visited as part of this research have chosen to be identified directly, but they will see their views and work practices reflected in the text.

A number of key individual contributors within the trade union movement, IBEC, the IDA and several who work in the "disputes resolution" system shared their expertise and opinions. These people have had an enormous impact on the practical operation of the industrial relations system in Ireland, performing very critical (and often very difficult) roles. This book was put together over a long period of time and some of the contributors have "moved on" — to more senior roles, to political office, to academia etc. I have therefore taken the view that their contributions should be acknowledged, but their anonymity protected.

I am particularly indebted to Liam Doherty in IBEC who was hugely helpful in "sketching" the background and the practical operation of the more recent industrial relations legislation. Alastair Purdy of Analog Devices was also very helpful with the "technical stuff" (changes to the legislation around union recognition). Dr Tim Hastings shared his academic experience and practical application around developing "IR strategy options" within existing organisations.

Michael Barry of the National College of Ireland was very helpful in steering me towards useful sources of information and remains a passionate advocate of treating workers with fairness and dignity. Dr Ferdinand von Prondzynski, now President of Dublin City University, was immensely helpful during the research phase and has continued to be a good friend over many years.

Elaine Bracken, Georgina Buffini and Madeleine Patton did the marathon typing and retyping and loved every single minute of it! David Givens and the staff at The Liffey Press expertly guided the publication process.

A grateful thanks to all the above for the support and the time generously given.

Dedicated to
Amie, Cillian and Nicole

It must be considered that there is nothing more difficult to carry out, nor more doubtful of success, nor more dangerous to handle, than to initiate a new order of things. For the reformer has enemies in all those who profit by the old order, and only lukewarm defenders in all those who would profit by the new order . . .

This arises partly from the incredulity of mankind who do not truly believe in anything new until they have had an actual experience of it.

— Machiavelli

1

THE INDUSTRIAL RELATIONS SYSTEM: A PERIOD OF RAPID TRANSITION

THE DEVELOPMENT OF THE NON-UNION sector in Ireland is part of a profound set of changes taking place within the industrial relations system. These include the increasing use of part-time and contract labour which facilitates labour market flexibility and a general weakening of trade union power — underpinned by a steep decline in union membership levels and strike statistics.

The changes taking place in Ireland broadly mirror those which have occurred in other developed countries. For example, changes in the United Kingdom include the development of "new style" collective agreements with complete work flexibility, no-strike provisions and pendulum arbitration.[1] Research evidence demonstrates widespread implementation of flexibility and productivity agreements[2] and an attack on union-maintained job demarcations.[3] The industrial relations system within the US has encountered a range of similar initiatives, including giveback bargaining[4] the development of multi-tier wage rate systems[5] and the relocation of plants within the economically dynamic and non-union southern states.[6]

While the causes underlying the changes noted are complex, three have been particularly significant. Firstly, changes in the economic environment, in particular increased international competition, are at the root of many of the developments cited. Secondly, political developments (notably a rejection of consensus economic policy in the US and UK and the growth of anti-trade union legislation) have changed the general climate in which collective bargaining is conducted. Finally, the emergence of a high commitment model of work relationships has altered the context in which collective bargaining takes place at plant level. In order to understand the development of the non-union sector in Ireland, we firstly need to look at this broader canvas. As Gunnigle et al. argue:

> . . . the subject of industrial relations can best be understood and interpreted in the wider context of the historic, political, social and economic processes which have shaped the regulation of working lives.[7]

A pen sketch of each of these strands is attempted below.

CHANGES IN THE ECONOMIC ENVIRONMENT

> The most serious contemporary challenge to which the actors in the industrial relations system must respond is the economic and competitive one.[8]

International competition has had a marked influence on the industrial relations system in Ireland, forcing many companies to re-evaluate their traditional modus operandi. The ability to cope with a turbulent business environment is now a survival issue which has led to structural and procedural changes within many organisations. For example, the effect of virulent low cost competition (often from producers where labour exercises a very limited degree of collective power, for example, Korea, Taiwan) has led to a plethora of initiatives designed to enable companies to withstand the competitive onslaught ("you can't fight the market").

Across the developed economies trade union membership is in decline, reflecting the move towards service industries, a growth in part-time working and demographic changes in the workforce including rising educational standards. Changes in the economic environment have therefore played a key role in the transition taking place within the industrial relations system which create fertile soil for the non-union model of working.

CHANGES IN THE POLITICAL CLIMATE

The second factor influencing the changes occurring in the industrial relations system is a growing hostility to trade unionism at the political level (outside of Ireland). In recent years some key features of what may be termed the "post-war consensus" among governments, employers and unions have been broken. In the United Kingdom the government has attempted to curb inflation through fiscal rather than through negotiated incomes policies. For several years new policies have been aimed at making the labour market more competitive by reducing unit labour costs[9] and "unnecessary rigidities".[10] The break with post-war consensus politics is marked by the present Labour government's renunciation of any commitment to full employment. In practice, the Trades Union Congress has been edged to the side of the political stage with claims from government quarters that there is a "new realism" among the working population.[11] While in the Thatcher years the trade union movement in the UK arguably faced a more hostile climate than at any time since the defeats of the 1920s,[12] in economic, political, organisation and financial terms, the climate is no less precarious under Blair.

In order to understand current political developments and their influence on the collective bargaining process it is necessary to place them in historical context. According to the Webbs, the early historians of British trade unionism, employers:

> used their political and magisterial power against the men without scruple, inciting a willing Government to attack

> the men's combinations by every possible perversion of the
> law, and particularly in its administration.[13]

This state of affairs evolved over the following decades until in
the 1950s and 1960s a *modus vivendi* had been established between
labour and business. Earlier stages of distrust and hostility were
left behind as a result of the maturation of the parties, professionalism in negotiations and a solid, mutually satisfactory record of
progress.[14] In Ireland, the position of the union movement as a
major interest group mirrored this. As one commentator noted:

> From a small, relatively weak trade union movement in
> 1946, the movement today is probably the most powerful
> pressure group in Irish society with a membership which
> ranks Ireland as one of the most highly unionised countries
> in Europe.[15]

The strength of the trade union movement as an interest group
meant that it was courted by employers and government. In
McCarthy's terms:

> While the unions in the nature of things rarely offer posi-
> tive support to government, their acquiescence to govern-
> ment policies, even when it is somewhat negative, is highly
> valuable, and their goodwill is courted as a result.[16]

A MOVEMENT AWAY FROM CONSENSUS ECONOMIC POLICY

An alternative approach exemplified most sharply in the early
period of the Conservative Government (and in a gradualist
but more sustained form by the present Labour administration in
the UK) was legalistic and essentially coercive. Based on a conviction of overly powerful trade unions, it attempted to impose a restrictive statutory framework reducing union rights and immuni-
ties, particularly in the conduct of strikes, and gave doctrinaire
support for free market economics. As one commentator noted:

> . . . it would seem clear that union power, even if only a
> modest nuisance in the 1960s, has become a major obstruc-
> tion.[17]

When the Conservative Government was elected in the UK, it
moved decisively away from collaboration and openly declared
the switch to a monetarist strategy as a means of reducing inflation. Most importantly, the commitment to high employment,
perhaps the central imperative of economic policy since 1945, declined dramatically with the consequent negative implications for
trade union bargaining strength. As von Prondzynski highlighted:

> Where governments adopt Keynesian-type policies to alle-
> viate unemployment the negotiating strength of the union
> movement will tend to hold up; neo laissez faire policies,
> on the other hand, will completely undermine the trade un-
> ion-based structure of the industrial relations system.[18]

The Conservatives struck at the unions' *raison d'être* — representa-
tiveness. The effect was to change the way workers and the general public thought about unions. By the early 1990s, virtually
everyone, with the exception of the hardest of the hard left, accepted that ballots about strikes and for the election of union executives, the core of the Conservatives' most far-reaching piece of
labour legislation (1984 Trade Union Act), were a fixed part of the
industrial relations legal framework. These would not be swept
away by *any* government. Basic attitudes to trade unionism were
altered by the Conservative onslaught in what was little less than
a cultural remodelling of Britain. In Bassett's words, "the dog
would not allow itself to be wagged by the tail".[19] Overall, the
general climate for trade union activity in the UK became increasingly hostile:

> The economic recession, decline in union membership, a
> number of significant strike defeats, the dismissal of a
> number of leading shop stewards, the reluctance of work-

ers to hold union office and the populist attack on the legitimacy of trade unions suggest that trade unionists may be an endangered species.[20]

The changing political climate, of which developments in the United Kingdom provide a striking example, can be witnessed across several of the developed countries. While Ireland has not gone down the "anti-union" route politically, these developments nonetheless "spilled across" and began to influence the industrial relations system in Ireland, particularly around "what could be done" (a point we return to later). Through the mechanism of centralised pay bargaining, the union movement in Ireland has cleverly strengthened its hand with the government — reversing the international trend of a decline in union influence as the membership numbers fall.

A CHANGING COMPANY/EMPLOYEE RELATIONSHIP

The third explanatory factor in the development of the non-union sector in Ireland is the changing nature of the employment relationship. Many of the inherent assumptions in "traditional" industrial relations have been critically evaluated and revamped. An increasing number of companies are implementing what can be termed a "high commitment" model of workplace relations, moving away from the adversarial collective bargaining patterns which historically predominated. While some companies are involving unions in decision making, many are attempting to foster better relations *directly* with employees by excluding unions from the employment relationship.

The array and the complexity of the changes taking place pose tremendous interpretation difficulties. While there have been some attempts to quantify and analyse particular aspects of the changes noted, no global attempt has yet been made in Ireland to put these in an overall conceptual framework. Further, research on some of the areas touched upon has been limited. For example, while specific elements of the growth/operation of the non-union sector have been researched by a small group of contributors, the impact of this development on the general functioning of the industrial relations system has largely been ignored. This is partly a matter of history; when unions were powerful social institutions they merited close study. In part, it is also a matter of convenience. As one writer noted:

> It's simply easier to scrutinise shop stewards at a Coventry engineering factory . . . or the internal structures of the TGWU rather than the employment policies of IBM. You know how to find the TGWU, it's there, it's tangible. By contrast, non-unionism is amorphous, decentralised, inaccessible.[21]

The changing economic and political environment, coupled with the development of high commitment work systems, has led to what can be labelled the "new model" of industrial relations. The term is justified as we are witnessing an industrial renaissance, a radical reappraisal of the core values and assumptions of the traditional model of industrial relations along with the structures which supported it. The changes noted thus represent *fundamental* rather than peripheral change. The primary objective of this book is to explore one of these changes, that is, the development of the non-union sector, which is expanding exponentially.

THE NON-UNION SECTOR IN IRELAND

While there is very little formal research on the "size" of the non-union sector in Ireland, some historical data is detailed in Figure 1:

FIGURE 1: GROWTH OF THE NON-UNION SECTOR IN IRELAND[22]		
	Firm Size	*% of Firms in Sample which were Non-Union*
IMI Survey (1973)	500 +	0%
	100–499	4%
	25–99	32%
IDA Report (1984)	251 +	13%
	100–250	13%
	50–100	7%
Incoming Multinationals (1995–2005)	All sizes	90%+ take the non-union route[23,24]

Bottom line: The non-union sector has arrived and is here to stay. Before we explore this in more detail we will examine the "traditional model" of industrial relations which preceded it.

Endnotes

---

[1] Burrows, Giles. *"No Strike" Agreements and Pendulum Arbitration*. Institute of Personnel Management, London, 1986; Bassett, Philip. *Strike Free: New Industrial Relations in Britain*. Macmillan, 1987.

[2] Young, K. "The Management of Craft Work: A Case Study of an Oil Refinery". *British Journal of Industrial Relations* (24) 3, 1986.

[3] Millward, Neill and Stevens, Mark. *British Workplace Industrial Relations, 1980-1984. The DE/ESRCI/PSI/ACAS Surveys*. Gower, Hants, UK, 1987.

[4] Knack, Lee. "Collective Bargaining: Developments in the USA". Address presented to the FUE Industrial Relations Briefing Conference, Ireland, 1983; Gelfond, Susan. "A Pile of Cash that Doesn't Stack Up to a Raise". *Business Week*, 23 December 1985.

[5] Bernstein et al. "The Double Standard that's Setting Worker against Worker". *Business Week*, 8 April 1985.

[6] Arnold, Bob. "Eastern and Pan Am: Two Model Contracts Fly into Trouble". *Business Week,* 21 January 1985.

[7] Gunnigle, Patrick, McMahon, Gerard and Wallace, Joseph. *Industrial Relations in Ireland.* Gill and Macmillan, Dublin, 2004.

[8] McCormack, Janice and Mills, D. Quinn. Harvard University Discussion Paper on "The Industrial Relations System in Transition: Findings of a Three Year Study"; Kochan T. A., McKersie R. B. and Chalykoff, J. "The Effects of Corporate Strategy and Workplace Innovations on Union Representation". *Industrial and Labor Relations Review,* Vol. 39, No. 4, 1985.

[9] Tebbit, Norman, the Secretary of State for Employment, speaking at a conference of Scottish Engineering Employers. *Department of Employment Gazette* Vol. 90, 1982.

[10] Wakeham, John. The Minister for State at the Treasury, Hansard, *House of Commons Debates,* Vol. 13, 18 March 1983.

[11] Gennard, John. "What's New in Industrial Relations", *Personnel Management,* IPM, London,1985.

[12] Goodman, John F.B. "Great Britain Labour Moves from Power to Constraint". From Barkin, Solomon (ed.) *Worker Militancy and its Consequences: The Changing Climate of Western Industrial Relations,* Praeger, New York, 1983.

[13] Webb, B. and S. *A History of Trade Unions* (second edition), Longmans, London, 1920.

[14] Rosen, Sumner M. "The United States: American Industrial Relations System in Jeopardy?" From Barkin, Solomon (ed.) *Worker Militancy and its Consequences: The Changing Climate of Western Industrial Relations,* Praeger, New York, 1983.

[15] Hillary, Brian. "Industrial Relations Compromise and Conflict". From Nevin, Donal (ed.) *Trade Unions and Change in Irish Society,* Mercier, Dublin, 1980.

[16] McCarthy, Charles. "The Development of Irish Trade Unions". From Nevin, Donal (ed.). *Trade Unions and Change in Irish Society,* Mercier, Dublin, 1980.

[17] Minford, Patrick. "Trade Unions Destroy a Million Jobs". *Journal of Economic Affairs*, No. 2. 1982: 73.

[18] von Prondzynski, F. *Freedom of Association and Industrial Relations* Mansfell, London, 1987.

[19] Bassett, Philip. *Strike Free: New Industrial Relations in Britain*. Macmillan, 1987: 8.

[20] Fenley, Anthony. "Trade Union Activists - An Endangered Species". *Employee Relations*, Vol. 6, No. 3, 1984.

[21] Bassett, Philip. *Strike Free: New Industrial Relations in Britain*. Macmillan, 1987.

[22] McCann, J.J. "The New Industrial Relations Arena of Human Resource Management: Union–Non-Union". *Industrial Relations News Report*, 1988: 16.

[23] Based on estimates from officials in the Industrial Development Authority and members in the Chartered Institute of Personnel and Development. This "soft" data was empirically confirmed in the study of greenfield sites conducted by Dr. Paddy Gunnigle of the University of Limerick.

[24] Gunnigle, P. "Management styles in employee relations in greenfield sites: challenging a collectivist tradition", unpublished PhD thesis, Cranfield School of Management, 1995; Gunnigle, P. "Collectivism and the management of industrial relations in greenfield sites", *Human Resource Management Journal*, Vol. 4, 24-40, 1995; Gunnigle P. "Why Ireland? A qualitiative review of the factors influencing the location of US multinationals in Ireland with particular reference to the impact of labour issues", *Economic and Social Review*, XXXII/1, 43-67, 2001; Gunnigle, Patrick, Morley, Michael and Turner, Tom. "Challenging collectivist traditions: individualism and the management of industrial relations in greenfield sites", *Economic and Social Review*, XXVIII/2, 105-34, 1997.

2

THE TRADITIONAL MODEL OF INDUSTRIAL RELATIONS

THE FIRST CHARACTERISTIC OF THE traditional model of industrial relations was organisation and labour market rigidity. At plant level this can be defined as an inability to make product, process or conditions of employment changes in response to market demands. Change is usually a bargaining issue to be negotiated, often a lengthy process as the parties haggle over the "price of disruption". A key feature of the traditional model is the presence of a strong, unified trade union movement with power to back sanctions which gives respect at the negotiation table. Historically, the model was often played in a win/lose fashion. Over time, defined areas of territory and control become established. Expansion outside of this (by either party) was seen as a loss to the other side and strongly resisted, lessening the degree of responsiveness to the marketplace and resulting in organisation rigidity.

At the macro level inflexibility is closely aligned to job market norms, for example, the price at which labour can be bought. A monopolistic hold on the price of labour (through the establishment of closed shops and union rates) is a central feature of the traditional model of industrial relations. Under this model, pay norms are also related to the principle of equity rather than performance, being geared to the job rather than the jobholder.

In recent years these organisational and labour market characteristics have come under severe pressure. Increased competition and a rapid rate of technological innovation have meant that flexibility is now a key factor in business survival. The rate of product/process change, particularly within the high technology sector, is remarkable by traditional standards. For example, in one computer company a new product has been introduced, on average, every five months since the particular technology was developed in 1955. The American conglomerate 3M boasts that each year 20 per cent of its product line was not available the previous year, an astonishing rate of innovation within this huge corporation.[1] Many similar examples could be cited. Organisations are becoming market-driven production units in which flexibility and quick response time is not simply a bonus — they must be able to withstand a "quickened pace" of product and process development simply to survive.[2] To cope with the combined effects of economic and technological developments, flexibility has become a key business requirement which has fundamentally impacted the conduct of industrial relations. The rigidity of the traditional model, possibly more than any other single element identified, was the primary influence in the movement towards non-union operations.

ADVERSARIALISM UNDERLIES THE UNION/MANAGEMENT RELATIONSHIP

Oppression may its hostile front display,
And tyranny exist its short accursed day,
But unashamed virtue and the cause of right,
Shall stand undaunted, nor will yield to might[3]

The second element of the traditional model of industrial relations is what Barbash has described as the "adversary principle".[4] Here industrial relations can be understood as an armed truce with occasional "warfare" between opposing interests. Employers manage their businesses through minimising the interference of both employees and trade unions, to greater or lesser degrees of success in individual organisations. Unions, in the main, operate as reactive organisations which attempt to protect employees from the worst excesses of employers (for example, arbitrary dismissal) and to extend employees' share of the profit distribution process (one former Irish trade union leader memorably defined profits as "undistributed wages"). The role of management is "to manage" (that is, plan/organise/lead/control) while the unions, historically, would oppose management strategy where it runs counter to the stated or felt needs of employees. The adversary principle can be summarised as:

- A feeling on the part of management that unions and collective bargaining are, at best, necessary evils in a modern industrial society.

- A conviction on the part of the labour leadership that the union's main job is to challenge and protest particular managerial actions (much like the "opposition" parties in the political arena).

- Basic disagreement between the parties over the appropriate scope of collective bargaining and the matters which should be subject to joint determination.[5]

Conflict between the two groups is thus inherent in the separate definitions of roles — employers and employees are seen to have conflicting interests where benefits for one party are considered to be detrimental to the other. Under the traditional model, industrial relations can thus be described as "the science of confrontation".[6]

Differences in Political Orientation

While unions are primarily economic institutions, the labour movement may also be understood as an instrument or vehicle for political and social change. This viewpoint was succinctly stated by Hugh Scanlon when, as President of the AUEW, he commented that:

> There are irreconcilable conflicts between capital and labour — between those who invest their labour and those who invest money. It is management's job to look after the shareholder's interests and the Trade Unions' to look after labour's interest.[7]

The outward conflict between the two groups is thus explained by an underlying divergence in political orientation. As Schlotfeldt argues:

> It is, of course, highly doubtful whether consensus can be reached at all with unions or labour leaders who pursue declared political objectives in contradiction to our free democratic system and to private enterprise.[8]

This is very much the case in Europe generally, where unions have been closely aligned to parties on the "left" of the political stage. The fact that in America unions have shown a reluctance to challenge the traditional two-party system (or to outwardly favour one party over the other) should not obscure the basic point that they have consistently put forward a particular political philosophy. While it is difficult to define that philosophy with any precision, perhaps a description not far amiss would be that it rests on the utilitarian principle of the greatest good for the greatest number. The unions have readily identified themselves with the greatest number and have, on that ground, insisted on a right to determine the greatest good.

In Ireland the trade union movement has its closest links with the Labour Party.[9] Funding support is provided along with party membership posts being held by individual officials (for example, Pat Rabbitte was a former senior trade union official). In contrast, business interests have traditionally supported Fianna Fáil, Fine Gael and, more recently, the Progressive Democrats. A divergence in underlying political philosophy therefore separates unions from management and is used to justify the oppositionary stance taken.

"Peace" is Maintained through Procedures and Institutions

Despite the political differences noted, the adversarial nature of the employment relationship is kept in check through collective bargaining. Equilibrium is maintained through an elaborate system of procedural rules and third party institutions which regulate and diffuse conflict. For example, where the ultimate sanction of withdrawal of labour or lock-out is brought into play, few combatants "fight to the death". However, while most conflict is diffused, it is seldom eliminated. The system is kept in balance through a massive expenditure in time and effort. Even where the parties outwardly move away from their oppositionary mode, as under the national pay agreements, the fundamental adversarialism which underlies the bargaining relationship remains in place. These agreements closely equate to what Crouch has described as "bargained corporatism",[10] where unions continue to be the active voice of organised labour as an interest group. Initiatives at national level are pursued less on the basis that a new collaboratist view of the union role has emerged, but rather that the changed bargaining structures gives them more clout[11] — the same issues are negotiated, albeit on a higher level stage. Trade unions in Ireland have very cleverly used this political connection to drive a

pro-union agenda (see later section on the range of legislative initiatives which have taken place in recent years).

A NARROW VIEW OF THE POTENTIAL
WORTH OF EMPLOYEES

The third element of the traditional model of industrial relations is the narrow view of the potential worth of employees
held by many companies. The notion of industrial relations as a
system of control is central to any understanding of the traditional
model.[12] Two core philosophical tenets are often held:

- Most employees do not wish to contribute to the success of
  organisations and thus need to be tightly controlled.

- Even where employees identify with a company, the value of
  their input is limited by educational constraints.

These views are particularly potent in relation to employees lower
in the organisational hierarchy. Under the traditional model of
industrial relations all employees (other than senior management)
are seen to suffer from both of the above "weaknesses" and their
views, opinions and ideas on the management of enterprises are
largely left untapped. The organisational solution to overcome
these supposed defects has been to design jobs in such a way that
employees have little autonomy in carrying them out. They are
supervised either by direct management control where tasks cannot easily be prescribed (for example, maintenance craftsmen) or
by the technology employed (for example, a narrow sub-division
of tasks in an assembly line). While few firms would articulate
this perception of employees, the way in which work is organised
under the traditional model of industrial relations clearly supports it. In the US, Robert E. Cole argued that management dis-
misses workers' co-operation because it is essentially seen as ir-
relevant other than to ensure stability of supply.[13]

Industrial Apartheid Exists in Many Companies

Within many organisations the equivalent of a caste system, or what can be colourfully described as "industrial apartheid", is in place.[14] Paul Tansey, a former Industrial Editor of the *Irish Times*, made the point that the marketing manager in Company A often has more in common with the marketing manager in Company B, a competitor, than with the production employees in Company A.[15] These attitudes often lead to a marked stratification within plants between various grades of employees. The system is maintained through such differences in conditions as "clocking in", longer working hours, different colour protective clothing (unrelated to the nature of the work performed) and even separate dining facilities. Finbar Flood, former chairman of the Labour Court and ex-Managing Director of Guinness Ireland, humorously tells the story that at one point Guinness had seven canteens. That's not seven "locations", but seven "levels"!

THE LOW STATUS OF THE PERSONNEL FUNCTION

A central feature of the traditional model of industrial relations was the low status (and in some cases the complete absence) of the personnel function. In organisations where little value is placed on employees' input (other than in a narrowly defined industrial engineering sense) the personnel function is downgraded. Under the traditional model, personnel management can be likened to a prison warden function, that is, containment of a potentially disruptive group. The term "hire and fire", so long used to describe the function, denotes this status through a narrow conceptualisation of the HR role. The productive lifespan of employment (that is, the time which lies between "hire and fire"), and the link between organisational climate and productivity, are either completely ignored or delegated to line management. Under the traditional model personnel staff were often glorified welfare officers, a view shared by many trade union leaders.

The narrow view of the personnel function is compounded by the lack of clout of incumbents. Even within companies where personnel is organised as a separate function, many personnel managers do not report directly to the chief executive. The fact that personnel management was not a "profession" until comparatively recent years[16] further impaired its status. As one manager described it, personnel executives were seen to "bring little to the organisation party".[17] Some writers even argued for the total abolition of the function on the basis of its supposed uselessness.[18]

INDUSTRIAL RELATIONS: THE SCIENCE OF CONFLICT CONTAINMENT

Despite their supposedly low status, formal industrial relations matters (for example, wage negotiations) are usually handled by personnel departments which may seem to contradict the points noted above. Here, it would seem, lay a direct opportunity for the personnel function to underscore its worth in the achievement of low cost settlements, enhanced flexibility agreements and so on. Yet industrial relations in many organisations is limited to a reactive, fire fighting exercise. The goal or output of such departments has historically been addressed in negative, conflict containment terms rather than in efforts to extract a greater degree of commitment or flexibility from employees. In one company, where no industrial relations problems had occurred for a considerable period of time, the industrial relations manager was asked by the managing director, "what do you do all day"? The presence (not the absence) of conflict was seen to provide the rationale for personnel staff. While most companies subscribe to the view that good industrial relations is a key part of their business strategy, the concept is usually narrowly defined.

Under the traditional model of industrial relations "good" means "mute".

In contrast, under the new model, which will be discussed in the next chapter, the notion of industrial relations as tactical planning to overcome obstacles has given way to a broader view of HR management as an integral business function. Crisis management has given way to proactivity as organisations seek to engage and energise the workforce.

EMPLOYEES' LOW COMMITMENT TO ORGANISATIONAL GOALS

The final characteristic of the traditional model of industrial relations is that employees, in the main, exhibit a low commitment to organisational goals. Even where such goals are known, the adversarial nature of the relationship precludes their being interpreted in a mutually beneficial way. This is not simply a misconception on the part of employees. Ample evidence to support this win/lose view is provided through redundancies, lay-offs, wage/benefit freezes and organisational changes which negatively impact the workforce. The idea that the organisation's and employees' interests are divergent is not a theoretical construct of militant employees, but often a realistic interpretation of a lack of commitment to them. For example, demarcations in many cases help to support job security and overtime earnings. Collective bargaining, understood here as a "rule making process",[19] gives employees some degree of control over their working lives. Conflict is thus inherent in the relationship between organisations which seek to control the productive process and employees who try to achieve a greater degree of self-control.

Limited in their potential contribution, often conforming to narrow job specifications and operating within the "industrial apartheid" context outlined earlier, many employees use union membership as a power lever, as the only available method to achieve an input into decision making. Under the traditional model "organisation voice", a mechanism for employees to influence business decisions, can generally only be achieved through trade union clout. As the late Professor Charles McCarthy graphically described it:

> There is a kind of hopeless conviction in Ireland that even if one could articulate one's problems, there is no one there to listen. This is how many people from the unskilled worker to the bank official see it. The complaint is not so much that there are faceless men, but that the men who command power regard you as faceless. This is what becomes unbearable.[20]

Under the traditional model the narrow view of employees and the lack of effort to tap into their talent corresponds well with McCarthy's notion of "facelessness". It is not surprising therefore that employees often exhibit a low commitment to organisational goals:

> Men respond to low trust with low trust. In an increasing number of situations, employees responded by withholding moral involvement in their employers' objectives; working indifferently and with little personal commitment, seeing the employer as pursuing his own interests to the exclusion of theirs; feeling used, therefore, in the service of goals not their own; manipulating the work situation for their benefit if opportunity permitted; practising restrictionism and obstructionism; organising themselves collectively, if they could, to force the employer to pay attention to their needs as well as his and in general by refusing to conduct their relationship with him in the full spirit of high-trust problem-solving. Like him, they adopted the stance of contractual calculation.[21]

The factors outlined above, when taken together, describe the traditional model of industrial actions. The common themes are to establish order, exercise control and achieve efficiency (in industrial engineering terms) in the application of the workforce — precepts which depend upon a stable environment to function efficiently. The model's antecedents include the bureaucratic organisations of the military and the church. The early writers on organisation efficiency[22] probably also deserve some credit for developing those elements of the model which have led to a narrow view of employee worth through focussing on specialisation and a narrow subdivision of tasks. Because it was consistent with the prevailing ideology in society (the "inspired" and the "perspired") and because it worked satisfactorily for many decades, the traditional model of industrial relations was internalised by successive generations of managers. While social science research has consistently shown many of the central tenets to be flawed from a social engineering perspective,[23] it has proved remarkably resistant to change. The core features of the traditional model of industrial relations are summarised in Figure 2.

FIGURE 2: THE TRADITIONAL MODEL OF INDUSTRIAL RELATIONS	
Key Elements	*Denoted By*
• Rigidity of organisations and labour markets	• Rigid demarcation/"territorial" • Resistance to change/change as a bargaining issue • Long lead time in response to marketplace developments • Inflexibility of wage structures • Pay geared to job rather than job holder • Strong/active trade union movement at local and national level
• Adversarial nature of the employment relationship	• Difference in political orientation • Win/lose bargaining • Conflict accepted as normal • Command and obey structures • Control through rules and procedures
• Narrow view of employee worth	• Employees seen as a factor of production/variable cost. • Link between organisations climate/productivity downgraded • Limited employee influence • "Doing"/"thinking" separated • Limited communication of business information/"need to know" basis
• Low status of personnel departments	• Low staffing levels • Lack of "clout" • Non chief executive reporting status • Non "professional" image • Industrial relations unmeasured
• Employees: Low commitment to organisational goals	• Individual and organisational goals seen to conflict • Efforts made to subvert management process

Endnotes

[1] Peters, Thomas A. and Waterman, Robert H. *In Search of Excellence: Lessons From America's Best Run Companies*, Harper and Row, New York, 1982.

[2] Naisbitt, John and Aburdent, Patrica. *Re-Inventing the Corporation*, Warner Books, New York, 1985.

[3] Kerr, George. "Kerr's Exposition of Legislative Tyranny and Defense of the Trades Union". Pamphlet written in 1834 dedicated to the trades unionists of Great Britain and Ireland. From Boyd, Andrew, *The Rise of the Irish Trade Unions*, Anvil Books, Dublin, 1985.

[4] Barbash, Jack. "Values in Industrial Relations: The Case of the Adversary Principle". Presidential Address at the 33rd Annual Meeting of the Industrial Relations Research Association, Denver, Colorado, 1980.

[5] Harbison F. H. "Collective Bargaining and American Capitalism". From Kornhauster, A., Dubin, R. and Ross, A.M. (eds.). *Industrial Conflict*, McGraw-Hill, New York, 1954.

[6] "Trade Union Official E". Points made during interview with author.

[7] Scanlon, Hugh, President of the AUEW. Speech made at the North London Polytchnic, 1977.

[8] Schlotfeldt, Walter. "Industrial Relations in a Recession". Address given to the FUE Industrial Relations Briefing Conference, Dublin, 1987.

[9] The voting patterns of individual trade union members may not reflect this. (See, for example, Plunkett, James, "Changed Times", from Nevin, Donal (ed.) *Trade Unions and Change in Irish Society*, 1980: 136).

[10] Crouch, Colin, *The Politics of Industrial Relations*, Fontana, London, 1979.

[11] Roche, Bill, "From Social Contract to Economic Brinkmanship: Trade Unions and the State in Britain", *Industrial Relations News Report*, Ireland 1981.

[12] Walton, Richard E. "From Control to Commitment: Transforming Workforce Management in the United States". Paper prepared for the Harvard Business School's 75th Anniversary Colloquium on Technology and Productivity, 1984.

[13] Cole, Robert E., "The New Industrial Relations", Special Report, *Business Week*, 11 May 1981.

[14] Murray, Sean. Survey of Employee/Industrial Relations in Irish Private Sector Manufacturing Industry Report Commissioned by the Industrial Development Authority, 1984.

[15] Point made in conversation with the author on 28 July 1988.

[16] In recent years the growth in membership of the Chartered Institute of Personnel and Development with professional exams as an entry requirement, the growing complexity of the area (for example, increased labour legislation) and an influx of multinational investment has meant that the lowly status of the function is slowly being reversed.

[17] Tom O'Brien, Former Personnel Director of General Electric Superabrasives, speaking to the author on 22 May 1987.

[18] Townsend, Robert. *Up the Organisation*, Coronet Books, London, 1971.

[19] Flanders, Alan. *Industrial Relations: What's Wrong with the System?* Faber and Faber, London, 1965.

[20] McCarthy, W. E. J. and Collier, A. S. *Coming to Terms with Trade Unions*, Institute of Personnel Management, London, 1973.

[21] Fox, Alan. *Man Mismanagement*, Hutchinson, London, 1974.

[22] See, for example, Taylor, Frederick Wilslow. *Scientific Management*. Harper and Row, New York, 1947.

[23] McGregor, Douglas *The Human Side of Enterprise*, McGraw-Hill, New York, 1960; Likert, Rensis. *New Patterns of Management*, McGraw-Hill New York, 1961.

3

THE NEW MODEL OF
INDUSTRIAL RELATIONS

A KEY INFLUENCE IN THE MOVEMENT towards the "new model" of industrial relations has been the growth in competitive pressures within the international marketplace.[1] While competitiveness is denoted by several factors (design, quality, after sales service, pricing and so on) we are here solely concerned with labour competitiveness, that is, productivity, flexibility and relative wage costs. The car industry in the US clearly illustrates this point.

For many years the operating practices of established US car manufacturers were geared toward servicing a domestic market. The absence of external competition, coupled with a high domestic demand for cars, meant that core manufacturing measures were often poorly controlled. The lack of international competition and the steady demand for new cars caused an insular focus with low pressure for productivity improvements.[2] The power of the unions within this sector led to high relative wages/conditions of employment and the car industry became firmly established in the top quartile of the pay league. Into this protected environment came virulent, mainly foreign, competition, which eroded the market domination of existing (unionised) manufacturers.[3] The economic challenge came both from new competitors and new conditions of competition, for example, the substitution of plastics for metals and the growth of the non-union sector. With lower labour costs and new production facilities, an increasing share of the US and world markets was lost to foreign competition.[4]

Intensified competition forced many organisations to re-evaluate their traditional modus operandi. Efforts to weather the economic storms were reflected in a range of industrial relations initiatives throughout the developed economies. Collectively these developments attempted to dismantle and deregulate collective bargaining structures which were seen to limit the ability of companies to respond to the competitive challenge. A central goal of these developments was the search for organisational and labour market flexibility. This, of itself, is not new. As Streek argues:

> At first glance, flexibility — its ugly opposite being "rigidity" — seems to be a catch all term for everything that employers find desirable and in fact complaints by employers of industrial relations rigidities are nothing new.[5]

Yet while the goal of flexibility is not a recent development, its attainment has become much more important. The issue has been given prominence by the introduction of new technologies which offer fresh possibilities for organising work. Increased investment often demands greater utilisation of capital-intensive plants and a labour force with new skills. As one report noted:

> A major requirement for the growth of employment and flexibility in the labour market is a working population which has both the skills and flexibility needed in order to cope with a period of rapid change caused mainly by the growth of modern technology.[6]

Such is the link which existed between the traditional model of industrial relations (with a strong, unified trade union movement) and organisation rigidity that the achievement of labour force flexibility was seen to be an almost impossible goal:

> The search for full scale flexibility seems certain to remain
> for personnel managers for many years the search for the
> Holy Grail. It is to be desired devoutly but never quite
> attained.[7]

Many companies are no longer able (or are simply unwilling) to
accept workforce rigidity. Changes in the economic environment
have therefore led to a renewed focus on organisational flexibility.
The non-union model is seen to deliver this and as a consequence
has been actively embraced by employers.

EMBRACING ORGANISATIONAL FLEXIBILITY

Organisational flexibility is a somewhat amorphous concept. It
is useful to classify the different approaches taken by organisations to achieve it under two separate headings: (a) functional
flexibility and (b) financial flexibility.[8]

Functional flexibility denotes the first key element of the so-
called "flexible firm" model. For example, the agreement which
covered Sony's greenfield site at Bridgend in the United Kingdom
specified no demarcations except on the basis of individual capa-
bility and safety. Manufacturing workers (whose jobs were
graded A to F with a three-line job description) could be moved
from production to warehousing to incoming inspection. If necessary, clerical workers and even senior managers, it was claimed,
could be put on a production line.[9] While the flexible firm model
includes the traditional notion of moving employees between different sections of a plant, it extends beyond this. Within companies, integrated labour markets are giving way to segmented ones.
Employers are beginning to re-organise their manpower resources
into fixed and variable components, core employees and peripheral supplementary labour, somewhat akin to what is generally
described as the "Japanese model". Core employees have a
greater degree of job security as other grades are used as a buffer

against business downturns. Peripheral workers conduct less critical activities and are hired on contracts which permit easy adjustment of their numbers as the scale of operation changes. External workers (contractors) conduct those activities from which the firm has distanced itself and are not employees at all in the traditional sense. The core workers are at the centre, the peripherals surround and, to some extent, insulate them and the externals are deployed around the outside.[10,11] One industrial relations commentator made the point that employers can now buy labour on a "retail" rather than a "wholesale" basis.[12]

Double-Breasted Wage Strategies

Another element of the financial flexibility model is provided by the growing number of companies pursuing so-called "double-breasted" wage strategies. Under this heading core (unionised) facilities have different terms and conditions to satellite (non-union) facilities. Within the US, "unionised" companies have acquired or started up non-union subsidiaries. Years of profit-draining assaults from an army of non-union competitors forced companies to consider this.

William M. Legg, Managing Director of Alex Brown and Sons Inc., a Baltimore brokerage, argued that the establishment of non-union subsidiaries was the only way to compete in the largely non-union south and southwest states, where drivers earned 30 per cent less than Teamsters members.[13] Companies such as Consolidated Freightways, IU International and Roadway Express, which together employed about 40,000 Teamsters, bought or started up 15 non-union subsidiaries. While it was extremely difficult to calculate reliable figures, the union reckoned that most of the 20 largest unionised carriers, representing half its trucking membership, had non-union operations where base pay rates and general conditions differed from their unionised operations.[14] Despite its small size, this trend towards "double-breasted" strategies has begun to occur in Ireland, with several "established" manufacturers, and even some semi-state companies, commencing new operations on a non-union basis (albeit the core rationale is to remain union-free rather than to pay lower wage rates).

Trade Unions are Seen to Impact Negatively on Competitiveness

Increasing competition puts pressure on wage rates and on general labour productivity, forcing companies to maximise labour utilisation. Plants that cannot compete are either shut down or have investment diverted elsewhere. While there had always been a difference in wage rates between unionised and non-union US workers (and between unionised US workers and those in other countries) what changed is that this difference became the key competitive factor.[15] Stressing the importance of the wage cost relativity factor, Fisher notes:

> . . . being competitive has become so difficult that better, more effective, and less costly use of people is a challenge that can no longer be relegated to second or third place on the list of corporate priorities.[16]

While increases in competitive pressures affect *all* companies, a key point is that trade unions are seen to have a negative influence on competitiveness by establishing and maintaining high wage levels and restrictive working conditions. Unionised organisations are forced to maintain high relative wage and benefit rates, sometimes established in a more favourable business environment. Unions act as a ratchet mechanism ("what we have we hold") on wage rates and working practices and unionised companies are stereotyped as being less able to respond to changes in the marketplace (a "double whammy"). Despite downturns in sales or profitability, wage levels do not descend. The classic notion of supply and demand holds that where supply increases price falls, but this situation of perfect competition does not apply in a highly unionised labour market. When the supply of labour increases (due to the growth in unemployment, higher birth vs. death rates, the increasing participation of women in the labour force and so on) the price at which labour can be bought does not fall. Indeed, the traditional labour market has shown itself to be highly resistant to such changes. As Brown notes:

> . . . workers who seem incapable of combining to press for a
> rise will spontaneously unite to refuse work at less than the
> customary rate, even when jobs are scarce. [17]

Increases in competitive pressures may also have presented some companies with an opportunity to reassess their modus operandi. One respondent argued that the majority of American managers never abandoned their philosophical opposition to unions,[18] a point supported by other research evidence:

> In the end, what may be most surprising to an observer of
> American management is the degree to which opposition to
> unions seems to be a matter of general doctrine rather than
> of analysis of the specific situations involved. If there are,
> as is sometimes argued, benefits of being unionised in some
> instances, American managers do not seem to investigate
> them.[19]

THE DECLINING MEMBERSHIP LEVELS OF THE TRADE UNION MOVEMENT

> It would appear that the union movement is now a mature
> product that is losing its market share.[20]

The decline in trade union power is central to any understanding of the transition taking place in the industrial relations system in Ireland. Throughout the western economies the influence of the union movement has been radically pared back in recent years. In Britain, union activity is at its lowest level since the second world war — with fewer than 30 per cent of employees being union members (down from 58 per cent in the late 1970s). In the private sector the picture is bleak for the unions, with less than one in five people in employment being union members. [21] Labour leaders are watching helplessly as their membership rolls decline and their political influence withers. Instead of fighting to get higher membership unions are struggling, and often failing, to hold on to existing members. At the time of writing, there is a strong rumour that Liberty Hall (for a long time the tallest building in the capital and the architectural embodiment of trade union power in Ireland) is to be put up for sale.

Most of the trade union membership losses can be attributed to the fact that countless "traditional" jobs have simply disappeared. While some compensatory gains have been achieved in the white collar area, these have not been enough to stem the tide of membership losses. Most ominous for the unions is the changing nature of many of the available jobs.

The Steady Development of the Service Sector

Jobs are shifting from blue collar to white collar industries, many of which rely heavily on part-time workers and women. The white collar worker is less ideological, looking toward their own career rather than solidarity, argues Roger Blanpain, Professor of Industrial Relations and Labour Law at the University of Louvain in Belgium. The big industrial plants that used to supply the shock troops of trade unions are slowly disappearing. Replacing them are smaller assembly plants, high technology companies and service industries. In these new facilities there is no legacy of conflictual labour-management relations upon which union organisers can depend for continued support.[22]

In recent years there is also the new phenomenon of a growth in the number of workers doing the jobs they once did at the factory or office at home through computer terminals. This "terrifies" union leaders who feel such workers will be almost impossible to unionise.[23] As Visser notes:

> The overall direct impact of these changes on trade unions is that the domains in which they have strongholds are shrinking. [24]

Decline in Trade Union Membership Levels in Europe

> There is a theory that all cartels come to an end. It's a miracle how long OPEC has lasted and a greater miracle how long Fleet Street has lasted.[25]

In common with most other western countries, trade unions in Ireland have experienced a decline in membership penetration levels. Overall trade union membership in the Republic has declined to an estimated 39 per cent of the workforce. This is from a historically "high" position of 55 per cent in 1980 (see Figure 3).

Michael Barry of the National College of Ireland has always made the point that trade union power is not simply a "numbers game". In Ireland, trade unions have an input into tax and a range of other social issues, including fiscal policy, which may be the envy of union movements in Europe. For example, during the last 20 years while the level of union penetration has been in decline, Irish unions have had enormous influence on developments at the national level. Since 1990, incredibly 19 individual pieces of pro-employee legislation have been passed by the Irish Government on minimum wages, equality, family-friendly and collective bargaining issues.[26] Regarding the demise of trade unions, D'art and Turner counsel that "the evidence is sparse and inconclusive".[27] While the trend is towards declining penetration levels and individual organisations deciding to operate on a non-union basis, trade unions in Ireland are far from a spent force.

FIGURE 3: TRADE UNION MEMBERSHIP AND DENSITY, 1925–2003[28]			
Year	Membership	Employment Density (%)[a]	Workforce Density (%)[b]
1925	123,000	21.2	18.7
1930	99,450	20.0	20.0
1935	130,230	22.6	18.6
1940	151,630	26.2	23.0
1945	172,340	27.7	25.3
1955	305,620	45.7	41.6
1965	358,050	52.4	48.8
1975	449,520	60.0	53.2
1980	527,960	62.0	55.3
1985	485,040	61.3	47.5
1990	474,590	57.1	45.0
1995	504,450	53.1	41.1
2000	586,944	43.2	38.8
2001	595,086	44.2	38.3
2002	644,400	44.7	40.6
2003	641,633	43.6	39.0

[a] Employment density: The percentage of civilian employees who are trade union members.

[b] Workforce density: The percentage of the total civilian workforce, that is, including those employed and those seeking employment, who are trade union members.

THE EMERGENCE OF HIGH COMMITMENT WORK SYSTEMS

A major factor underlying the development of the new model of industrial relations is the growth of high commitment work systems. A reassessment of the value of employees to organisations is taking place with many of the core assumptions of the traditional model being challenged and rejected. The common denominator of the range of programmes under this general heading is that they are directed towards achieving higher productivity levels *and* employee motivation.

Distinguishing between Systems and Value Changes within Organisations

In order to understand the move towards high commitment work systems it is important to differentiate between systems and value changes within organisations. System change, as the phrase implies, simply encompasses changed methodology or ritual. For example, if at a particular company the number of communications meetings with employees was increased or their format revised this would represent system change. Value changes involve a refocus on fundamental business tenets. The change from the control (traditional) to the commitment (new) model of industrial relations is of the second order. While systems changes (for example, the development of participatory structures) accompany the new emphasis, they are driven by a revised understanding of workplace relations.

This concept is, of itself, hardly revolutionary. Within all societies, rituals are not "stand alone" but are based on deeply held beliefs and convictions.[29] Rituals and the institutions to support them reflect underlying values in a society or, for the purpose of our focus, in an organisational setting. The way in which modern business is organised is similarly based on deeply held values, beliefs and convictions about people at work, even if they are not always fully articulated.

The value placed on the commitment of the workforce provides a key conceptual difference between the traditional and the new model of industrial relations. The notion of an employee as "a machine babysitter"[30] has given way to a view that people work is important and want to contribute to it. Productiveness cannot simply be measured in narrow industrial engineering terms but is influenced by the total workplace environment. In contrast, the design of work systems under the traditional model encouraged the perception that "head work" was the responsibility of managers only. As Alfred S. Warren Jr., Industrial Relations Vice-President of General Motors Corporations, put it:

> We're still living in the 1930s, paying for the use of a worker's hands and not what he can offer mentally.[31]

In similar vein, Michael Sonduck, Corporate Manager of Work Improvement at Digital Equipment Corporation remarked:

> One of the most dehumanising assumptions ever made is that workers work and managers think. When we give shop floor workers control over their work, they are enormously thoughtful.[32]

The most dramatic evidence of changes in workforce management strategies appeared in manufacturing plants built in the US during the 1970s.[33,34] However, such systems are not exclusive to the US. The Scandinavian job enlargement projects, the most publicised being the experiments at the Volvo plants, were both similar in design and orientation and pre-dated the developments in the US. The key point here is that these no longer represent isolated examples but are becoming widespread across a range of industries throughout the developed countries.

FROM CONTROL TO HIGH COMMITMENT

> Every employee comes equipped with a mind . . . at
> absolutely no extra cost.[35]

The broad concept of levels of commitment is comprised of four types of involvement which vary in terms of orientation and intensity. The most positive (highest level) involvement has been termed "moral", reflecting a sense that what one is doing is morally correct, perhaps even morally superior. Religious organisations, arguably, provide the best example of this. Positive, but less intense, is "spontaneous–expressive" involvement which conveys the idea that what one is doing is enjoyable, gratifying, even fun (for example, the pursuit of a leisure activity). Relatively neutral involvement is "calculative", that is, pursued to achieve a specific outcome (in the economic system this is most often wage/salary payments). The most negative (lowest level) is "alienative" involvement in which organisational membership is either against one's will (for example, a prison) or simply a means to some other end (working for a living in a job that a person does not enjoy). Etzioni had earlier identified moral, calculative, and alienative as elements along a continuum of membership involvement. Walton's work provided the addition of "spontaneous/expressive" involvement which neatly captures the transition from the traditional to the new model of industrial relations. Viewed in these terms, high commitment work systems are characterised by spontaneous–expressive involvement and may even be seen by members as morally superior. They are marked by moderate amounts of calculative behaviour and relatively little alienative feeling. The rationale for creating high commitment work systems is that it tends to be accompanied by motivational energy, by responsiveness to the needs of business, by identification with unit members/goals and by other indices favourable to the quality of work life.[36]

The key ingredient of such systems is the high commitment expended by members. It is not simply that commitment is sought by planners to promote a productive and healthy work place, for that would also be true of conventional work organisations. Rather, high commitment by workers is presumed in the basic design of the work structure. If high commitment is not forthcoming, the system is vulnerable as companies could revert to a control model of industrial relations. By way of contrast, a conventional operation that provides close supervision, simplified tasks, narrow job descriptions, detailed procedures and relies heavily on formal controls is designed to function adequately even when member commitment is moderate to low. It provides few ways for the organisation to benefit from high commitment, however.[37]

Employees are Becoming Less Submissive

The development of high commitment work systems, in part, reflects changes in society. To take a simple example, I have no memory of negotiating what brand of clothes I would wear to school or of my mother cooking different menu options to suit a variety of tastes among my brothers and sisters. Yet, one generation later, my own children have an expectation of this. High commitment work systems are more closely aligned to the way we now run "family organisations" and are more likely to meet the needs of employees who bring these new expectations to the workplace. Changes in society have changed expectations from work — employees are less frightened and submissive, more self-affirmative and critical of inequity. The suggestion here is that industry is beginning to organise work and incentives to appeal to new worker values rather than trying to fit people to work designs from an era when expectations were fundamentally different. As Young notes:

> At the moment too many of our workplaces stifle enterprise and initiative. The result is that people go

elsewhere — to their pigeon lofts, to their do-it-yourself, to betting shops, where they show far more skill in manipulating numbers than most employers encourage them to show at work.[38]

The development of high commitment work systems is also explained by rising educational standards. Better educated workers seek more challenge on the job and more involvement in the decision making process. In more sophisticated technological companies, of which there are many in Ireland, the actual jobs often demand third level education. Given these changes the traditional form of organisation, based on command/obey tenets, is simply inappropriate. Core societal changes have meant that people will no longer accept the authoritarianism associated with the traditional model.[39] A workforce which is better educated, more articulate and assertive must be involved in the decision making process both to avoid potential frustrations and to tap into the creative energy which exists. As Fox argues:

> Rising living standards, better education, and growing aspirations among ordinary men for self-respect and dignity have all contributed to a widening disinclination to accept without scrutiny the commands, policies and decisions of officially constituted authority. Increasingly men ask "Why?"[40]

Does Better Education Reduce Unionisation?

Changing educational levels may also influence the process of de-unionisation. Studies in the US support the point that unionisation and educational level are negatively correlated.[41] Complimentary research conducted in the UK showed that as the level of education rose (beyond secondary school), the level of union membership fell dramatically.[42] As Hundley argues:

> . . . it is likely that workers on jobs requiring more schooling will be less inclined towards unionisation.[43]

While it is difficult to generalise with any exactitude, experience suggests that "higher status" employees perceive themselves as better able to negotiate with employers directly, while "lower status" employees perceive themselves as being less able to negotiate with employers directly. It follows that changing education levels in Ireland has quite likely supported the development of the non-union sector.

Do High Commitment Work Strategies Pay Off on the Bottom Line?

A key question raised by sceptics is, "does it really work"? Evidence is growing that high commitment work designs can meet the twin goals of increasing job satisfaction and improving quality and productivity. The driving force is not altruism but business pragmatism. Commitment to employees pays off on the bottom line, a phenomenon that has received academic support for some time and is now achieving growing recognition within the business community. The development of high commitment work systems denotes a recognition that in most business organisations the outputs from employee commitment fell short of expectations. In relation to the US, Walton notes:

> A broad consensus has emerged that US managers generally have come to rely upon poor models for managing their workforces; to expect and accept much less from workers than is potentially available.[44]

In part, the focus on high commitment work organisation design also emerged when the supposed productivity gains of new technology were not realised by companies. As one report noted:

> The solution to fading competitive ability, sluggish
> productivity growth, and poor quality cannot be found in
> the mythical black box of a miraculous technology. To
> realise the full potential of automation, leading edge
> companies are integrating workers and technology in
> "sociotechnical" systems that revolutionise the way work is
> organised and managed.[45]

For its potential to be realised, new technology must be combined
with an organisation of work that utilises worker's skills, mobi-
lises commitment to quality, encourages self-discipline and per-
mits decentralisation of responsibility.[46] Thus an acceptance of the
limitation of technological developments, in part, explains the development of high commitment work systems. Organisations that
have implemented them have proven the value of the approach.
Yet if the supposed higher productivity and loyalty which such
work structures generate is a reality, the question remains as to
why so few organisations, in a relative sense, have followed this
route? In general, communications on company successes have
not been highlighted; the adoption of high commitment work systems has been a quiet revolution. The answer probably lies in the
fact that many of the leading companies have not trumpeted their
findings because it is too early to predict if there would be a long-
term success, and possibly also hoping to gain a competitive advantage. However, some of the pioneering companies are now
communicating their experiences and the evidence of superior
performance is impressive. For example, while Procter and Gamble, which established its first team-based plants in the 1960s, has
always refused to comment publicly on the matter, remarks made
by Senior Vice President David Swanson (in a closed meeting at
Harvard) confirmed the success of the new strategy. Swanson said
P & G's teamwork plants were:

. . . thirty to forty per cent more productive than their traditional counterparts and significantly more able to adapt quickly to the changing needs of the business.[47]

Ten years ago, fewer than two dozen manufacturing plants in the US organised work on a team basis. Today teamwork is used in thousands of offices and factories, especially new, highly automated plants with small workforces of 25 to 500 people.[48]

SUPERVISORY STRAIN: A DIFFICULTY FOR NON-UNION COMPANIES

High commitment work strategies put considerable strain on supervisors and the middle management group as they call for particularly well-developed human relations skills. To relinquish their former role, supervisors need both an understanding and acceptance of the new managerial philosophy, combined with sufficiently developed personal skills to cope:

> The commitment model implies a new set of role requirements for first-line supervisors; they should facilitate rather than direct the work force, impart rather than merely practice their technical and administrative expertise, and promote the development of self-managing capabilities of individual workers or work teams. In short, supervisors should delegate themselves out of their traditional functions — if not completely, then almost.[49]

The supervisory role in a high commitment strategy thus requires relatively sophisticated interpersonal skills and some conceptual abilities often not present or even potential in a company's existing workforce. A particular conceptual hurdle to be overcome concerns the exercise of power. Despite top-down commitment, the fundamental process of sharing organisational control is often not accepted at the middle management level. Many participatory experiments start off well, only to fail because they expose a company whose dominant culture is authoritarian. Poole, supporting this point, argues:

> Authoritarian methods are generally preferred to democratic ones by the great majority of management and their objections to participation are frequently based on ideological considerations in which the concern for industrial efficiency is of a lower order than the maintenance of a particular pattern of domination.[50]

In larger companies, if the local management team has not been initiators of, or at least party to, the new direction, they may search for ways to ensure that the policy will fail. As one writer noted:

> Fearing a loss of power, many middle managers torpedoed early participative programmes . . .[51]

Lyman Ketchum helped design one of the first sociotechnical plants in the US, a Gaines Food Inc. plant that opened in Topeka, Kansas. She noted that under the high commitment model the old idea that a manager's main function was to control workers is replaced with the concept that a manager should encourage employees to use initiative, which contradicts much traditional management training. The modern conception of management is analogous to an orchestra conductor. While continuing to direct operations, the central purpose has been redefined as bringing about the best performance from the individual players. This represents a fundamental conceptual change. Under the traditional model the "players" were not seen to have a significant contribution to make. Attitude change is a slow process and cannot simply be directed at shopfloor employees. In order to progress toward the high commitment model, companies need to develop the underlying concepts with the supervisory/middle management groups, which has proven to be one of the more problematic aspects of making the transition.[52]

THE CHANGE FROM PERSONNEL TO
HUMAN RESOURCES MANAGEMENT

While the absolute growth in the personnel function represents a quantitative change, underlying it a qualitative change has also taken place. The concept of strategic planning provides a good example. While forecasting and budgeting are long accepted exercises in the financial area, personnel management was traditionally considered to be a reactive function. A key emerging difference is that companies are actively beginning to look at long-range human resource planning. This is not simply an extension of the financial focus (that is, relating to longer-term wage/benefits costings), but addresses issues like organisation development and climate building. The welfare officer status of personnel practitioners is slowly giving way to the concept of the social engineer.[53] Traditionally, the personnel perspective was short term, reactive and ad hoc. In contrast, the human resource management approach, characteristic of the new model of industrial relations, is long term, proactive and integrated with the real business needs.

Turning Japanese

In a paper entitled "Toward Convergence of Japanese and American Management Practices", Yoshi Tsurumi writes:

> Traditionally, in any Japanese firm, the personnel department is very close to the president who is, in turn, expected to maintain a personal interest in individual employees. The personnel department (and the personnel manager) is indeed a power centre within the Japanese firm. Therefore, there is very little chance that the initiative and authority of the personnel department might be undermined or over-ridden by other departments.[54]

An active and influential personnel department is an important element in the development of high commitment work systems and was a clear pattern among the non-union plants visited. Such departments provide the key link between senior management attitudes and values and the achievement and maintenance of the desired organisational climate. The influx of multinational companies has been particularly influential in this development. Along with the introduction of new technology, a philosophy of people management has been imported which is very different to the core assumptions of the traditional model of industrial relations. The focus is on "employee relations" (an internal focus on the relationship between the company and the employee) as distinct from "industrial relations" (which focus on the institutions which regulate the relationship, for example, trade unions and collective bargaining).

The development of high commitment work systems, combined with the economic and political changes sketched earlier, have led to the development of a "new model" of industrial relations. The key elements of this are summarised in Figure 4.

FIGURE 4: THE NEW MODEL OF INDUSTRIAL RELATIONS	
Elements	*Denoted By*
1. Flexibility of organisation	• Market orientation • Change accepted as a constant • Maximum mobility of labour • Multi-tier wage rate systems • Pay linked to skills bank • Job design based on multi-skilled assumption • Increasing use of contract/part-time labour
2. Decline in trade union power	• Growth of non-union sector • Decline in membership levels • New style collective agreements • Rejection of consensus economic policy • Emergence of "macho management" • Changes in legislative base • Individual rather than collective concept • Give-back bargaining
3. Less overt control	• Control through shared goals/values • "Flat" organisation with abandonment of supervision in some cases • Informality in relationships • Increase in consultative strategies
4. Wider view of employee worth	• "Stretch" objectives set • High commitment to job security • Increased sharing of business data • Participative structures/problem solving groups to tap creativity • High expenditure on training/re-training
5. High status of personnel departments	• More resource (Human/Financial) • Recognition of "professional" status • Reporting to Managing Director • Personnel presence on shifts
6. Employees: High commitment to organisations	• Top quartile pay • Stock ownership plans • Acceptance of shared responsibility • Desire for challenging work • Suggestion plans/methods utilised

Endnotes

---

[1] Kochan T.A., McKersie, R.B. and Chalykoff, J. "The Effects of Corporate Strategy and Workplace Innovations on Union Representation", *Industrial and Labour Relations Review,* Vol. 39, No. 4, 1985; Fisher, Ben. Discussion paper on Kochan et al. "The Industrial Relations System in Transition: Findings of a Three Year Study" Carnegie-Mellon University. 1985.

[2] "Human Resources Director A" (US-based). Points made during interview with author.

[3] Miljus, J., Professor of Organisational Behaviour, Ohio State University, 1986, in conversation with the author.

[4] McCormack, Janice and Mills, D. Quinn. Harvard University Discussion paper on "The Industrial Relations System in Transition: Findings of a Three Year Study" Kochan et al. 1985.

[5] Streek, Wolfgang. "The Uncertainties of Management in the Management of Uncertainty: Employers, Labour Relations and Industrial Adjustment in the 1980s" *Work, Employment and Society* Vol. 1, No. 3, 1987.

[6] European Commission. "Internal and External Adaptation of Firms in Relation to Employment". Memorandum from the Commission of the European Communities, Brussels, 23 April 1987.

[7] Peach, Len. "Flexibility: The Flavour of the Future", *Personnel Management,* Vol. 17, No. 10, 1985.

[8] Cassells, Peter. "Flexibility in Industrial Relations". Lecture delivered to the Irish Association for Industrial Relations, 1988.

[9] Institute of Manpower Studies (IMS). "Changing Work Patterns". Report (360) prepared by the Institute of Manpower Studies for the National Economic Development Office, UK, 1986.

[10] Atkinson, John and Meager, Nigel. "Is Flexibility Just a Flash in the Pan?" *Personnel Management,* 1986.

[11] In relation to craft workers three levels of functional flexibility can be differentiated. At the first level core skills remain but the craftsman gains an "appreciation" of skills required in other jobs. At the second level the craftsman becomes proficient in a different discipline (for example, a mechanical craftsman undergoing an electrical training module). The

third level can be denoted as multi-skill, involving craftsmen using a number of wide ranging skills. The research evidence from the nine companies visited during this study (where practises within the maintenance function were analysed) highlighted the fact that a significant trend towards multi-skilling is emerging in Ireland.

[12] Jim O'Brien, Former FUE executive. Paper on labour market trends presented to the Institute of Personnel Management, Mansion House, Dublin, January 1987.

[13] Arnold, Bob and Dubin, Reggi Ann. "A Pioneering Pact Promises Jobs for Life", *Business Week*, 31 December 1984.

[14] Ibid.

[15] Kochan T.A., McKersie, R.B., Chalykoff, J. et al. "The effects of Corporate Strategy and Workplace Innovations on Union Representation" *Industrial and Labor Relations Review*, Vol. 39, No. 4, 1985.

[16] Fisher, Ben. Carnegie-Mellon University. Discussion Paper on Kochan et al. "The Industrial Relations System in Transition: Findings of a Three ;Year Study", 1985.

[17] Brown, Wilfred. *Exploration in Management*, Penguin, London, 1962.

[18] "Human Resource Director A". Points made during interview with author.

[19] Steiber, Jack, Mckersie, Robert, E. and Mills, D. Quinn. *U.S. Industrial Relations 1950–1980: A Critical Assessment*, Madison, WI Industrial Research Association, 1981.

[20] Foulkes, Fred. "Large Non-Unionised Employers" From Jack Stieber et. Al. (eds.) *U.S. Industrial Relations 1950–1980: A Critical Assessment* Madison, WI, Industrial Research Association, 1981.

[21] Machin Steplon. "Trade Union Decline, New Workplaces and New Workers". From *Representing Workers: Trade Union Recognition and Membership in Britain*, Gospel, Howard and Wood, Stephen (eds), Routledge, London, 2003.

[22] *International Business Week*, 19 November 1984: 38.

[23] *Newsweek*, 9 December 1985: 12.

[24] Visser, Jelle. "European Unions in Retreat". Paper delivered to the Department of Industrial Relations, University College Dublin, 30 October 1985.

[25] Murdock, Rupert, quoted in *Time* 1986.

[26] John Horgan. Address to CIPD members. National College of Ireland, Dublin, 23 February 2005.

[27] D'Art D. and Turner, T. *Irish Employment Relations in the New Economy*, Dublin, Blackhall, 2002.

[28] Gunnigle P., McMahon, G. and Wallace, J. *Industrial Relations in Ireland*. Gill and Macmillan, Dublin, 2004.

[29] Malinowski, Bronislaw. *Magic, Science and Religion*, Souvenir Press, London, 1982.

[30] Braverman, Harry. *Labour and Monopoly Capital: The Degradation of Work in the 20th Century*, Monthly Review Press, New York, 1974.

[31] Warren, Alfred, Industrial Relations Vice President, General Motors, quoted in *Business Week*, 1981.

[32] Sonduck, Michael, Corporate Manager of Work Improvement, Digital Equipment Corporation, quoted in *Business Week*, 1981.

[33] Lawlor, Edward E. "The New Plant Revolution", *Organisation Dynamics*, 1978.

[34] Walton, Richard E., "Establishing and Maintaining High Commitment Work Systems". From Kimberly John R. (ed.) *The Organisational Life Cycle*, Jossey-Bass, San Francisco, 1980.

[35] Undated 3M advertisement.

[36] Walton, op. cit.

[37] Walton, ibid.

[38] Young, Lord. Address given to the Institute of Personnel Management. *Personnel Management*. London 1987: 9.

[39] "Industrial Relations Expert A". Points made during interview with author.

[40] Fox, Alan. *Man Mismanagement*, Hutchinson, London, 1974.

[41] Schmidt, P. and Strauss, R.P. "The Effect of Unions on Earnings and Earnings on Unions: a Mixed Logit Approach", *International Economic Review* Vol. XVII, 1976; Schmidt. P. "Estimation of a Simultaneous Equations Model with Jointly Dependent Continuous and Qualitative Variables: The Union-Earnings Question Revisited", *International Economic Review*, Vol. XIX 1978.

[42] Guest, David and Dewe, Philip. "Why Do Workers Belong to Trade Unions? A Social Psychological Study in the UK Electronics Industry", *British Journal of Industrial Relations*, Vol. XXVI, No. 2, 1988.

[43] Hundley, Greg. "Education and Union Membership", *British Journal of Industrial Relations*, Vol. XXVI, No. 2, 1988.

[44] Walton Richard E. "From Control to Commitment: Transforming Workforce Management in the United States". Paper prepared for the Harvard Business School's 75th Anniversary Colloquium on Technology and Productivity, 1984.

[45] *Business Week*, "Management Discovers the Human Side of Automation", *Business Week*, 29 September 1986.

[46] Streeck, Wolfgang. "The Uncertainties of Management in the Management of Uncertainty: Employers, Labour Relations and Industrial Adjustment in the 1980s", *Work, Employment and Society*, Vol. 1, No. 3, 1987: 298.

[47] Swanson, David, Senior Vice President, Proctor and Gamble, quoted in *Business Week* 1986: 64.

[48] *Business Week*, "Management Discovers the Human Side of Automation" *Business Week*, 29 September 1986: 61.

[49] Walton, Richard E., op cit.

[50] Poole, Michael, *Theories of Trade Unionism: A Sociology of Industrial Relations*, Routledge and Kegan Paul Ltd., London, 1981: 89.

[51] Saporito, Bill, "The Revolt against Working Smarter", *Fortune*, 1986: 46

[52] Walton, Richard E. "Do Supervisors Thrive in Participative Work Systems?", *Organisational Dynamics*, Winter 1979; Schlesinger, Leonard A. and Klein, Janice A. "The First Line Supervisor: Past, Present and. Fu-

ture". From *Handbook of Organisational Behaviour*. Lorsch J. (ed.), Prentice-Hall, New York, 1987.

[53] For a more comprehensive discussion on this see Mooney, Paul, *Turbo-Charging the HR Function*, CIPD, 2004.

[54] Tsurumi, Yoshi. "Towards Convergence of Japanese and American Management Practices". From *Multi-National Management: Business Strategy and Government Policy*, Ballinger, Cambridge, MA, 1977: 213.

4

INDUSTRIAL RELATIONS: STRATEGIC OPTIONS FOR COMPANIES

GIVEN THE CHANGES DETAILED, several industrial relations "strategic options" are now available to organisations. A strategy in the sense used here can be defined as "a consistent approach over time which is intended to yield results in the medium and long-term for a specific problem.[1] While a degree of choice has always existed in this area, it has expanded considerably including the very real possibility of establishing and maintaining a non-union operation. This chapter summarises the options now available to companies locating in Ireland or for existing organisations who wish to explore their current industrial relations structures. In simple terms, four alternative strategic options are available.

- Option #1: Maintain the status quo

- Option #2: Pursue a policy of union minimisation

- Option #3: Establish a co-operative bargaining relationship

- Option #4: Operate on a non-union basis.

THE FIRST STRATEGIC OPTION: MAINTAINING THE STATUS QUO

The first option open to existing companies is that they can decide to maintain the status quo. In some companies where the union(s) are particularly strong, where the need for change is not apparent to the management team, or where the political will or skills to implement an organisation development process are absent, this may be the most rational choice. Organisational change is a difficult process and is not something which can be easily achieved or should be attempted half-heartedly. Indeed, unsuccessful change attempts can damage the existing industrial relations climate. Unless the will is in place to provide the necessary financial, human and even emotional commitment to the change process, it will almost certainly fail.[2] A further rationale for the adoption of a status quo stance is outlined by Fox:

> The new managerial stratum of industrial relations and personnel specialists certainly contains some who will have warned their line colleagues against too fierce an exploitation of coercive possibilities, on the grounds that there is a future as well as a present. Firms who enjoy what they judge to be a satisfactory pattern of labour relations may well have chosen not to prejudice it for the sake of short-term advantage.[3]

In some circumstances the "do nothing" strategy may therefore be the most logical choice. However, this choice is often made by default. It seldom follows a structured process in which the range of available options has been considered. A lack of conceptual foresight, an acceptance of mediocrity in organisational performance, a hankering for traditionalism or simply a lack of managerial commitment all negate the route of organisational change being chosen.

THE SECOND STRATEGIC OPTION: UNION MINIMISATION

The second option open to companies is to pursue what may be termed a policy of "union minimisation". Under this heading, companies work at building a communications and participation bridge with existing employees through decreasing the relevance of trade unions in the employment relationship. The primary motive here, and the core distinction between this and the co-operative bargaining strategy noted below, is the attempt to by-pass the unions through a form of consultation without negotiation. Efforts are directed towards cementing the direct relationship between companies and employees at the expense of the unions and traditional collective bargaining structures.

Companies may attempt to minimise the power of the unions either overtly or covertly by stealth. Examples of the first route are evidenced by the growth of so-called "macho management" policies where the power of organised labour is challenged directly and attempts made to win back ground lost in times more favourable to the union movement. An example of a covert strategy is the move toward the employment of contract and part-time labour which lessens representational rights at particular locations. While such changes are often justified under the heading of cost efficiency (which may be true in individual cases), the central value to the organisation is often the accompanying decline in trade union influence. Covert strategies may take a number of forms. Companies may try to identify areas or groups of employees whose position in the organisation gives them the potential to disrupt the business. The organisation may have to make a basic choice of breaking up a strategically powerful group or, if that is not possible, of isolating it geographically and organisationally from other sections.[4] Initiatives to reduce the dependency of organisations on particular groups through inhibiting the development of solidarity, or through changing work methods or arrangements, are both examples of covert strategies designed to minimise the power of unions.

The obvious risk in a union minimisation strategy is that the unions may perceive the threat posed and find ways to block it. Yet while this may be the case in established companies, those creating personnel policy on a greenfield site have an obvious advantage in this regard.

A Polaroid Snapshot: "Union Minimisation" in Practice[5]

An interesting historical example of this policy was the position taken by Polaroid at Newbridge, Co. Kildare (the plant is now occupied by Wyeth Medica, a Pharmaceutical company). Polaroid manufactured film-processing equipment but subsequently closed due to market difficulties. During the start-up phase a pre-employment agreement was negotiated with the Federated Workers Union of Ireland (FWUI) for general workers and with the National Electronic and Electrical Trade Union (NEETU) for craftsmen. Although the plant never became fully operational, it provided an excellent example of the successful pursuit of a "union minimisation" policy.

Employee relations at Polaroid were characterised by a strong bond of identity between the company and the workforce. The structure in place was a system of interlocking work groups which generated strong teamwork, employee loyalty and operations flexibility (broadly similar to the high commitment work systems described earlier). A great deal of effort was invested in establishing a positive climate and in maintaining it through open communications. Of more immediate relevance to the current focus was the attitude of the company toward the unions. While Polaroid chose the route of negotiating a pre-employment agreement (very much the "norm" at the time), their operational style could not be described as traditional in any other sense. A former general secretary of SIPTU who negotiated the pre-employment agreement was told by Polaroid's managing director that the union "had no role" in the internal affairs of the company. The company would meet the union once each year to re-negotiate the contract of employment; outside this they would manage their own affairs.

As the plant closed after just three years in operation it is not possible to predict how successful the union minimisation policy would have been in the longer term. Several other companies have consciously (and covertly) chosen this route. Understandably, those who pursue this strategy have asked that they remain anonymous. What seems to be the case is that the route of union minimisation is achieving a growing number of adherents in Ireland. As the power of unions has declined in recent years, it allows companies more scope to alter their existing collective bargaining framework. Many companies have taken the initiative in tackling former strongholds of union power under the guise of responding to increasing marketplace pressures.

Employee First, Union Member Second

The underlying philosophy within Polaroid was that employees were firstly part of the company team and secondly union members. Recourse to the union was seen to be legitimate only when the relationship between the company and the employee had broken down. The prime concern of the company was to ensure that this did not occur. Thus, while Polaroid operated a unionised facility they did so with an employee relations philosophy which closely resembled that which prevails in the non-union sector. Polaroid operated on a non-union basis at most of their US plants, and in essence retained this general philosophy despite the fact that the workforce in Ireland was unionised.

The union official, supporting the broad thrust of the direction taken at Polaroid, stated that companies should manage their employees in such a way that they do not have to resort to a trade union. He was scornful of the type of problems that trade unions normally become involved in as a result of mismanagement, asking rhetorically, what did he know about individual companies, about who should get promoted or what is the correct job grade for a particular position? Yet, "that's the sort of shitty issues we got dragged into".[6] Unions were said to spend an inordinate amount of time "mopping up" management mistakes and the official was supportive of the efforts made to establish a closer company/employee identity bond (albeit, not at the expense of trade union membership).

THE THIRD STRATEGIC OPTION: CO-OPERATIVE BARGAINING

The third strategy option available to companies is to work toward a new understanding of the bargaining relationship with both unions and employees. Successful change strategies in this area can be seen within industrial relations systems outside of Ireland, for example, concession bargaining in the US and the development of "new style" collective agreements in the UK. The various "partnership arrangements" in Ireland fall under this umbrella. In essence this is an attempt to solicit the co-operation of both unions and employees in limited areas of business decision-making. In some companies this has been achieved through negotiating trade-offs with the unions. For example, facilitation of union membership growth, through concession of closed shop arrangements and the check-off for union dues, allows the building of a co-operative climate with the unions and also potentially benefits the organisation in stability terms. As Purcell argues:

> . . . in the corporation where the bulk of employees are already unionised, groups of workers who do not have a collective voice by virtue of not being union members become a source of difficulty. They are essentially disenfranchised.[7]

Other elements of this policy address the strengthening of the procedural and institutional machinery for the resolution of conflict, a point explored in some detail later. Through accepting the role of unions at the workplace (albeit in a limited capacity) conflict is diffused before class consciousness and solidarity have time to develop.[8] Attempts are made to build constructive relationships with the unions and incorporate them into the organisational ethos. Broad-ranging discussions take place with unions where extensive information is provided on a whole range of decisions and plans, including aspects of strategic management. Typically, the right of "last say" or ultimate decision-making rests with the management team. Emphasis is also put on techniques designed to elicit employee commitment and the need to accept and connect with the requirement for ongoing change. These often include share option schemes and gainsharing, briefing or cascade information systems, joint working parties or the creation of quality councils.

The central difficulty of this particular strategy lies in moving both sides away from the adversarial nature of the employment relationship (which typifies the traditional model of industrial relations) towards a more integrative, collaborative one. Yet the question "quo bono" is raised here. The attempt to work "with the unions" may underscore a genuine commitment to a new order of industrial relations or may represent a covert attempt to overcome the perceived constraints of the traditional model. Rather than overtly challenging union power, some companies decide to work towards minimising it in the guise of a new found commitment to employee relations.

Co-operative bargaining is based on the accepted psychological premise that change is usually more effective when the parties involved have achieved a position of medium security.[9] When change is attempted where the base level of trust between the parties is low, it is usually defensively resisted. The difficulty for the unions is to assess the true motives underlying particular initiatives. The philosophy of union representatives, the prior history of industrial relations (particularly the level of trust between the parties) and the core skills of the management group in highlighting and "selling" the necessity for structural and attitudinal change determine the success or failure of this strategy.

The Institutionalisation of Industrial Conflict: An Argument for Granting Recognition

The decision to grant union recognition can be described as the "least worst" option for incoming companies. A counter (Marxist) view was that the decision to unionise plants was actually taken on a positive basis. Contrary to the popular notion that trade unions are antagonistic to the capitalist order, this view was that they "oil the wheels of industry". While outwardly unions provide a forum for employees to have a voice at the workplace this normally poses little constraint for companies.[10] Negotiations range over a limited number of bargaining areas — none of which pose a fundamental challenge to the "right to manage". This follows from the narrow definition by trade unions of their area of responsibility and authority (they get locked into the "teas, towels and toilets issues"). A fundamental questioning of managerial authority in areas like the distribution of profits or the role of unions in the initiation of change is seldom addressed. Companies should therefore grant recognition to trade unions to create a forum through which conflicts at the workplace can be channelled and diffused.

Implicit in the argument for the co-option of a trade union presence was the notion that a "moderate" union helps to exercise control over the membership, thereby acting as an extension of management. In essence, the industrial relations arena simply provides a "talking shop". The illusion of participation satisfies employees' needs for representation while the constraints imposed on companies through the granting of recognition are "marginal".[11] Another respondent, supporting the above, stated that unionisation offers a mechanism to resolve disputes which does not exist in the non-union sector. Part of the rationale for recognising a trade union, therefore, was seen to be the establishment of formal industrial relations procedures through which grievances or issues of concern can be processed and resolved.[12] Support for this view was evidenced by the fact that, in eight years of operation as a full-time union official, this person had never had to visit particular companies. Any disputes which had arisen during this period had been resolved internally.

A further supposed benefit of trade union organisation was that it lessened the influence of individuals. Unionisation was seen to be more democratic as, in a non-union situation, "small groups can bring a whole plant out".[13] The benefits of trade union recognition were therefore stated to be twofold: (a) unionisation leads to a more formal procedural framework which "rationalises" the industrial relations structure and results in industrial peace and (b) unionisation leads to greater democratic control over the membership.

THE FOURTH STRATEGIC OPTION: UNION AVOIDANCE

The fourth industrial relations strategy option is a straightforward policy of union avoidance. Companies can decide to operate on a non-union basis, attempting to convince employees that they do not have a need for the services provided by a union. The likelihood of employers being able to maintain a non-union status has increased considerably in recent years. In the US the experiences of several early pioneer companies has led to what has been termed "a fully fledged, non-union resource management system".[14] Research evidence suggests that the long-standing willingness of employers to oppose unions has been reinforced in recent years with the availability of union avoidance expertise.[15] There is a growing fraternity in Ireland who possess expertise in the union avoidance area and the developing non-union sector provides an expanding market for this. At the present time, the union avoidance option is generally only available in a greenfield setting. To my knowledge there is, as yet, no significant evidence of union "de-recognition" occurring in Ireland. However, the success of a high percentage of new companies in maintaining their non-union status offers a degree of comfort to employers contemplating the non-union route.

In recent years, the non-union option has increasingly been chosen by companies setting up manufacturing facilities in Ireland. The almost automatic option of conceding recognition to blue collar workers in pre-employment agreements is no longer the case. The growth and successful maintenance of the non-union sector highlights this as a realistic policy option for companies, with existing non-union companies providing role models for others to follow. The lessons of several companies which commenced operations on a non-union basis and subsequently conceded recognition also allows an insight into failed policy options.

*   *   *

The scenarios sketched above represent, in simple terms, the choice options available to companies on a plant-by-plant basis. For multiple location employers, a number of sub-strategies are also possible. In what may be termed a dual, or double-breasted, strategy some firms seek to operate on a non-union basis in new plants only while continuing to invest in existing unionised plants. Other companies shift product lines away from core (unionised) to satellite (non-union) facilities. In this way, the unionised plants come to have an ever decreasing share of investment and the companies rely less on these plants for production.[16]

Each of the strategies outlined has particular strengths and weaknesses, not least being the risk potential of failed policy options. The outlook of key decision makers, the risk preference and the counter strategies available to the unions involved are all factors influencing the particular route chosen.[17] Further, the options outlined are not equally available in all settings. In particular, it is difficult to achieve value or structural changes at plants which are already established. As one source described it, "birth is easier than reincarnation".[18] Companies commencing operations from a greenfield site have an obvious advantage in implementing some of the strategy options outlined. However, while organisation development is a difficult process, it is not impossible for established companies to reformat their current industrial relations strategy.

The significant point which emerges is that the union minimisation, co-operative bargaining and union avoidance options are being increasingly chosen in Ireland as a sophistication gap emerges between companies and unions with regard to human resource management policies. The industrial relations strategy options available to companies as a result of the developments sketched are outlined in Figure 5.

FIGURE 5: INDUSTRIAL RELATIONS STRATEGIC OPTIONS FOR COMPANIES	
1. Union Acceptance	Maintain status quo — no change requirements.
2. Union Minimisation	Attempt to build direct relationship with employees at the expense of existing collective bargaining framework.
3. Co-Operative Bargaining	Attempt to build relationship with employees and trade unions through stressing the mutuality in the employment relationship.
4. Union Avoidance	Cement core relationship with employees. Exclude third party representation.

So Which Option is "Best"?

In practice, the strategic option chosen is influenced by several factors: the different stages of the business life-cycle, policy considerations (for example, Ryanair's "low cost" strategy), the competence of the management team and their appetite to pursue particular approaches, the type of people employed in the organisation and the industry or sector within which it operates.

In greenfield sites, policies will depend on the assumptions and beliefs of the new management team alongside the "imported" philosophy of the parent organisation. In a mature business that has been in existence for some years, IR policies will be a function of its own core values and management style as well as depending on the actual or perceived balance of power between the management and the unions. Choices can depend on how willing management is to face industrial turbulence to depart from a "historical model" which may be damaging competitiveness. It follows that industrial relations policies reflect the particular circumstances of the firm, its history/traditional practices, management values and the power of the trade unions to exert influence. Policies can change as new situations emerge (typically the most potent issues are competitive pressures, new management teams or a takeover situation). In effect, there is "no one best way".

"Forcing Strategies": Sidelining the Unions

In terms of the choices available, two keys issues emerge. Firstly, what is the desirability of the particular change associated with the new strategy? Organisations really need to be clear on the "desired end point" that they wish to achieve, for example, in what way would "sidelining" the unions offer competitive advantage (and would the gain outweigh the pain)? A second highly practical issue is the feasibility of successfully implementing any new strategy, that is, even if you want to pursue a particular strategy, what is the likelihood of actually pulling it off? Under this latter heading a central issue is the relative power of the management and their determination or ability to steer the organisation (and the existing conflictual relationship with the unions) through a series of tactical manoeuvres. Serious scoping of the likely response of the union or unions is required to ensure success.

In the context of the four choice options outlined earlier (avoidance, minimisation, acceptance or co-operation) an attempt to marginalise the unions and limit their power can generally be described as "forcing" and falls within the "minimisation" approach detailed. The strategy of forcing change is heavily used by management. It is generally aimed at gaining economic concessions and changes in work rules and behaviour. Underpinning this ability to force issues is a mixture of bargaining power and evidence about the necessity for changes in work practices or rules (that is, there has to be a visible "wolf" at the door, for example, the threat of competition from a low-cost supplier which is clearly understood by the workforce). This is sometimes called a "burning platform", or as one HR manager colourfully described it, "you have to back up the hearse and let them smell the flowers".

Unions Will Resist this Attempt at Change

Generally where management in a brown field or mature industry seek to initiate so-called forcing or union marginalisation strategies, unions seek to maintain their relative power and develop an armoury of defence mechanisms to protect it. Responses can take the form of covert or overt concerted actions (strikes, work to rules and so on). Unions in a number of cases recognise the limitations of strike action as an economic lever and often look at non-traditional ways of "taking on" the company (for example, Aer Lingus pilots taking out full page ads in the newspapers to explain their "safety concerns" about new rostering arrangements). It can and often does become a "war" of sorts. Not all management teams have an appetite for this (and it can "unnerve" HQ personnel in other countries who are not familiar with the territory).

Common Tactical Approaches in Sidelining the Unions

In one study of companies where so-called "forcing" techniques were used a number of common tactical approaches and processes emerged:[19]

- In terms of pay, management often build and tactically exploit bargaining power in order to achieve changes and substantive savings. In some cases management teams seek to demonstrate the fact that the power balance has shifted significantly in their favour. A good example was the dispute at Bailey's Irish Cream. The company decided to build another plant in Northern Ireland in order to move away from the dependency on a single source of supply in Dublin (and a high overtime culture). Union resistance led to strike action, which the management team had spent many months preparing for.

  Message — If you go down this route you need to be prepared for a "hard road ahead".

- Managing internal differences becomes crucial: management usually seeks to ensure that members of its own organisation understand and support the objectives of a forcing strategy. Here the key issue of winning over and ensuring explicit support from middle management grades is crucial. This is dependent on a clearly articulated logic connecting the business requirements with the approach chosen — it has to "make sense". Union efforts to increase worker solidarity in the face of sidelining threats occasionally go hand-in-hand with efforts to weaken the consensus on the management side.

  Message — "Get on the same page or get out of the way."

- Clear and well articulated inter-group hostility and hostility aimed at management is an inevitable outcome of a forcing approach. Union personnel generally seek to promote anger and hostility towards the company (and specific personnel) in order to promote solidarity. For example, in An Post the union group produced a poster entitled "Miss Management" (a spoof on the hit musical *Miss Saigon*), where the leading "stars" were the senior management team who were trying to force a change strategy at the time.

Message — Pick an "emotionally tough" manager or team to lead the change process.

Forcing approaches generally place management in the driving seat in terms of initiating and making demands. Management has to be willing to manifest a strong readiness to operate during a strike. Management must appear willing to tolerate new levels of antagonism in employee relations as a price for achieving concessions or regaining the "upper hand".

The Sidelining Approach Poses a Number of Risks

In terms of risks for management a number clearly exist:

- The fact that the forcing approach might not result in a re-balancing of the power relationship (you can't just "bluff"; you have to be prepared to really follow through).

- Management can face an escalation of industrial conflict as it begins to exert its influence unilaterally.

- Forcing strategies usually involve "high stakes" bargaining where, by definition, one or other side has to win rather than a "win-win" scenario.

- The risk of a legacy of mistrust, a residue of bitterness, can be created which makes it difficult to create partnership activities further down the road.

The Genius is in the Details

Sometimes the process of mobilising and deploying bargaining power involves making various tactical assessments with regard to the future operation. Management may use the threat to leave the country or "escape" the relationship as a platform to rebuild its relative power position. The choreography and tactical postures and "positioning" adopted require serious advanced thinking and strategising among senior management. Different scenarios need to be detailed and considered in the light of intelligence on the likely union responses. Companies preparing for such "escape" scenarios often move contracts to other facilities to signal their intent without actually activating the "escape plan" itself. Postures range from actions designed to signal "serious intent" to actual market withdrawal.

Strike Planning — A Key Tool

Strike preparation is a device which can be instrumental in building up an employer's relative power base. It is part of a well-developed arsenal of preparations to regain and restore power. Preparations are sometimes used as part of an articulated and well-orchestrated manoeuvre to intimidate the unions — sometimes as much as the event itself. In one documented case of power rebalancing in the US, the company set up various management teams to oversee different aspects of the re-positioning. One group was set up to maintain and reinforce the post-strike changes, another team focussed on communications with its own workers and the local media while another team looked at the issue of plant security both during and after a strike. Preparing to hire replacement employees for the duration of the strike also sent its own message. Such "forcing" periods in management strategy are aimed at restoring power and leverage. This tough stance may not last indefinitely but simply be a precursor to a later more integrative style which seeks to involve staff and unions in a different way.

"CONSENSUS STRATEGIES": TAKING THE PARTNERSHIP AND CONSULTATION ROUTE

From the 1980s onwards different terms have been used to describe ways of involving employees and union representatives in information sharing and problem solving in the workplace. Among the early terms for this process were quality of working life, co-operative programmes, labour-management co-operation and constructive participation. More recently many such activities have been fused under the umbrella term "partnership."[20]

What is Partnership?

Partnership in a unionised setting is generally described as a "co-operative" effort between union representatives and plant management *outside* of the collective bargaining process. It generally has formalised mechanisms for some input by employees into management decisions. Such arrangements are intended to improve performance either through direct efforts aimed at improving productivity and efficiency (for example, local teams working on reducing waste) or through indirect efforts aimed at improving employee well-being. Descriptions of partnership generally factor in:

- A firm commitment to mutual gains for all within the organisation — managers, employees and trade unions.

- The importance of improving organisational productivity.

- Direct and indirect ways to improve the climate for management/union bargaining.

- Continuous exchange of information.

Partnership is a Voluntary (Not an Imposed) Exercise

Partnership requires the commitment of the management team and the trade unions to embrace it voluntarily. The most com-

monly cited factor favouring partnership is competition, for example, new manufacturing processes and technologies to stay
competitive. Economic crises of some magnitude typically play a
part in re-casting workplace practices, as have major strikes or
disputes and efforts to build a "better tomorrow". Sometimes the
greater the external pressures the parties are experiencing the
more likely they are to look to partnership as an alternative to
traditional collective bargaining.

In Ireland there is clear evidence that the changing nature of
competition has influenced some companies to adopt partnership.
For example, the country's largest union, SIPTU, explicitly associ-
ates partnership with competitiveness and has clearly stated this
in its various outputs on the subject. Organisations which espouse
values based on employee well-being (such as employment security, high wages and training and development) will be more
likely to go down the partnership road than companies who do
not. As with all change programmes, positive commitment and
endorsement from the chief executive or strong figures at a senior
management level is critically important. Overall "trust" appears
to be an important factor in the switch into partnership. While low
trust itself can be a spur to new thinking about how to improve
the workplace, it can also represent a formidable hurdle to be
overcome in the initiation of the process (one which requires considerable thought and innovation).

Outcomes

In terms of outcomes it is clear that few companies are committed
a priori to partnership in advance of it actually being tested.
Rather they remain to be persuaded when they see what benefits
will follow. In general, it is argued that there are significant gains
available to employers from the adoption of partnership approaches. Managers often report that companies become more
competitive (faster order processing, production processes

speeded up, improved quality and so on). One of the most significant outcomes reported is the extent to which companies have
been allowed to expand their "decision space" by bringing in a
wider range of perspectives and by allowing them to harness the
tacit knowledge and innovative potential of the workforce.[21]
However, there is also a realisation that the rewards and benefits
from partnership can sometimes be slow to emerge and that the
type of serious top level commitment from both staff and unions
is not easily won.

Risks Associated with the Partnership Approach

Several risks are also associated with this strategy:

- Giving additional power to the unions without the potential
  gains to the company can be risky (that is, the process can be
  hijacked by traditional collective bargaining). While it is common for trade unions and management to keep the agendas of
  collective bargaining and partnership separate in the early
  stages of development, over time this separation frequently
  becomes blurred.

- Starting partnership and not giving it the time or resources to
  flower can result in a lowering of morale and trust within an
  organisation.

- Partnership involves some sharing of decision-making and
  power and sometimes places middle management in an un-
  comfortable position in which they can feel disempowered or
  undermined.

- Partnership may not deal with sufficiently important issues to
  give it a profile and allow it be seen as a valuable avenue (it
  can become a "fishing for minnows" forum).

While established companies have a range of strategic choices,
what is crystal clear is that more and more companies are choosing the non-union route.

Endnotes

---

[1] Thurley, Keith and Wood, Stephen. "Business Strategy and Industrial Relations Strategy". From Thurley et al (eds.) *Industrial Relations and Management Strategy,* Cambridge University Press, 1983: 197.

[2] Likert, Rensis. *New Patterns of Management,* New York, McGraw-Hill, 1961.

[3] Fox, Alan. *Man Mismanagement,* Hutchison, London, 1986: 64

[4] Purcell, John et al. "Power from Technology: Computer Staff and Industrial Relations". *Personnel Review,* Vol. 7, No. 1, Winter, 1978, pp. 31/39.

[5] While the Polaroid example might seem like "old news", because of the sensitivity of the topic it is not possible to identify companies who currently pursue this strategy.

[6] "Trade Union Official F". Points made during interview with author.

[7] Purcell, John. "Management Control through Collective Bargaining: A Future Strategy". From Thurley, Keith and Wood, Stephen (eds.) *Industrial Relations and Mnagement Strategy.* Cambridge University Press, 1983.

[8] Ibid.

[9] Brown, Paul. *Managing Behaviour on the Job,* John Wiley and Sons, New York, 1982.

[10] "Trade Union Official B". Points made during interview with author.

[11] "Trade Union Official B". Points made during interview with author.

[12] "Trade Union Official C". Points made during interview with author.

[13] "Trade Union Official C". Points made during interview with author.

[14] Kochan, Thomas A. and McKersie, Robert B. "The Industrial Relations System in Transition: Findings of a Three Year Study". From Barbara D. Dennis (ed.) Proceedings of the 37th Annual Meeting, Madison WI, IIRA 1985: 265

[15] Verma, Anil. "Union and Non-Union Industrial Relations Systems at the Plant Level". Unpublished Ph.D. Dissertation. Sloan School of Management, MIT, 1983.

[16] Gennard, John. *Multi-National Corporations and British Labour. A Preview of Attitudes and Responses,* British/North American Committee, Alfred H. Cooper & Sons Ltd. London, 1972: 5/6

[17] Kochan T.A., McKersie T.B. and Chalykoff J. "The Effects of Corporate Strategy and Workplace Innovations of Union Representation". *Industrial and Labour Relations Review,* Vol. 39, No. 4, pp 487-501, 1985.

[18] Naisbitt John and Aburdent, Patricia. *Re-Inventing the Corporation,* Warner Books, 1985.

[20] One of the confusions here is that the single term "partnership" has different meanings for different people.

[21] John O'Dowd's research on 88 companies in Ireland found that workforce productivity improved in just over 70 per cent of the companies and that 65 per cent reported that business had also improved overall.

5

THE DEVELOPMENT OF THE NON-UNION SECTOR IN IRELAND

"Traveller, there is no path, paths are made by walking".[1]

WHILE THERE HAD BEEN A FOREIGN multinational presence in Ireland for many years, a huge influx of manufacturing companies occurred from the early 1960s onwards. The invest-ment was encouraged by the then Taoiseach, Séan Lemass, and the policy of industrialisation pursued has remained a central element of Ireland's economic policy to this day. A number of structures were developed to attract this investment including the establishment of the IDA and the Export Tax Free Relief Zone at Shannon, run by the Shannon Free Airport Development Com-pany. The purpose of both organisations was to encourage over-seas manufacturers to locate in Ireland by offering a range of fi-nancial and service incentives. This was to lead to the establish-ment of a manufacturing sector which would provide employ-ment for the expanding workforce and, in relation to the elec-tronic industry, the efforts were directed at promoting Ireland as the "Silicon Valley of Europe".[2] While the influx of multinational investment did not receive unqualified support, in general it was welcomed by the economic partners on the basis of the employ-ment possibilities created. As Fintan Kennedy, then general secre-tary of the ITGWU, stated:

> Let me make it clear at the outset that we in the Irish
> Transport and General Workers' Union welcome foreign
> industry to Ireland. We do so because we firmly believe
> that it can help very considerably in the expansion of our
> industrial and economic development. Not only do we
> welcome foreign industry, but we have also gone out of our
> way — literally gone out of our way — to attract it.[3]

While the multinational companies were welcomed on the basis of
providing employment opportunities, this was equated with increased membership levels for the unions. Without denying the
positive social intent, there was also a high degree of self-interest
in such lobbying. It is less certain if the unions would have been
as actively involved in encouraging non-union multinationals to
locate in Ireland. Yet, even non-union companies may have been
welcomed on the basis of providing "membership potential".
While there were some documented cases of multinational companies refusing to recognise trade unions, the overall picture
which emerges from that early investment period is one of widespread union acceptance.[4]

THE UNATTRACTIVENESS OF THE IRISH
INDUSTRIAL RELATIONS ENVIRONMENT

The success of the IDA in attracting foreign investment was
admirable given that Ireland, from a labour relations perspective, offered several potential negatives. In particular, the existing
legal framework must have seemed somewhat irrational to industrialists schooled in a more formalised environment. Patrick
Kneafsey, President of Fulflex International, stated at a National
Management Conference in Dublin that most international companies, used to operating in a well legislated and regulated industrial society where the rights and obligations of trade unions,
management and employees are defined and protected:

> ... would find it difficult, if not impossible, to contemplate a serious financial investment in a lawless industrial society where contracts and agreements have no force of law; minorities can intimidate employees into unofficial work stoppages costing millions of pounds and where the rulings of the Labour Court are not binding, so that what little industrial relations legislation exists cannot be enforced.[5]

The view that the Irish industrial relations environment provides a disincentive for investment is still strongly held within employer circles. IBEC and other employer bodies lobbied for some years for changes to the legal system (particularly the 1906 Trade Disputes Act and the exemption provided therein for cases in tort being brought against the unions for industrial action) which would supposedly bring greater industrial relations stability. Industrial relations in Ireland is based on the principle of voluntarism; collective bargaining is conducted on the basis of agreements voluntarily reached. While at times recourse to the courts is taken (breach of contract suits, injunctions against picketing and so on), the nature of the employment relationship (for example, the fact that the parties must work together at some future point) means that legal remedies are infrequently used. However, the fact that a significant number of multinational companies have located in Ireland suggests that considerations other than the IR environment are of primary importance in the investment decision. In practice, the multinationals attempted to minimise what were perceived as the negative constraints of the Irish environment through the establishment of pre-employment agreements.

PRE-EMPLOYMENT AGREEMENTS: MINIMISING THE NEGATIVE ELEMENTS OF THE IR ENVIRONMENT

The existing legal environment was simply one of several potential negatives of locating in Ireland. Companies also wished to circumvent the industrial relations ills which could attach to a poor union/management relationship. For example, they wished to avoid inter-union hostility where a number of unions competed for the same grades of employees. Further, companies in the high technology sector needed to achieve substantial operational flexibility. In the 1960s/1970s the route chosen by the vast majority of the multinationals to achieve these objectives was to negotiate pre-employment agreements. Given the particular constraints of the Irish industrial relations environment, pre-employment agreements seemed to provide a solid option. These became the "norm" for incoming companies offering several specific benefits including the avoidance of multi-unionism, the selection of a "moderate" union and the establishment of a contractual-type relationship which included formal disputes procedures and flexibility clauses. These and a number of subsidiary benefits have been extensively detailed in earlier research conducted by myself and others.[6]

Yet while most companies establishing plants in Ireland negotiated pre-employment agreements, it should not be implied that they welcomed a trade union presence. Union recognition was essentially seen as the "least worst" option as there was a lot of suspicion about unions and union officials,[7] particularly where companies operated on a non-union basis in their "home country". American companies, in particular, were said to be uneasy about conceding recognition. When they went to the ICTU to meet the officials they were said to "examine the head for horns and the feet for hoofs".[8]

To Unionise or Not to Unionise? *That* is the Question

The decision to grant union recognition is seldom taken lightly as it has fundamental and irreversible effects on the structure of power and authority within a company.[9] Yet despite the misgivings expressed by some companies, the vast majority of incoming multinationals granted union recognition during that period. This was in keeping with the IR "culture" in Ireland and ensured that the companies were not a target for trade unions to solicit members. For a period which spanned more than 20 years (circa 1965–1985), approximately 90 per cent of incoming companies established such agreements and granted sole negotiation rights to one union or to a fixed "group" of unions.[10]

An important point to be made in relation to pre-employment agreements is that recognition rights were largely confined to "blue collar" employees, as "staff" (white collar workers) were perceived as being less likely to seek union recognition. One former union official in Cork made the point that no employer has ever "put on a plate" clerical, technical or administrative employees in a pre-employment agreement. These are organised on the same basis as "our forefathers pioneered back in the early 1900s".

Why "Blue Collar" Workers were Unionised

Multinationals accommodated trade union recognition within "blue collar" grades for a number of reasons. Firstly, many incoming companies had little history in dealing with white collar grades on a unionised basis. The already low levels of unionisation within the US were largely confined to the blue collar sector and this is still largely the case in manufacturing industry.[11] Secondly, the notion has continued to prevail that white collar employees have a closer identity with management and are therefore less likely to seek union recognition. This reflects the view, supported within the trade union movement itself, that white collar workers have less affinity with the union movement. A former general secretary of SIPTU made the point that Irish workers (blue collar) join a union as a normal sequence of life events, like "getting a job, or getting married". White collar workers were said to have a much more instrumental attitude to unions, a point supported by research conducted in the US.[12] For most of the rank and file, trade unionism is simply a device by which they can pursue objectives more effectively than if they stand alone as isolated individuals. It is an "instrumental" collectivism rather than one which invests the collective with transcendent value in its own right.[13] In other words, most employees see unions as a method to achieve specific objectives and are not ideologically committed to the *concept* of trade unionism. The central point here is that while pre-employment agreements gave a significant boost to union membership levels generally, the profile of membership largely remained unchanged. Divisions between unionised blue collar and non-union white collar employees remained in place (leaving aside the high levels of white collar unionism in the Irish public sector).

A further factor in steering incoming companies towards granting recognition was the perceived difficulty in maintaining non-union status. The general level of union membership, the constitutional position with regard to freedom of association and the acceptance of trade unions as an integral part of Irish society posed high instability risks. Further, the advice received from both the IDA and IBEC (then FUE) steered the companies towards the co-option of a trade union presence. In addition, the Labour Court had also shown itself to be in favour of collective bargaining through consistent support for the view that union recognition should be conceded (a bias which continues to this day).[14] In numerous cases where "union recognition" was sought by employees (even a small percentage of employees), the Labour Court invariably made a recommendation in favour.

PERSONNEL POLICY FOR INCOMING COMPANIES: THE ROLE OF THE IDA

The role of the IDA in promoting Ireland as an investment location is multidimensional; advice on industrial relations is simply one aspect. Companies interested in establishing plants in Ireland look to the IDA for the whole gamut of business advice including financing, materials procurement, transport and so on. The research focused on the IDA's role, if any, in encouraging companies to operate on a unionised or a non-union basis.

Some of the respondents interviewed made the point that the IDA is neutral on the question of union recognition and send companies to IBEC for detailed advice in this area. Three reasons were put forward. Firstly, the IDA does not have the expertise to give anything other than a general overview of industrial relations in Ireland. Secondly, union recognition is a politically sensitive issue. The IDA, as a state-run organisation, attempts to distance itself from this aspect of advice to incoming companies, simply highlighting the legal position and the demographics of the trade union movement in Ireland.[15] The role of the IDA was therefore put forward as that of an "honest broker", helping companies understand the Irish industrial relations environment without in any way steering or influencing them towards a unionised or non-union status.

The final reason put forward to support the assertion that the IDA plays a relatively minor role in influencing personnel policy is that most incoming companies already have a well established personnel policy derived from their home base. Organisation culture, which underpins specific policy decisions, was stated to be pre-set. Incoming companies import their personnel philosophies and policies in the same way that they introduce their particular technology.[16] The point is valid to the extent that there is good evidence to suggest that operating norms in the home country do indeed spill over into subsidiary operations.[17] Yet there are limitations to this analogy. Companies cannot simply transplant an entire mode of operation from one country to another. It is highly unlikely that any company working in a different cultural and legislative setting would decide personnel policy without taking account of the local environment. While the broad thrust of a company's personnel policy may be pre-set, this is dovetailed into the particular operating environment. Indeed, the very success of the multinationals is partly accounted for by their ability to operate effectively in cultural environments as diverse as the Far East, North America and Ireland (the "think global, act local" slogan captures this point well). For example, a number of US companies which operate on a non-union basis at their parent plant negotiated pre-employment agreements in Ireland. Advice from some quarter, therefore, influenced these companies towards the view that a unionised status made more business sense in the Irish environment. The question posed here is to what extent the IDA was involved in this process.

The IDA Traditionally Supported the Granting of Union Recognition

The IDA, both in the current and earlier research conducted, denied that it attempts to influence incoming companies' decisions on the question of union recognition. While this formal response is not surprising, the evidence from earlier research indicates that it may be somewhat less than a neutral intermediary.[18] Perhaps the clearest indication of IDA support for union recognition can be taken directly from IDA sources:

> In the IDA we go to considerable pains to persuade incoming manufacturers at all levels of the importance of establishing early relationships with trade unions . . . in our experience Irish unions have shown considerable sympathy with genuine difficulties or teething troubles that can arise with a new export industry.[19]

Several conditioning factors were brought to bear to influence companies towards granting recognition. Firstly, the right of Irish citizens to form or join trade unions, enshrined under the constitution, is highlighted to incoming companies. A briefing document on industrial relations issued to potential investors states:

> It is the policy of the IDA to require of the firms that it grant aids that they recognise the constitutional right of

workers to be members of trade unions holding negotiating licences to carry on negotiations on behalf of their members.[20]

While highlighting the constitutional position does not make union recognition compulsory or "grant conditional", it sends a strong signal to potential investors of the preferred option. Further evidence for the argument that the IDA supported the granting of recognition rights is provided within the same policy document, which noted that as 75 per cent of workers (hourly paid) in manufacturing industry were unionised (at that time) it "is not realistic" for a manufacturer to successfully maintain a non-union operation. The written statement of support for the concession of union recognition is reinforced in informal interviews with industrialists where the problems of multi-union encroachment (a key potential disadvantage of commencing operations on a non-union basis) were stressed.

The IDA's support for the granting of union recognition is partly explained by the fact that the social partnership status achieved by the trade unions has elevated the movement to an influential position in Irish society. Yet the major influence on the pro-recognition policy almost certainly derived as a consequence of the recognition dispute which occurred at the E.I. Company in Shannon. It marked a watershed in the IDA's stance on union membership at a very early stage in Ireland's industrial development. The dispute largely explains both the IDA's policy in this area and the almost automatic granting of union recognition in pre-employment agreements by incoming companies for many years subsequent. The negative publicity generated (underscored by the fact that a Commission of Inquiry was set up to explore the issues involved) influenced IDA policy in a pro-recognition fashion. Because of the critical importance of this dispute, it is outlined below in some detail. While this dispute may seem like "an-

cient history" now, it seems clear that its influence drove industrial relations policy in the country for a period of over 20 years.

The E.I. Company: The Flagship of the Non-Union Sector

The E.I. Company[21] manufactured radio and electronic components. The company commenced operations in 1962 in the Shannon Industrial Estate. The recognition dispute at the plant was
particularly significant in that G.E. was the first non-union multi-
national company which located in Ireland. Initially employing
about 50 people, by early 1968 approximately 1,200 were on the
books, of whom about 70 per cent were female. From the outset
the E.I. Company operated on a non-union basis. Trade unions
were not formally recognised for the purpose of collective bargaining although employees were free to join a trade union on an
individual basis if they so wished. In mid-1966, the ITGWU
served a claim on the company for revised wages and conditions
for its members. The company refused to enter into negotiations
with the union and thus began the preliminaries to the dispute.

On 30 August 1967, members of the ITGWU in E.I. passed a
resolution which called on their executive council to serve strike
notice on the company in support of the claim issued and because
of the failure of the company to formally recognise the union. After further correspondence between the company and the union,
on 6 October 1967 strike notice was served. The Labour Court in-
tervened and the strike notice was not acted upon. Instead, direct
discussions on the question of recognition took place with representatives from the parent company in the US participating. It was
eventually agreed that a referendum of all employees concerned
(general workers) be held to establish whether they desired to
have the ITGWU accepted as the sole negotiating body. The company agreed that if a majority of employees voted for representation it would grant recognition rights to the ITGWU and that the
union would be recognised as the sole negotiating agent for all

general workers (whether unionised or not). The union accepted this with the proviso that, regardless of the outcome of the referendum, it would continue to represent the interests of union members at E.I.

Prior to the ballot being held, the ITGWU withdrew its acceptance of this position. The union alleged that the company had violated an important part of the conditions to be maintained, that is, that employees could exercise their free choice "in an atmosphere devoid of force, threat or fear".[22] The union's true motives may have been somewhat different. It was suggested that they recognised, at this stage, that the vote would probably go against them thereby decreasing their general level of support.[23] Despite the union's withdrawal a ballot was held on 14 March 1968 (supervised by a firm of chartered accountants) which resulted in a majority decision in favour of the status quo (599 employees voted to continue with the existing arrangement, 404 voted to be represented by the ITGWU).

In the meanwhile, the ITGWU had decided to reactivate the demand for a strike. Formal notice was again served on the company and despite the efforts of the Labour Court to defer the strike pending investigation, a stoppage commenced on 19 March 1968. Thus began one of the most publicised recognition disputes which has ever occurred on Irish soil. The strike continued for over three months during which time a substantial number of employees remained at work. It received significant negative publicity due to the picket line violence (which included the burning of buses taking non-striking employees to work). Without doubt the severity of the strike was in large part due to G.E. deciding to contest the granting of recognition. The union equally took a rigid stance, possibly seeing the loss of the dispute as being the "thin end of the non-union wedge". A return to work finally took place on June 29, a condition of the return being that the then Minister for Labour would appoint a Committee of Inquiry to make a study of the issues raised in the dispute. The report issued had a substantial bearing on the IDA's subsequent policy with regard to advising incoming companies on the question of union recognition.

Appointment of Committee of Inquiry into the E.I. Dispute

In July 1968 a Committee of Inquiry into the E.I. dispute was set up with the following terms of reference:

> To make a study of the issues raised in the recent dispute between the ITGWU and the E.I. Company Ltd., Shannon, and to make recommendations on the procedures which ought to be operated for dealing with representations made by or on behalf of the company's employees in relations to their terms and conditions of employment.

The findings of the Committee of Inquiry were of central importance to the development of the non-union sector. It highlighted that the goal of the E.I. Company to remain non-union was essentially seen as illegitimate in the Irish industrial relations environment at that time.

The company argued against union recognition on the basis that its viability and operating efficiency would be impaired by a union presence. As wage rates were set with regard to the local (unionised) norm, and as the company had "always been sensitive and responsive to the needs of its personnel",[24] there was no need for "third party" intervention. The Committee of Inquiry, in rejecting these arguments, strongly supported the granting of union recognition. Their recommendations, and the underlying philosophy on which they were based, could hardly have been made clearer:

> ... part of the E.I. Company's case is that its employees are not in need of the assistance of a trade union, as the Company itself is at all times solicitous for the welfare of those it employs. We respect the sincerity of the Company in professing this principle, but we do not accept that

benevolence on the part of any employer renders trade union membership superfluous.[25]

The Committee underscored their belief that companies locating in Ireland should operate on a unionised basis:

> . . . we conclude that the E.I.'s Company's policy on trade union recognition is not appropriate to the circumstances of this country. We consider, too, that policy is in conflict with this country's basic concepts of good labour relations and that the Company's refusal, in accordance with policy, to negotiate with the ITGWU on the terms and conditions of employment of the Unions' members in E.I. constitutes a threat to industrial peace in the whole of the Shannon Industrial Estate, if not in the whole country.[26]

Impact of the Findings on the IDA

Given the strength of the recommendations it is not surprising that the case had a profound effect on the policies of the IDA. The findings were all the more important when one considers that the Committee was comprised of two Managing Directors (Martin F. McCourt and Paul Werner) and Con Murphy, the well-known Rights Commissioner, who at that time worked for the Irish Sugar Company. The point here is that there was unlikely to be a trade union bias from such a group. The views expressed reflected those held on *both* sides of the industrial divide (at that time), that within the Irish industrial relations environment there was no alternative to the granting of union recognition. The absolute acceptance of the legitimacy of trade unions is peppered throughout the report:

> The E.I. Company is proud of its success at Shannon and, indeed, justifiably so. But we do not accept that a policy of non-union working was a factor in this success; the implication that trade union intervention is detrimental to

the maintenance of maximum efficiency is not sound. Such a philosophy implies a lack of confidence in the ability or willingness of Trade Unions to act in a responsible fashion. Trade Unions exist to protect their members' interests, not to create situations by which such members may be left jobless.[27]

The Committee's report was also critical of the IDA's role in communicating to industrialists the prevailing industrial relations environment in Ireland:

The IDA recollects that the subject of labour relations was discussed during the preliminary talks which led to the establishing of the E.I. factory. Through some unfortunate breakdown in communications the information did not, apparently, reach those in the General Electric Company directly concerned; had it been otherwise, subsequent distressing events might not have taken place.[28]

They went on to suggest that the IDA should develop a brochure or handbook setting out details of the legal and industrial relations environment in Ireland to be distributed to all potential investors.[29] This indeed did subsequently occur and the document has been quoted earlier (highlighting the fact that the report was taken seriously and acted upon).

As a result of the dispute, and not least as the ITGWU were seen to be the victors, significant negative publicity occurred for the IDA within the United States. As one person described it, the dispute became "disproportionately conspicuous".[30] It upset the promotion of Ireland as a stable industrial relations environment suitable for investment. In terms of policy, what seems to have developed is that the IDA took the stance that Ireland (as a nation hoping to attract investors) could not afford the bad publicity which would attach to another "E.I.-type" dispute. From that point onwards they steered incoming companies towards granting union recognition. The E.I. case was therefore a watershed in influencing the pro-recognition attitude which persisted for a number of years subsequent to the publication of the report. The Committee's findings very clearly unveil the attitudes which prevailed at that time and served to highlight the potential disastrous effects of a policy of fighting recognition, which, given the strength of union opposition, was felt to be futile. Irrespective of whether or not they had a history of unionisation at their parent plants, IDA policy was directed towards convincing companies that they should interview a union and "have them in from the start".[31] The suggestion that incoming multinationals were steered towards granting recognition is given credence by the fact that the vast majority of the more than 700 multinationals which invested in Ireland (up to the publication of the Telesis Report) chose to unionise their workforces.[32] The E.I. dispute, because of its length and the adverse publicity generated, conditioned incoming multinationals that a policy of non-unionism was "unrealistic in the Irish environment".[33]

For a number of years subsequent to the E.I. dispute, few incoming multinational companies risked the establishment of a non-union plant. While it remains conjecture, we can speculate that had the outcome of the E.I. dispute been different, that is, if the committee's report had supported the company in its stance, then the development of the non-union sector would have occurred both earlier and more vigorously. Almost certainly the E.I. case acted as a brake on this development and it is only in comparatively recent years that the non-union sector has become firmly established. It follows that despite assertions that the IDA plays a neutral role on the question of union recognition it was almost certainly the case, until relatively recent times, that the granting of union recognition was strongly supported.

The IDA Stance Today

Pro-union for many years, the IDA stance on the granting of recognition rights in start-up industries can now realistically be described as "neutral". One of the respondents, admitting that his
knowledge of the area was anecdotal, also perceived a change in
emphasis with a movement away from suggesting the automatic
concession of union recognition.[34] Supporting this view, another
respondent argued that there was a general change in the thrust
of IDA policy. They now essentially view trade unions as "back-
ward institutions" that hold policies contrary to the industrial relations scenario which the IDA is attempting to market. While it is
very difficult to quantify this change (and outwardly IDA policy
has remained static) informally the non-union option can now be
highlighted as a realistic alternative. For example, several of the
non-union plants are regularly visited by potential investors on
the advice of the IDA.

The most likely explanation for the policy change is business
pragmatism. The IDA has not reversed its pro-recognition policy
for ideological reasons but has attempted to neutralise as many
constraints as possible in order to attract investment in the face of
increasing foreign competition. As the function of the IDA is to encourage industrialists to locate in Ireland (on the basis of which it is
judged as being either successful or unsuccessful) every attempt
would be made to remove obstacles. The imposition of pre-
conditions, such as the almost automatic granting of union membership, may well have lessened the attractiveness of Ireland to
some industrialists. It is therefore likely that IDA executives attempting to market Ireland as an investment location welcome the
broader range of choice options with regard to unionisation status.
The fact that a relatively stable (and growing) non-union sector can
now be presented "helps the IDA's sales pitch".[35]

ASSISTING INCOMING COMPANIES TO ESTABLISH PERSONNEL POLICY: THE ROLE OF IBEC

As noted earlier, IBEC usually meets incoming industrialists on recommendation from the IDA and offers detailed advice on the Irish business and industrial relations environment. The research attempted to establish the precise role of the employers group in relation to directing personnel policy within these companies and, particularly, their influence in helping companies to decide on a unionised or non-union status.

A strong consensus existed within the respondent group that IBEC[36] historically encouraged companies to grant union recognition where a union was reasonably representative of particular categories of a majority of employees or of all employees. However, companies were likely advised to grant recognition chiefly on the basis that it provided the most stable industrial relations environment. There was no suggestion that IBEC ever supported the granting of union recognition against the better interests of the companies involved. Indeed, given the particular constraints of the Irish industrial relations environment until relatively recent years (and the core IBEC view that the quality of industrial relations is determined more by management attention to human resources than a union or non-union status), the promotion of pre-employment agreements was probably the correct approach. Some of the senior personnel argued that companies decide their own stance on recognition which is then simply supported by IBEC. To some extent this formal response is what would be expected; given the sensitivity of the area it would be difficult to express any other position. However, a strong consensus existed among the remaining respondents that IBEC did play a partisan role in influencing companies towards granting recognition during the 1970s and 1980s.

IBEC Traditionally Supported the Granting of Union Recognition

In advising incoming multinationals IBEC proposed union recognition on grounds similar to those outlined by the IDA. The culture of unionisation among "blue collar" workers, in particular, posed a continuing threat to the stability of non-union operations. Several examples could be cited where recognition was conceded after start-up with the negative consequences of partial or multi-union encroachment. The negotiation of a pre-employment agreement overcame many of the potential problems for incoming companies and also offered a degree of representational choice. A bargaining relationship could be established with a "selected" union rather than the choice of the union lying outside of the company's control.[37] IBEC therefore supported the granting of union recognition as this provided industrial relations stability. In promoting the granting of union recognition, IBEC was likely conditioned by the existing industrial relations system which accorded unions an established role. Indeed, the existence of the trade union movement may be said to provide the *raison d'être* for an employer body. While at times IBEC may seek to limit the power of the unions, it is unlikely to wish to see the movement decimated. One respondent made the point that if there were no trade unions there would not be an IBEC "as we know it".[38]

Apart from recommending recognition on the basis of industrial relations stability, IBEC may also have supported this stance from their business perspective. The reasoning here is not difficult to comprehend: there is arguably less need for the services of IBEC where a company operates on a non-union basis. Advice on the broader area of employee relations was less critical than on industrial relations which needs to be dovetailed to the specific legislative and cultural environment. Incoming companies already have a degree of human resources expertise from their home country of operation. While this may not be completely

"cross cultural", employee relations issues are likely to be somewhat universal. Through the 1990s, the most important aspect of
IBEC's advice therefore related to the specific industrial relations
environment in Ireland, advice which was also tailored to suit the
needs of non-union organisations. It made better business sense
that companies should grant union recognition as they were likely
to become members of the employer body on the basis of achieving ongoing advice. In the 1970s and 1980s membership of IBEC
was "sold" on the basis that companies needed to understand the
subtleties of dealing with Irish trade unions or even the best way
to work with individual officials.

Highlighting the link between union recognition and IBEC
membership, one trade union official maintained that he had organised more members for IBEC (then FUE) in Cork than they
had themselves. Unions were said to be "recruiting agents" for
the employer body.[39] Another agreed, stating that if the non-union
sector became widespread it would have very serious implications for IBEC "in terms of the shillings".[40] Overall there was a
consensus that on business grounds there was no advantage to
IBEC in the growth of the non-union sector. While one respondent
suggested that there may be some "new" business for IBEC (in
advising companies on how to remain non-union) this was a mi-
nority view which received little support.

The fact that a number of the non-union companies initially
remained outside IBEC would seem to give credence to this view.
The point was made that there is somewhat of an ideological dilemma for non-union companies in being members of IBEC, an
employers' organisation. Secondly, it was argued that membership may limit their autonomy in steering an independent policy
course (in particular on wage rates). Finally, on a more pragmatic
basis, the non-union companies, given their own large and qualified human resource departments, simply may not need the services provided.

IBEC Now Encourages Membership by Non-Union Companies

Similar to the earlier points made on the policy change which took place within the IDA, IBEC's stance on the question of union recognition has also undergone a transition. A shift in policy has occurred in recent years as a result of the changing industrial relations environment and the general decline in trade union power. The change in policy has two notable effects. Firstly, IBEC no longer expects member companies to automatically recognise trade unions and is happy to accept into membership those who do not wish to establish a collective bargaining relationship. The overwhelming majority of large and medium-sized non-union companies in Ireland are now members of IBEC. Secondly, the advice given to incoming companies now encompasses the full range of strategic options and is accompanied by a wide range of human resource service support for members. With an established non-union sector it can no longer be held that the non-union route is a "non-runner".[41]

A sub-feature of this policy change is that IBEC can be said to be taking a more proactive stance in the general area of employee relations, assisting companies in making the transition from "industrial relations" to "employee relations". Where historically IBEC may have stressed to companies that they should "cement" their relationship with full-time officials, the current focus in many organisations is towards establishing a more direct relationship with employees. Indeed, IBEC has championed the need for a greater recognition by the state of the legitimacy of the direct employment relationship in the framing of labour regulation and policy. The traditional company/union industrial relations divide was seen to cause a polarity of roles between the industrial relations manager position and that of the full-time official. The thinking now is often to retitle the position "employee relations manager" and switch the primary focus towards internal plant relationships. Through encouraging the non-union companies to become members, IBEC is both shaping and adapting to the changing environment of industrial relations in Ireland.

UNION RECOGNITION: THE SUPPORTIVE ROLE OF THE LABOUR COURT

The Labour Court has played a partisan role in supporting the granting of union recognition rights. Where the question of recognition has come before the Court, it has not been an independent arbitrator but an active supporter of collective bargaining. The pro-recognition orientation of the Court was starkly highlighted in research conducted on Labour Court decisions in union recognition cases. This showed that the Court was in almost all cases supportive of recognition and recommended accordingly.

There should be little surprise that the Labour Court is supportive of union recognition when the background of its officials is considered. These are drawn from the ICTU and IBEC, organisations which are locked into the existing industrial relations structure. Yet the rationale underlying the Labour's Court's stance runs deeper than simple conditioning on the basis of traditionalism. A former Chairman of the Labour Court, and one of the respondents in this research, stated that it is "very clear" that the Court is in favour of collective bargaining and that effective collective bargaining implies the presence of independent trade unions of the members' choice. The Labour Court is therefore not neutral on the question of union recognition. Both the Irish Constitution and the legislation on which the Court was established support a pro-recognition philosophy. If there were now a consensus to change this "they had better update the Act".[42]

An attempt was made to establish whether the level of employee support for recognition was an important criterion for the Court in its deliberations. For example, one view put forward was that the Labour Court independently established if the majority of employees wish to achieve union recognition and, where this is the case, it would normally be granted.[43] However, the notion of "majority" is difficult to quantify and is not a simple 51 per cent. The chairman was quite explicit on the philosophy of the Court in this regard stating that if an individual employee wants to join a union, they can do so. If the union is incapable of getting more than one member out of 100, it bargains with one per cent strength and so on. It is left to the union through its own efforts to improve its power through getting a greater proportion of the potential members.[44] Thus the Labour Court orientation was pro-recognition regardless of the numbers involved. There is no doubt then that the Court has been an active supporter of collective bargaining and companies who wish to establish and maintain non-union plants can derive little comfort from the Court's stated position and previous judgements in this area. While a company may be able to maintain a general consensus among its workforce that they should remain non-union, the likelihood of a 100 per cent consensus on this point makes the non-union status unstable.[45]

Labour Court Criteria for Rejecting Recognition

Given the strength of the pro-recognition stance, it is interesting to investigate the circumstances, if any, in which the Labour Court would reject union recognition. Two specific criteria were outlined: (a) if there is already adequate means for the independent expression of trade unionism, that is, if recognition of an additional union would disrupt the existing industrial relations structure, or (b) if the granting of recognition would fundamentally contradict the aims of the organisation. On the first point the example given was that the Court may rule against the concession of recognition where other unions are already recognized, that is, if employees are seen to have adequate industrial relations machinery already available to them. While the Labour Court has as a central tenet the task of establishing collective bargaining procedures, it also has the objective of supporting good industrial relations practices. The contradiction between the two roles is highlighted when companies, or other unions, argue that the granting of recognition may be disruptive to the industrial relations stability of a firm. Where this is the case, the Court has decided in a number of its judgements to limit recognition to the union(s) already in place. On the second point, the example given was if union recognition were sought by army personnel. This would so undermine the purpose of the organisation (where a single unquestioned authority source is essential to its correct functioning) that the Court would almost certainly recommend against the granting of recognition rights. It is extremely difficult to convince the Court on this second point; the criteria applied were said to be "rigorous".[46] For example, the fact that a management team was strongly opposed to the granting of recognition, or argued that the needs of the business demanded high flexibility, would not provide sufficient weight. The Labour Court has never yet rejected recognition on these grounds.

The Labour Court's stance on the granting of recognition rights is absolutely clear. Without doubt the strong support by the Court on the question of recognition rights (which both the IDA and IBEC are fully aware of) was a further influential factor in steering the majority of incoming multinationals along the union recognition route. The central point is that historically there was almost no support for companies who wished to set up a non-union operation in Ireland. The entire institutional "machinery" (IDA, IBEC, Labour Court) supported the granting of union recognition. In the face of such cohesive support, few companies chose the route of establishing a non-union operation. In the late 1980s I tried to convince my then employer, Sterling Drug, to set-up a non-union facility in Dungarvan, Co. Waterford. Mike Burke, then General Manager, who was a very talented but conservative man, remarked, "I came to Ireland to make Panadol, not history". It was a brave management team indeed who would attempt to break this consensus.

THE NEW WAVE: BREAKING THE MOULD OF
AUTOMATIC UNION RECOGNITION

While the majority of incoming multinationals unionised "blue collar" employees in pre-employment agreements, a core group of non-union manufacturing companies established a foothold in Ireland. The break in the "go union" consensus came in the form of Digital Equipment, Amdahl and Wang Corporation. While initially small in relation to the total multinational group, the significance of these pioneering companies should not be understated. Trade unions held an established place within Irish society with the union movement having a history which predated the foundation of the state itself. In short, Ireland had a culture of unionisation among general and craft workers which was "bone deep". As we have seen, the majority of multinationals locating in Ireland recognised this and, through the establishment of pre-employment agreements, followed the existing pattern. If the situation had remained unchanged, that is, if the influx of some non-union multinationals had not occurred, the likelihood is that the unions would have managed to deepen their overall penetration levels by extending recognition into white collar grades. Indeed, the vertical extension of unionisation into technical, professional and managerial grades did occur in many areas.

Yet the expansion of union penetration was disturbed by a new development: the establishment of large manufacturing plants operating on a completely non-union basis, a radical departure from the norm. Schooled in a different cultural environment, a small group of companies set up non-union plants and broke the mould of automatic union recognition. The possibility of operating on a non-union basis probably found some support within the Irish management circuit. While union avoidance was an imported philosophy it was said to "fall on fertile ground" as many Irish managers had a distaste for trade unions.[47] As the possibility of operating on a non-union basis became a reality, many companies who were ideologically opposed to trade unionism supported this new direction.

Distinguishing between the "Historic" and the "More Recent" Non-Union Sectors

Any analysis of the non-union sector in Ireland needs to distinguish between that which historically existed and the developments which have come about in more recent years. As the level of unionisation has never risen above 50 per cent, it follows that there has always been a large non-union sector in Ireland. However, there are several qualitative differences between the historical non-union sector and the more recent one which the simple membership statistics disguise.

Prior to the influx of multinational companies into Ireland the private sector Irish workforce was fairly readily divisible into two groups, non-union "white collar" and unionised "blue collar" employees. A number of factors combined to ensure that the typical white collar worker (often termed "staff") remained non-union. Firstly, the white collar worker traditionally operated as an individual employee, closely identifying with the employer. Unionisation within white collar grades was partly seen as inappropriate by the employees themselves. In contrast, the attitude towards blue collar workers which prevailed was that "management" and "men" were two distinct groups.[48] White collar workers generally held the belief that they were closer to management and consequently did not identify themselves with the trade union movement. To support the non-union status, a clear gap in pay and conditions was maintained between staff and manual grades. Better pay, sickness benefits, pension rights, job security and shorter hours all marked out a superior social and financial position which, to a degree, obviated the need for unionisation. In order to sustain the divisions between the unionised and non-union groups, companies "looked after" the staff group. In what can be termed a phenomenon of "vertical non-unionism", membership was thus closely linked to work grade — the higher the status of the job the less likely was union membership.

The non-union status of staff was also supported by a general bias by employers against trade unions which was said to be "widespread".[49] Supporting this point, one trade union official related an amusing incident which occurred some years ago at Bantry General Hospital in Cork, where the then ITGWU was attempting to organise hospital workers. During the campaign, a senior nun at the hospital called a meeting of employees and supposedly told them it was a "mortal sin" to join a union.[50] While this particular incident could not be verified, without doubt opposition from employers was traditionally a limiting factor in the growth of white collar union membership levels. As Hawkins notes:

> There is little doubt that in the past the active hostility of employers has, at least in certain industries, proved to be a powerful obstacle to the expansion of union membership.[51]

Because of the inherent bias, from both employers and employees themselves, for many years the unions made little membership headway above the "lower" employee grades. Yet while the unionised blue collar/non-union white collar divide represented the general position, there were exceptions. Draughtsmen were recruited by the AUEW on the Clyde in Belfast as early as 1913 (the union was then known as the Association of Engineering and Shipbuilding Draughtsmen). Although draughtsmen were said to have now become relegated to "run of the mill" technical staff, at that stage they were "high grade labour".[52] Yet such groups were an exception; white collar work in the private sector was almost synonymous with being non-union. While this scenario may have changed somewhat, it is only in comparatively recent times that white collar workers have unionised in large numbers.[53] Changes in job security patterns and the erosion of differentials between blue and white collar grades in recent years partly explains the growth of white collar trade unionism.

The Importance of Industry and Company Size

Two further distinctions can be made between the historical non-union sector and that which has come about in more recent years due to the influx of multinational companies. The first relates to company size. The historical non-union sector was primarily associated with smaller companies (that is, less than 100 employees). In part this reflected the fact that specific industries (for example, retailing) were involved. It also underscores the point that where larger groups of people were employed, the likelihood of union membership was greater.[54] The newer non-union sector differed from its historical counterpart on both of these points. Firstly, many of the more recent non-union plants employed large workforces. The maintenance of a non-union status was no longer confined to small pockets of isolated employees. Secondly, the more recent non-union sector was primarily located within the manufacturing sector, previously the heartland of unionisation. Non-union operations were therefore no longer solely identified with the services sector or small units.

A Two-Tier Structure of Non-Union Companies Always Existed

A final distinction needs to be made in relation to the development of the more recent non-union sector. While the term "non-union" is applied globally to all employments where trade union recognition is not conceded, within this overall grouping two separate types of companies can be differentiated. The first type, what can be termed "bottom tier" non-union companies, operate at the lower end of the labour market, generally paying poor wages and conditions of employment (for example, retail workers in small newsagents). In contrast "upper tier" non-union companies operate at the top end of the labour market paying high levels of wages and conditions of employment (for example, solicitors, accountants).

Bottom-tier non-union companies primarily resist unionisation because of the low wage rates paid. The granting of recognition would likely bring increased labour costs and a decrease in competitiveness.[55] Resistance to unionisation is underpinned by fear that such companies would be driven out of business if their competitive position worsened vis-à-vis non-union employers in the same sector.[56] Unionisation in the bottom tier non-union sector may also be resisted for a second reason — the close association between owners and employees. Many small companies are owner-managed and resistance to union recognition is often based on a personal opposition to trade union "interference" in the decision-making process. In contrast, unionisation in the upper-tier sector is primarily resisted on the basis of limiting a company's "freedom to manage" rather than on any supposed negative impact on wage costs. Employer resistance to unionisation in this sector may also be explained on the basis that higher level employees would normally have access to sensitive information (salary surveys, company profitability figures, etc.) which would increase their bargaining leverage should they become organised.[57]

While the divisions between the upper and lower tiers of the non-union sector may not, in reality, be as clearly defined as outlined above, the central point is that it is not possible to speak of the non-union sector as a single entity, as a homogenous group of employers or employees. Account must be taken of the very different traditions which comprise the total non-union grouping. Both the traditional upper and lower tier non-union sectors must in turn be differentiated from the non-union sector which developed in recent years due to the influx of multinational companies. While the more recent non-union companies essentially fall into the upper tier grouping in relation to wages/conditions of employment, similarities between the two types cease to exist at this point. The non-union status in the historical upper tier sector was maintained primarily due to sociological reasons. As earlier shown, for many years white collar workers did not seek to unionise for reasons of status. Union membership was seen as a working class phenomenon and "inappropriate". The newer non-union sector (in which blue collar employees predominate) does not enjoy the advantage of a "natural" non-union status. This must be maintained by companies through the continuous application of advanced personnel policies. While the non-union sector (in trade union imagery) is most often associated with the bottom tier grouping (that is, the notion of "sweatshop" conditions and exploitation of workers), the companies visited during this research are "excellent employers" by all objective standards.

The core differences between the traditional and the more recent non-union sectors are outlined in Figure 6.

FIGURE 6: DISTINCTION BETWEEN THE TRADITIONAL AND MORE RECENT NON UNION SECTORS	
Traditional	*More Recent*
• Non-union status was based on job grade: "white collar" bias.	• Non-union status irrespective of job grade: blue and white collar.
• Mainly service industry.	• Manufacturing and service industries.
• Smaller companies (< 100).	• No size limitations.
• Upper tier/lower tier divide.	• Good conditions apply to all employees.
• "Sophisticated" HRM practices were under developed (albeit some company had paternalistic HR cultures).	• Can either follow "sophisticated" HRM practices (e.g. involvement) or "harder" HRM practices (e.g. outsourcing).

In summary, the traditional labour market/unionisation profile in Ireland has changed markedly in recent years. Irish industry can

no longer be simply divided into a unionised and a non-union sector along "job grade" lines. While historically this may have been
the case, the employment of hourly paid workers on a non-union
basis, and the extension of trade unionism into white collar, professional and managerial grades, has meant a substantial blurring
of the traditional union/non-union divide. Figure 7 captures the
points detailed above. It provides a categorisation of the labour
force unionisation profile and highlights changes in union membership levels which have taken place within the various sectors.

FIGURE 7: UNIONISATION PROFILE/MEMBERSHIP TRENDS OF THE IRISH LABOUR FORCE				
Sec-tor	Sub-section	Employee/ Company Profile	Conditions of Employ-ment	Union Membership Trends
N O N U N I O N	**Group A**			
	"Upper Tier" Non-Union	Higher status/level employees in all companies i.e. "lateral non-unionism".	High pay rates and conditions of em-ployment.	Growth as socio-logical and organ-isational changes favour white-collar unionisation. Movement to a ser-vice based economy also influential. As the number of jobs in this sector in-creases, unionisa-tion becomes more likely.
	Group B			
	"Upper Tier" Non-Union	All employees in the multina-tional non-union compa-nies i.e. "verti-cal non-unionism".	High pay rates and conditions of em-ployment.	The steady growth of the non-union multinational sector has meant a decline in union penetration levels.

Group C			
"Bottom Tier" Non-Union	Tends to be confined to particular industries e.g. retail, clothing, footwear. Often small companies. All grades of employees.	Typically poor wage rates and conditions of employment.	Service sector likely to grow as the economy develops. Net effect equals falling union membership levels.
Group D			
"Partially" Unionised Companies	All company types: membership most often associated with blue collar workers i.e. "lateral unionisation". White collar workers comprise an increasing percentage of this group.	Mixed – from poor to good.	Falling union membership levels (blue collar) due to redundancy (close-downs of "smoke stack" industries) and increasing use of labour saving technology. Some growth as the unions penetrate into white collar areas.
Group E			
Fully Unionised Companies	Some public sector areas and limited number of companies operating closed shop agreements, e.g. craft contractors.	Mixed – from poor to good.	Penetration percentage stable in the public sector. Private sector: Closed shop agreements becoming very unusual.

(Left vertical label spanning Groups D and E: **UNIONISED**)

Endnotes

---

[1] Williams, Bruce. "Living with Technology". Boyer Lectures, the Australian Broadcasting Commission, Sydney, Australia. 1982.

[2] Cogan, D.J. and O'Brian, Ronan. "The Irish Electronics Sector: Technical Manpower as an Indicator of Structure and Sophistication". *IBAR Journal of Irish Business and Administrative Research,* Vol. 5, No. 1, April 1983: 3.

[3] Kennedy, Fintan. "Multi-National Companies and Conglomerates: The Problems for Trade Unions". From: "1968 Dispute between the I.T.G.W.U. and the E.I. Company Limited, Shannon". Commission of Enquiry Report, Stationary Office, Government Publications, April 1969: 3.

[4] Bergman, L. "Multi-National Corporations and Labour in the E.E.C: A Survey of Research and Development." *International Institute of Labour Studies,* 1973; McCrea, N. "Report on Research Finding Relating to Great Britain", *International Institute for Labour Studies,* 1973; Stopford, J.M. "Employment Effects of Multi-National Enterprises in the U.K.". *ILO Working Paper No. 5* Geneva, 1979; Liebhaerg, B .*Industrial Relations and MNCs in Europe.* Gower. UK, 1980; Kelly, Aidan and Brannick, Teresa. "Industrial Relations Practices in Multi-National Companies in Ireland". *IBAR Journal of Irish Business and Research* Vol. 7, No. 1, Spring, 1985.

[5] Kneafsey, Patrick. President of Fulflex International. Quoted in *Management,* Irish Management Institute, Dublin, May, 1983.

[6] Mooney, Paul. "The Development of Pre-Employment Agreements in Irish Industrial Relations". Unpublished postgraduate dissertation submitted in fulfilment of a Diploma in Industrial Relations, Trinity College Dublin, 1984.

[7] "Trade Union Official A". Points made during interview with author.

[8] "Trade Union Official B". Points made during interview with author.

[9] Hawkins, Kevin. *The Management of Industrial Relations.* Penguin, UK, 1979; Department of Employment, "Industrial Relations Procedures", Manpower Papers, HMSO, London, 1975: 514.

[10] "Industrial Relations Expert B". Former IBEC official, now retired.

[11] Miljus, J., Professor of Organisational Behaviour, Ohio State University, 1986, in conversation with author.

[12] Mills, C. Wright. *White Collar*. Oxford University Press, New York, 1958: 308.

[13] Fox, Alan. *Man Mismanagement*. Hutchison, London, 1974: 20.

[14] On several occasions I have worked with companies trying to maintain a non-union status, who've constructed Labour Court submissions which would "make James Joyce proud" in terms of writing standards. The outcome is easy to predict, regardless of the merits of the particular arguments made. The Court has shown a consistent bias in favour of granting union recognition (see later detailed point on this).

[15] "Trade Union Official C". Points made during interview with author.

[16] "Trade Union Official C". Points made during interview with author.

[17] Heenan, D.A. *Multi-National Organisation Development: A Social Architectural Perspective*. Addison-Wesley, 1979.

[18] Mooney, Paul. "The Development of Pre-Employment Agreements in Irish Industrial Relations". Unpublished postgraduate dissertation submitted in Fulfilment of a Diploma in Industrial Relations. Trinity College Dublin, 1984: 75/76.

[19] Walsh, John, IDA Executive. From: "1968 Dispute between the I.T.G.W.U. and the E.I. Company Limited, Shannon". Commission of Enquiry Report, Stationary Office, Government Publications, April 1969: 45.

[20] Industrial Development Authority, "Guide to Irish Industrial Relations" Industrial Development Authority, Dublin 1980: 3.

[21] The E.I Company is a wholly owned subsidiary of the American conglomerate General Electric. It was the first G.E. company to commence operations in Ireland. Since that time several other G.E. businesses commenced operations in Ireland. E.C.C.O. in Dundalk (1971) Atlantic Plant Construction in Bray (1974), G.E.I.S.C.O. in Dublin (1976), Speciality Materials Ireland in Dublin (1981), etc. It is not a coincidence that all of the G.E. manufacturing plants which located in Ireland, subsequent to the E.I. dispute, negotiated pre-employment agreements for their hourly paid workforces rather than attempt to operate on a non-union basis.

The dispute had the effect of sending a signal to this and other multi-national companies that the non-union mode of operation was particularly difficult to support in the Irish environment. In contrast, several of the "newer" (post-1990s) G.E. businesses are non-union which reflects the changing marketplace.

[23] Mangan, Tom, former G.E. employee, in conversation with author.

[25] Committee of Inquiry 1968: 17 (33) "1968 Dispute between the I.T.G.W.U. and the E.I. Company Limited, Shannon". Commission of Enquiry Report, Stationary Office, Government Publications, April 1969.

[26] Ibid: 22 (54).

[27] Ibid: 15 (28).

[28] Ibid: 15 (36).

[29] Ibid: 15 (18).

[30] McCann, J.J. "The "New" Industrial Relations Arena of Human Resource Management — Union–Non-Union" *Industrial Relations News Report* 1988: 15.

[31] "Trade Union Official F". Points made during interview with author.

[32] Bell, R.M. "The Behaviour of Labour, Technical Change, and the Competitive Weakness of British Manufacturing". A report prepared for the Technical Change Centre, England, 1983: 19.

[33] "Trade Union Official E". Points made during interview with author.

[34] "Trade Union Official G". Points made during interview with author.

[35] "Trade Union Official E". Points made during interview with author.

[36] Previously the organisation was called FUE (Federated Union of Employers) which changed to the Federation of Irish Employers (FIE) in 1989. In 1993 the FIE merged with the Confederation of Irish Industry to form IBEC (Irish Business and Employers Confederation).

[37] This may be somewhat of a misnomer as it pre-supposes that the conduct of union members can be directed by the union officialdom, suggesting a degree of control over the membership which may have little practical reality. In reviewing industrial relations within the ESB in what has now become something of an industrial relations case study classic,

Fogarty et al. stated, "We have heard a number of times in our evidence the phrase, 'the unions must bring their members under control'. Unions, as we have said, do not control their members in the sense in which managers control their subordinates. Union members owe loyalty to the rules of their club, both as a matter of solidarity and responsibility for the welfare of others and in their own long-term self interest. For without loyalty to a union constitution and procedures effective long-term action through the union becomes impossible. But whereas the manager has behind him the authority of a job to be done, the customer comes first, in a union the members feel something of a customer's freedom in relation to their officials."

[38] "Trade Union Official C". Points made during interview with author.

[39] "Trade Union Official A". Points made during interview with author.

[40] "Trade Union Official C". Points made during interview with author.

[41] "Industrial Relations Expert B". Points made during interview with author.

[42] "Industrial Relations Expert C". Points made during interview with author.

[43] "Industrial Relations Expert D". Points made during interview with author.

[44] "Industrial Relations Expert C". Points made during interview with author.

[45] It should be recognised that the Court's recommendations do not have any legal standing except in certain very specific circumstances. It follows that where the Court supports the granting of recognition rights, a company has the option to ignore this. Nonetheless the point remains that the Court's general pro-union bias poses a continuing risk to a non-union strategy (as a positive recommendation lends strong moral support to a union campaign for recognition). See detailed points on the changing legislative environment covered elsewhere.

[46] "Industrial Relations Expert C". Points made during interview with author.

[47] Personnel Manager: Company E. Points made during interview with author.

[48] "Trade Union Official E". Points made during interview with author.

[49] "Trade Union Official B". Points made during interview with author.

[50] "Trade Union Official A". Points made during interview with author.

[51] Hawkins, *Trade Unions*. Hutchison and Company, London, 1981: 95.

[52] "Trade Union Official E". Points made during interview with author.

[53] Kelly, Aidan. "The Effects of Personal Characteristics on the Process of Unionisation among White Collar Employees". *IBAR Journal of Irish Business and Administrative Research*. Vol. 2, No. 2, October 1980, pp. 78-84.

[54] Bain, George Sayers. *The Growth of White-Collar Unionism*. Oxford University Press, 1970.

[55] "Industrial Relations Expert A". Points made during interview with author.

[56] "Industrial Relations Expert D". Points made during interview with author.

[57] "Industrial Relations Expert C". Points made during interview with author.

6

ADVANTAGES/DISADVANTAGES FOR COMPANIES OPERATING ON A NON-UNION BASIS

"A non-union workforce is flexible, innovative and responsive. Therefore it is less costly and more productive. Being non-union offers us a major competitive advantage."
— Non-Union Company Briefing Document for Executives

WHILE THE RESEARCH WAS CONDUCTED across a divergent group in terms of company age, size and technology employed, the answers given under the heading of the advantages/disadvantages for companies operating on a non-union basis were remarkably consistent. A consensus on the following points existed within the companies surveyed.

THE FIRST ADVANTAGE: LABOUR/OPERATIONAL FLEXIBILITY

The single most important advantage in operating on a non-union basis was seen to be operational and labour flexibility. This includes individual labour mobility (employees in IBM jokingly insist that this stands for I've Been Moved)[1] and a lack of demarcation between work groups. The fact that method and process changes do not have to be continually negotiated with a union allows companies to respond quickly to changing market conditions. While a good degree of time is invested in the non-union sector in communicating organisation/process changes to employees, the potential disruption where unions challenge or disagree with specific initiatives is by-passed. Changes can therefore normally be accommodated very quickly. Non-union companies enjoy a high degree of operational flexibility or what can simply be termed "freedom to manage". One trade union respondent, agreeing that such flexibility existed, stated that "unfettered freedom" formed the mainstay in the ideology of non-union companies. As Foulkes notes:

> When a company has to deal with union representatives rather than directly with its employees as individuals, it needs to be much more careful and consistent in its actions and in how it develops policies. Its actions will be scrutinised and subject to review, its discretion limited by a contract.[2]

While all organisations require some degree of labour and operational flexibility, this is seen as a fundamental requirement in a high technology environment. Indeed, the expenditure and effort in maintaining a non-union status (see later points) is partly justified by the achievement of maximum flexibility in the utilisation of people and equipment. Unionisation is seen to lead to inflexibility in direct contradiction to the operational requirements of companies in this sector.

The Practical Implications of Labour Flexibility

Flexibility of labour, in practical terms, means the mobility of employees within different sections of a plant with no demarcation between grades except on the basis of job competence. It may be as simple as "asking someone to do a bit of cleaning and tidying around the place" or it may extend to areas like production operatives doing machine repairs, helping with photocopying if the office staff are busy and so on. The example below from the United Kingdom highlights this point.

When Nissan concluded an agreement to build Japanese cars in England, it signed an agreement with one union, the AUEW, to cover the entire unionised workforce. Speaking with the personnel manager about flexibility in a Japanese context, one foreman stated that when a maintenance man needs assistance then "obviously" the operators will help him as they know more about the job than anyone else. In contrast under the traditional model of industrial relations a maintenance man would regard it as an erosion of his skills if an "unskilled" worker was able to contribute to a technical problem. Further, the unskilled man will often regard the breakdown as an opportunity to rest and not a chance to "work on wall charts, paint the railings, write a process note or help maintenance".[3]

The situation outlined above is comparable with industrial relations practices in Ireland. Most unionised companies experience, to a greater or lesser extent, demarcations between work grades which are supported by the unions. Operating on a non-union basis offers one route to overcome this. For example, in one of the non-union companies visited during this research the personnel executive had just spent two weeks on the shop floor packing finished goods to meet an end-of-quarter target. In a unionised environment it is highly unlikely if this could have been done as work normally completed by union members is jealously guarded on the basis of maintaining job security.[4] Indeed, given the rigidity of roles under the traditional model, it is unlikely if a member of the personnel department *would* do such work, even if it were possible. Operating on a non-union basis provides the opportunity to lower the "traditional" barriers between work grades. Criticism was levelled against the unions on this basis, that is, their focus on the status quo often causes them to "miss the woods for the trees" with job enrichment opportunities being lost to employees.[5] Yet the core objection to the traditional rigidity of roles was that companies become hidebound and cannot compete effectively against international competition. Inflexible work practices sound the death knell for companies in an environment where "the only certainty is constant change".[6]

The Trade Union View: Labour Flexibility Disadvantages Employees

While the argument that operating on a non-union basis maximises labour flexibility was accepted by most of the union respondents, the point was made that this in turn disadvantages employees. Flexibility of operations is viewed by some as "a licence to exploit workers".[7] Within the non-union sector, no bargaining or negotiation rights exist and employees do not benefit from the productivity gains which result from efficiencies achieved.[8] A further objection to flexibility hinged on the fact that employees in the non-union sector were outside the decision-making process in that they did not have the opportunity to challenge particular changes. The concept of a "divine right to manage" struck a raw nerve with many of the trade union officials interviewed. Flexibility was seen as a euphemism for unilateral management control.

Yet these observations decry rather than deny the fact that operating on a non-union basis allows a greater degree of flexibility for organisations. In contrast, some of the respondents challenged the core view that flexibility is related in any way to a unionised or non-union status. One view was that the argument is "poppycock", particularly in relation to white collar employees who were stated to be totally flexible, mobile and interchangeable. They themselves try to avoid stagnation by "moving around the system".[9] Another respondent put the case a little stronger, stating that the higher level of flexibility in the non-union sector argument is "crap" and that good management practices can determine any level of flexibility within reasonable parameters.[10] The higher level of flexibility which can supposedly be achieved in the non-union sector is therefore put forward as a "smokescreen" for an anti-union stance by companies and is used to justify unilateral management control. To support this, the point was made that flexibility of operations features strongly in the unionised sector.

While the operational flexibility of the non-union companies was widely recognised, whether this is markedly superior to that which exists in the unionised sector is a moot point. Typically flexibility clauses are inserted in union/management agreements to cater for this. These can be quite elaborate as can be seen from the example shown below.

Flexibility Clause in a Union/Management Agreement[11]

It is agreed by the signatories in this Agreement, that flexibility of Labour is fundamental to the continuing progress of the company. Employees are expected to adopt a positive attitude to establishing a co-operative working environment. Therefore, it is a condition of employment that there will be genuine co-operation and maximum flexibility among employees within the craft areas, and also among employees within the non-craft areas.

The company depends upon product and process innovation for its continued success. Accordingly change is an ongoing feature of the business. This will include the introduction of new technology, manufacturing methods, processes and equipment.

It is company policy, where possible, to rotate all team members through the various group tasks both for business purposes and to provide maximum opportunity for job enrichment. This will occur in two ways.

A   Rotation through all the tasks in a defined work area.

B   Rotation through work areas.

The Company cannot guarantee that an employee will remain on the work, or in the area where first engaged. The Company reserves, at its absolute discretion, the right to select, determine or amend the number of employees necessary to carry out the business of the Company in an efficient manner.

Given the scope of flexibility clauses in union/management agreements (similar to that outlined above) it can be argued that the notion of greater flexibility within the non-union sector is overstated. The decision to operate on a non-union basis is fundamentally ideological but is given a commercial rationale for the purpose of outward respectability. In my own experience it is certainly true that the non-union companies are "anti-union", in the sense that they do not wish a union presence. However, the issue of flexibility cannot be written off so easily. Flexibility of operations ranked as the number one advantage at all of the non-union companies visited (a view which also received support from personnel respondents within the unionised plants). Further, the degree of labour and organisation flexibility achieved at the non-union plants visited during the research was, in my experience, far superior to that which generally exists within the unionised sector. However, the pivotal question of whether this follows from the fact that the companies operate on a non-union basis or is an outcome of the quality of the management/employee relationship remains open.

Does the "Quality of Management" Explain the Level of Flexibility Achieved?

Within the high tech sector a heavy demand is placed on the ability of companies to respond to rapidly changing market conditions. Flexibility of labour is therefore a critical factor in enabling companies to survive in this environment. Yet the marketplace environment does not, of itself, provide the explanation for the levels of flexibility achieved. Many unionised companies operate in similar volatile environments and have not, on the whole, been able to achieve the same degree of flexibility. In attempting to understand the key difference between unionised and non-union companies, the question is whether it is the absence of trade union organisation or a difference in the quality of "people management" practices which provides the answer. Despite attempts to have well defined agreements, a high degree of flexibility derives more from the quality of the management/employee relationship than all encompassing clauses. In short, it is not possible to "legislate" for flexibility. It is dependent on the degree of mutual trust and co-operation within an organisation. Industrial relations agreements simply set the parameters for this relationship and, in many cases, the maximum standard which can be achieved. Their practical application is heavily dependent on the goodwill to support them.

During earlier research conducted,[12] a divisional director of IBEC supported the point that it is the degree to which flexibility of operations is pursued by companies which determines the level achieved, rather than a union or non-union status per se. In essence this mirrors a broader point running throughout the book, that is, when the union/non-union debate is stripped away the quality of people management is the key explanatory factor in the climate (including the degree of flexibility) achieved at individual plants. It follows that organisational flexibility can indeed be achieved in a progressive unionised environment, and some unionised companies exhibit levels of flexibility which makes them "indistinguishable from non-union companies".[13] However, such examples remain notable exceptions. The adversarial nature of the role of trade unions limits the concept of mutuality within the employment relationship. The absence of a fundamental degree of trust between companies and unions (which characterises the traditional model) ensures that the debate on organisational flexibility often takes place in a climate of hostility. It follows that while the quality of management is the key factor in the achievement of a positive employment relationship, in relation to flexibility the absence of a trade union is hugely helpful, allowing a greater degree of unilateral control.

It is not simply that one practice, demarcation, has been slackened. Under the non-union model the very notion of management and employees as protagonists has been blurred. The non-union companies establish an environment in which the joint interests of the company and employees is continuously stressed — with employees' energy focused on the external environment rather than being absorbed in internal conflict. The non-union companies provide good benefits/conditions and job security for employees in return for a high degree of commitment to the organisation. The resulting flexibility of labour is seen as the primary advantage for companies operating on a non-union basis.

THE SECOND ADVANTAGE:
DIRECT COMMUNICATION/PROBLEM SOLVING
WITH EMPLOYEES

The second advantage in operating on a non-union basis is the ability to communicate directly with employees. "We don't use unions as our communications vehicle" was a common view expressed. The primacy of the management team in the area of problem solving (in the absence of a trade union) further strengthens the bond between the non-union companies and employees. For example, Flood and Toner concluded that the major advantages of union substitution lie not in clear economic "cost-benefit" criteria, but in allowing an organisation scope to develop a unitary company culture which fosters "warm personnel relations" between management and employees.[14]

A strong emphasis on communications featured at all the non-union plants visited and many structures had evolved to give it substance. A striking feature was that communications were formally planned. While there was some diversity in the actual methods employed, the concepts of openness and "employee voice" (in the sense of employees being able to comment on decisions taken) ran throughout the sector. Efforts made in the communications area were justified by the benefits which follow, that is, the achievement of output and productivity targets, less resistance to technological change and employee involvement in the resolution of business problems. While the link between effective communications with employees and productivity is by no means straightforward, a number of companies pointed to their successful business track record as evidence that a policy on employee communications and involvement spills over into business success.

Direct communications with the workforce has three particular benefits. Firstly, a strong communications link is seen as an essential part of the "motivational package". Employees cannot direct efforts towards an unmarked goal. Effective communication ensures that the goals of the business are made tangible to the workforce, highlighting how the IR efforts support business goals. Communications helps to make global statements on cost or productivity tangible by highlighting concrete examples of what can be done by individual employees. For example, one company had experienced a major problem in relation to product quality. Through specific communication efforts, the workforce understood the problem and became involved in efforts to overcome it. In just over two months a problem which had "dogged production for four years" was resolved.[15] While the view that involvement often leads to commitment is hardly revolutionary, the surprising fact is that so few companies manage to put it into operation.

An additional point put forward was that communications is a two-way process with information also being fed upwards by employees. A general view expressed within the non-union sector was that the management team does not have a monopoly on innovation or problem-solving ideas. Employees were viewed as a rich resource in cost reduction, method improvement, product development and so on. By establishing an open two-way communications process this resource can be "tapped into". This contrasts starkly with the view of employees and the mode of operation under the traditional model where problem solving and solution implementation are largely divorced entities. As one employee working in the food industry in the UK noted, "I make more decisions driving to work than I ever do once I get there".[16]

The third stated benefit of effective communications systems was that they provide a channel to tap into the mood of a workforce, ensuring that the negative potential of employees' dissatisfactions can be "headed off at the pass".[17] An ability to tap into the organisational grapevine is seen as a key problem-solving device which, in the non-union sector, has the additional benefit of highlighting potential unionisation issues. A range of individual methods has evolved to give this substance. Overall, good communications/problem-solving systems were seen as central pillars. A non-union status virtually forces management into direct communication with the workforce as otherwise a vacuum develops which can quickly be filled by a union. Through attention to detail in both communications and problem solving, a bond of trust develops in which "the non-union status is deepened".[18]

Most of the above stated benefits of effective communications could, in theory, apply equally well in a unionised environment. The question remains why, in a general sense, the efforts made in the non-union sector are markedly superior in this regard. The key explanatory factor seems to be the divergence in underlying philosophies between unionised and non-union companies. The efforts made in the non-union sector reinforce the point that effective people management is an issue of key concern to companies which understand the importance of a highly committed workforce. Yet, similar to the points made under the heading of flexibility, the very presence of a union may act as a stumbling block to direct communications with employees. An extreme example is where employees will not attend formal company communications sessions on instruction from the union because a particular issue is deemed *subjudice*.[19] However, a union presence may negatively impact the direct communications/problem-solving process in other, less obvious, ways.

The Presence of a Union Impedes Communications and Problem Solving

The presence of a union often impedes communications and the direct bond between a company and its employees. Several points can be put forward to support this assertion. Firstly, shop stewards often interfere with the direct company/employee relationship. Where a problem occurs at the workplace, employees are normally expected (under standard industrial relations procedures) to initially address the issue with their direct supervisor. If the relationship with the supervisor is poor, employees may be inclined toward discussing the problem with a shop steward. Where this occurs the role of the stewards is buttressed at the expense of the supervisory group who, over time, can become "bypassed". The level at which concessions are made in the problem-solving chain is thus an important factor. Where grievances are resolved in the later stages of procedure (when the union has become involved) this signals to employees that issues are best taken beyond the supervisory group to the stewards who have more "clout". Companies who, as a policy, do not concede issues until they have become formalised, in effect, steer all grievances into the collective bargaining forum, decreasing the role of supervisors in problem resolution.

Companies reinforce the role of shop stewards in other ways. For example, in communicating the outcome of negotiations or organisational changes through the union group (in advance of informing supervisors) the role of the stewards is again bolstered. While this point may seem rudimentary, few companies put the necessary effort into involving the supervisory group in industrial relations issues to ensure that they feel part of the management team. A further point is that supervisors, by the nature of their role, are involved in balancing both production and employees needs. Personnel issues take their place alongside a myriad of production-related problems in some priority ranking. Organisations, although often stating that employee relations/communications is an important function for supervisors, often solely measure the production aspect of their work (partly because this is more tangible). Companies which stress employee relations twice per year and production quotas twice per shift sow the seed of increased union power by pushing the supervisory group to prioritise "production" problems. In the words of John Powell, "sometimes what you do is ringing so loudly in my ears that I cannot hear what you say".[20]

A sub-point under this heading is that shop stewards are voluntarily elected while supervisors carry out problem solving essentially on a "conscript" basis. While the resolution of employee relations issues provide the raison d'être for shop stewards, it can be argued that many supervisors view employee relations problems as additional or ancillary work. Further, the fact that stewards usually need to be re-elected may provide a greater motivation toward resolving employee's problems. In contrast, supervisors are not dependent on an elected status and do not always believe that efforts to establish a positive industrial relations climate is a useful investment of their time.

The final point which arises in relation to the unions' role in communications/problem solving was that shop stewards may be more inclined than supervisors to involve themselves in problem solving due to the nature of their work. The pursuit of grievances may provide a diversion from the normal work, a break from routine. This is not to argue that every shop steward performs boring work or willingly takes on industrial relations problems. Neither is it suggested that all supervisory work is so interesting that diversions would not be welcomed. However, in the main, supervisors are likely to have a number of competing job responsibilities while the steward will normally have fewer and this assertion is "directionally correct".

Given the above it is little wonder that shop stewards often become a key link in the communications/problem-solving chain.

The central point is that the seeds of loyalty with a union are often inadvertently sown by organisations themselves. Companies, if they wish to retain the position of the supervisory group as the primary communications/problem-solving vehicle for employees, need to be acutely aware of these factors. Where a company "hands over" this process to a union (by communicating with employees through shop stewards or concession of issues solely through the collective bargaining forum), a shift in loyalty is the likely outcome. Operating on a non-union basis avoids these potential pitfalls. While a union presence need not *necessarily* mean that a shift in loyalty toward the union occurs, inattention to this critical area and the divergence in traditional shop steward versus supervisory roles often leads to this.

THE THIRD ADVANTAGE:
AUTHORITY ACCEPTANCE

The third advantage for companies operating on a non-union basis can be labelled authority acceptance. For example, in relation to unionisation among while collar grades, Bain has noted that "the most general fear is that ultimately staff unionism will restrict management's freedom to make decisions".[21]

As already highlighted, employees in the non-union sector do not have split loyalties to an alternative authority source. They tend to more readily accept direction given by the employer. The human resource respondents argued that the greater degree of authority acceptance does not indicate that the non-union companies are dictatorial, pointing to their efforts in the involvement/participation area. Authority is primarily accepted on the basis that a mutuality of interests in the employment relationship exists, a point continually stressed by the non-union companies and accepted by employees. Once the basic premise of a mutuality of interests is accepted, there is little dilemma for employees in accepting the legitimacy of managerial authority. A profitable busi-

ness was seen to provide good employment conditions and job
security. This is an "instrumental" view of the employment relationship. It focuses on the "deal" — whether this is good or bad.
Notions such as "unequal power relationships" are seen as the
domain of sociologists or political scientists, disconnected from
the day-to-day concerns of most employees.

Stressing the Mutuality of the Employment Relationship

Under the traditional model of industrial relations, where the parties view their interests as being divergent, tremendous potential
for conflict exists. The non-acceptance of managerial authority (to
determine manning levels, to implement change and so on) can
lead to endless conflict and debate when the legitimacy of managerial authority is challenged by employees. In contrast, non-
union companies experience fewer problems in the area of authority acceptance. They are generally more successful in promoting
the mutuality (win/win) argument. Authority acceptance follows
both from the greater efforts made by the non-union companies to
gain the willing compliance of employees *and* from the absence of
a countervailing authority source, a trade union.

A key point raised by the union respondents under this heading was that this simply represents an outward show of participation to mask the fact that employees have little actual control.
Flanders' comment that management "may only be able to regain
control by sharing it"[22] captures the essence of this argument. Yet
the non-union companies certainly create the perception that a
greater degree of participation exists than is the case in the unionised sector.[23] This follows from the beliefs highlighted that involvement of employees in particular changes both allows an easier passage and often results in a better overall decision. Regardless of the underlying motivation, the net effect of such efforts is
that managerial authority is more readily accepted.

THE FOURTH ADVANTAGE:
A DECREASE IN LEVELS OF CONFLICT

The fourth benefit for companies operating on a non-union basis follows directly from the greater acceptance of managerial authority noted above: where this exists a decrease in the levels of conflict at the workplace is a usual corollary. Under this heading, the absence of a trade union (as distinct from the employee relations practices of the companies), may lead to a decrease in the level of conflict experienced. Why? In simple terms, the goals of unions and companies are divergent. The traditional model of industrial relations is underpinned by this divergence of interests which the very presence of a union signifies. A union is a service organisation and must be seen, in the eyes of its members, to provide some quantifiable benefits to justify the subscriptions paid. The most tangible way to do this is to be seen to make gains at the expense of the employer. A union which did not provide such a service would not maintain credibility with its members. Unionised companies therefore have increased potential for friction at the workplace due to the very nature of the role conflict which characterises unions versus employers.

Where the union as an oppositionary force is removed from the equation, it decreases the level of conflict. However, this does not imply that conflict is eliminated in the non-union sector. One personnel respondent used an analogy with marriage. Where two people live under the same roof, supposedly with the same interests, conflict cannot be totally eliminated. With several hundred people under one "roof" the ideal of a conflict-free relationship remains nirvana.[24] Yet even where conflict does arise, non-union companies are better able to resolve issues in their favour due to the absence of an effective oppositionary force. A sub-benefit for companies operating on a non-union basis is a decrease in the level of *effective* opposition, allowing them more control over the outcome of particular disagreements.

Positive Relationships: The Management Team is the Primary Driver

To support the point that the quality of management was more important than a unionised or non-union status, reference can be made to the degree of influence which the management team controls in the overall employment relationship. Most unions operate in a reactive mode, responding to company initiatives. Companies therefore have a much greater degree of proactive control in the area of employee relations should they choose to utilise it. It is when they "hand over" the employee relations role to the unions that they begin to experience negative industrial relations.[25] This point is fundamentally important. As noted before, when the union/non-union debate is stripped away, what clearly emerges is that the ability of the management team and their commitment to effective people management is a key explanatory factor in the creation of a positive or negative industrial relations climate. While the influence of unions cannot be discounted, it may be somewhat less significant than is generally supposed.

This finding has both positive and negative implications for organisations. On the plus side it lends support to the view that a company's own employee relations philosophy is the primary determinant of the industrial relations climate achieved. Yet it effectively disallows the argument (for companies who have experienced poor industrial relations) that the "blame" for this lies at the door of the unions. Those companies which have in the past continually emphasised the negative influence of trade unions may have partly been scapegoating, using the phenomenon termed displacement by psychologists where weakness in oneself is rationalised as a weakness in some other person or institution.[26] However, while the primacy of the management team is accepted, the relatively small number of unionised companies which are noted for positive employee relations begs the question why many more do not achieve excellence in this area? Are we to believe that all the "good managers" are employed in the non-union sector? Hardly. Yet unionised companies which exhibit the key characteristics of organisational flexibility and low conflict remain a notable exception. On the surface this would seem to support the point that a union presence, of itself, it a negative influence on industrial relations. However, a better explanation is provided when the core philosophies of most unionised companies with regard to employee relations is examined in depth.

Disinterest in employee relations, a lack of understanding of the importance of people in the productive process or a lack of skills to implement a positive strategy often underpins conflict. The non-union companies do not enjoy the luxury of inattention to employee relations (if they wish to remain non-union). Good human resource management practices are therefore *forced* on these companies if they wish to maintain their status. In a sense then, some of the non-union companies can be said to "do the right thing" (focusing on employee relations) for the "wrong reason" (union avoidance). All other things being equal, where unionised companies support the core concepts of the high commitment organisation it is possible to achieve a broadly similar outcome. Given the above it is possible to classify "good"[27] and "poor" industrial relations climates as opposite ends of a continuum along which both unionised and non-union companies can be located. What seems to be the case is that while operating on a non-union basis offers the best possibility for the achievement of positive industrial relations (due to the absence of a trade union presence), the better-managed unionised companies overlap with these. This concept is expressed diagrammatically in Figure 8.

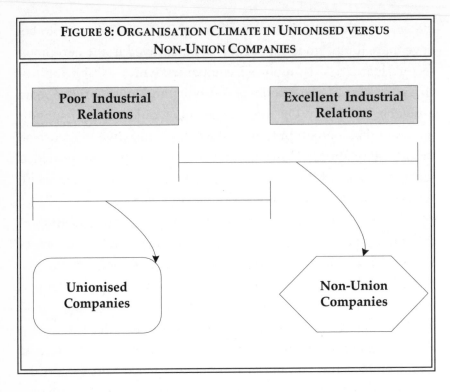

FIGURE 8: ORGANISATION CLIMATE IN UNIONISED VERSUS NON-UNION COMPANIES

It follows that many of the supposed benefits of operating on a non-union basis can also be achieved in a unionised environment. In some companies this indeed is the case with the personnel policies pursued and organisational climate being almost identical to that found within the non-union sector. For example, Analog Devices in Limerick was historically so well respected within personnel circles that it is often mistakenly classified as a non-union company. Glaxo Smithkline in Dungarvan is another example and many more could be cited. Once again, what clearly emerges from the research is that management style, commitment and skill in dealing with employee relations (whether in a unionised or non-union environment) is the key underlying factor in the development of a positive organisational climate at individual plants.

Does Unionisation Encourage Procedural Formality?

Some industrial relations observers equate operating on a non–union basis with a lack of procedural formality. As unionisation formalises the employment relationship this is a major benefit of conceding recognition. As Hawkins notes:

> The experienced manager hardly needs to be reminded of the vital contribution which an effective framework of procedure can make towards the general objective of orderly industrial relations.[28]

Clever use of procedures in the effective management of industrial relations is well documented in the research literature[29] and is not disputed. Rather, the problem lies in the notion that formal industrial relations procedures are equated with unionisation. There is zero evidence to support this. The non-union companies surveyed in the research have formal procedures which virtually mirror those in place in the unionised sector. Formalisation of industrial relations procedures is more a function of company size than unionisation status. The argument that unionisation brings about industrial peace through better procedural arrangements is inherently weak with procedural arrangements generally standard across both the unionised and non-union sectors. It follows that there is little validity in co-opting a union presence for this reason. However, there is a worthwhile point trying to "escape" under this heading. In the non-union sector employees must *believe* that the problem-solving machinery is fair and unbiased. Where management teams are both "judge and jury" this can create a perception of company bias. Several of the non-union companies are conscious of this and have sought to put alternatives into place (outside legal council, ombudsman structure and so on) in order for justice to be "seen to be done" (see later detailed points on this).

A sub-argument in support of unionisation was that shop stewards diffuse conflict through discouraging employees from pursuing "trivial" claims. While this may be the case in individual instances, in general terms shop stewards have little to gain in seeking to diffuse issues in this way. As they operate from a position of representative authority, such a strategy, pursued over a period, would lead to a decline in influence or even a replacement of the steward on the basis of being labelled "a management lackey".[30] Further, the supposed positive influence of a shop steward in relation to problem resolution has to be traded off against the negative impact of a shop steward presence (vis a vis the supervisory group) outlined earlier. Overall there seems little merit in co-opting a trade union presence in order to formalise industrial relations procedures or to put a representative structure into place.

Do Unions Bring about Industrial Peace?

Implicit in the arguments listed above was the notion that union recognition can indirectly bring about industrial peace through providing the structures to channel and diffuse conflict. As Hyman argues:

> Far from feeling threatened by a union presence, some companies may seek to incorporate unions within their industrial relations structures. Farsighted management's have little reason to resist, and some reason to welcome, the unionisation of their employees. By making explicit the very discontents which work in capitalist industry generates, unions help to make workers' behaviour more predictable and manageable. Resentment is not allowed to accumulate explosively, but is processed in a manner which facilitates at least temporary solutions; and union involvement in any settlement increases the likelihood that the members will feel committed to the agreed terms.[31]

The evidence uncovered during the research lends little support to Hyman's thesis. The assertion that unionised plants have lower conflict levels than non-union plants found no support from respondents on either side of the industrial divide. That a union official did not have to visit particular employments over several years of operation is inconclusive as an argument in support of granting union recognition. The fact that other employments *did* receive his attention during this period (presumably plants which were procedurally fully equipped) points to the industrial relations climate as being largely determined by internal relationships rather than by industrial relations structures or procedures.

Does Unionisation Lead to Greater Democratic Control?

The final point in support of unions providing a decreased level of conflict was that unionisation is more democratic. Operating on a non-union basis was said to create a number of problems as individuals or small groups of employees were not subject to the control of the wider group. Again, a questionable assumption is made here. Firstly, given the difficulty in organising opposition, the likelihood of small groups of non-union employees taking effective action is somewhat marginalised.[32] Thus, even if the point is accepted that individuals are not subject to the control of a wider group, the negative potential of this is offset by their lack of "clout". The non-union companies have an easier task in resolving contentious issues in their favour when dealing with employees on an individual basis and the potential disruption of dealing with "individuals" has little substance.

Secondly, the suggestion that smaller groups in a unionised environment are likely to be submerged by the wider group structure is also debatable. Numerical strength is not the sole power base for employees. Even where smaller groups may be outvoted, the possibility of unofficial industrial action is always open to particular interest groups and there are numerous examples of this occurring in Ireland. Indeed, the notion of strong centralised control of the membership may be overstated.[33] Given the democratic nature of union control the union "officialdom" is always subject to a challenge from the shop floor. In short, unions often cannot always deliver on the "control" aspect of the recognition bargain. While the general point that most employees will accept democratic decisions is accepted, there is little reason to doubt that this also applies in the non-union sector.

Overall, the core arguments in the "institutionalisation of industrial conflict" thesis are unconvincing. Contrary to the view that unionisation diffuses conflict at the workplace, the very presence of a union may well mean that more disputes arise. In what can be termed the "conflict generation process", the fact that a channel exists to process grievances gives rise to conflicts which would otherwise remain dormant or companies can become embroiled in external events over which they have little control.[34,35] Secondary picketing, the blacking of goods, sympathy strikes and so on can draw a company into areas in which they have no involvement, but also over which they may be powerless to exercise any degree of influence. The points put forward are better understood as a radical critique of the modus operandi of the union movement from within its own ranks, rather than a realistic argument for companies to concede recognition.

The logic of the argument is based on the premise that unions' successes to date have been marginal. Managers at the sharp end of industrial relations strongly argued against the thesis that trade unions are an impotent force. While it may be possible to minimise the role of unions in terms of their potential negative effect, they "should not be underestimated".[36] However, this view must be seen in the context of the job level of respondents. Without doubt unions are effective at the micro level (in having particular dismissal decisions reversed, gaining an extra percentage on a wage settlement and so on). For industrial relations or personnel managers it becomes difficult to disassociate such gains from the notion of effective union power. Yet the limitations of union power also need to be recognised. While they may be able to exercise some degree of countervailing force at a micro level their broader influence on industrial relations (given their reactive role under the traditional model of industrial relations) is more open to question. Union power is likely to be much less visible to the shareholder than to the personnel manager.

Negotiating with Individual Employees

It is sometimes argued that an additional disadvantage of operating on a non-union basis is the amount of time involved in dealing with employee relations issues. In a non-union company each individual was said to be "a negotiating unit". A greater amount of time is therefore taken up in resolving individual grievances/issues than is the case in the unionised sector.[37] The suggestion here is that issues are normally resolved in less time through a trade union channel, a point covered in some detail earlier. The assumption is that, given similar numbers employed, in a unionised environment time is saved by dealing with grievances on a collective basis. The logic of this argument is flawed on two counts. Firstly, it overstates the amount of managerial time invested in the non-union sector relating to problem-solving activity. Secondly, it overestimates the potential for problem resolution within a unionised environment.

The idea that non-union plants are much more "individualistic" is somewhat of a misnomer. The reality of personnel management in the non-union sector is not individual negotiating units. Policies are decided on a collective basis for the vast majority of issues. The confusion here possibly arises from the fact that the non-union companies continually reinforce the point that employees are *treated* as individuals. While this is a central theme of the union avoidance message it does not, in practice, translate into individual negotiations being conducted over the range of employment conditions. The notion that time is saved in grievance processing in unionised organisations is equally flawed. In a unionised environment the *structure* for handling grievances is simply changed. Instead of a company dealing with employees as individuals they deal with a shop steward representing those same individuals. The number of employees and the existing organisational climate are the key determinants of the amount of issues raised (and the time taken to resolve them), rather than the structure through which such issues are pursued. Additionally, the very "presence" of shop stewards can lead to a greater number of "grievances" — as pursuing such issues represents the reason d'être of the shop steward role, a point noted earlier. In my experience, this area *does not* represent a significant disadvantage for companies operating on a non-union basis.

*   *   *

The decision to go down the "non-union" route is not without downsides. There are a number of disadvantages for companies who decide to operate on a non-union basis. The "big issues" are detailed below.

THE FIRST DISADVANTAGE:
HIGHER COSTS INCURRED

The maintenance of high pay and benefits rates is a disadvantage for the non-union companies in an absolute cost sense and in the fact that it limits flexibility in deciding wage levels vis a vis unionised competitors. While there was general agreement across the respondent group that wage rates/benefits in the non-union sector tended to be "higher",[38] it is very difficult to be more precise. The best "guesstimate" is that compensation and benefits costs in the non-union sector are somewhere between five and ten per cent higher than in the unionised sector but it is difficult to prove these figures. One trade union official argued that the difference in wages levels is not very significant between the unionised and the non-union sectors. Another agreed, suggesting that the non-union companies keep "marginally ahead". Yet while the size of the cost burden was debated, there was no disagreement as to its existence. This potential disadvantage largely depends on the particular industry.[39] For companies where labour represents a small proportion of total costs, the burden is obviously lessened.

The rationale for maintaining high wage and benefit levels in a relative sense is not difficult to comprehend. Uncompetitive pay rates or conditions invite unionisation on the basis that the union could achieve *more* for employees. The non-union companies normally keep a sophisticated link with the marketplace to ensure that their ranking is maintained. Where individual rates fall out of line over a period they are addressed by paying higher increases to the particular grade at review dates to re-adjust them. If the anomaly is particularly large, some of the companies stated that they make automatic adjustments even mid-way through a re- view period. Yet this point should not be overstated. While pay rates in the non-union sector compare favourably with rates in the unionised sector, the notion that companies pay "an arm and a leg" to remain non-union is overly simplistic. High pay rates/benefits alone would not uphold a non-union status in the absence of the other support factors detailed. It is a single strand in a complex structure of actual and psychological rewards which together ensure that the non-union status is maintained.

The non-union companies need to constantly benchmark the unionised sector and this effectively puts the decision on wage increases outside of their control (that is, in relation to profitability of particular plants and so on). This was accepted as part of the price to be paid for the maintenance of their status. The disadvan- tage is somewhat marginalised by the fact that pay movements in most companies (whether unionised or non-union) are often driven by external wage trends, for example, national pay agree- ments. Further, in determining the actual cost of operating on a non-union basis, account needs to be taken of the savings gener- ated (through greater organisational flexibility and so on). Research conducted in the US highlighted that the majority of executives interviewed believed a non-union operation to be less costly when all factors were taken into account.[40] In the final analysis it's not clear how much it really matters. While outwardly it would seem that higher wage/benefit rates are a disadvantage of operating on a non-union basis, several of the respondents felt that their unit labour costs were reduced, albeit respondents from both sides of the industrial divide tended to hold contrasting views. It follows that while it is possible to state with some certainty that operating on a non-union basis translates into higher wage/benefits costs, the impact on total labour costs are more difficult to quantify (motivation, higher productivity and so on). In my experience, the decision to go "non-union" is often a philosophical one with the "business case" numbers used to support it.

Larger Personnel Functions

Non-union companies also incur higher costs as a result of the higher ratio of personnel staff employed. A heavily staffed and professional personnel department is required to maintain the demanding commitment to employee relations which is the hallmark of this mode of operation. The higher staffing requirements partly follow from an understanding of the role of the personnel officer in a non-union environment. Many of the companies see the role of the front line personnel staff as almost akin to that of a shop steward in a unionised environment.[41] In the best managed non-union companies, personnel officers act as mediators between employees and the company. It is very important that employees feel they can get "support" if they have a personal problem or grievance, partly in recognition that some conflicts of interest are inevitable in an industrial setting and partly on the basis that the attraction of unionisation is more potent in the absence of this structure. In the non-union sector front-line personnel officers take up the role, at least outwardly, of an "honest broker" rather than a spokesperson for the company. In addition to their heavy employee relations role, the generally higher level of sophistication within the non-union sector places a heavy burden on the personnel section. The combined effect of the difference in role conception and the wider range of techniques employed accounts for the larger numbers of personnel staff which need to be employed. Companies which opt for a non-union status therefore usually incur a significant cost burden in personnel staffing terms. Figure 9 contrasts the ratio of personnel staff to employees between the unionised and the non-unionised companies visited as part of this research. It graphically highlights the fact that the non-union companies employ significantly more staff, pro rata, in the personnel area.

FIGURE 9: RATIO OF PERSONNEL STAFF IN UNION VERSUS NON-UNION COMPANIES			
	Number Employed	*Personnel Staff*	%
Unionised Companies			
A	620	8	1.29
B	650	5	.77
C	98	0	0.0
G	1,200	8	.67
Weighted Average			.88
Non-Unionised Companies			
D	1,250	28	2.2
E	100	3	3.0
F	150	5	3.3
H	650	8	1.2
I	540	10	1.8
Weighted Average			2.0

THE SECOND DISADVANTAGE:
UNION ENCROACHMENT

The second major disadvantage of operating on a non-union basis was the ever present threat of unionisation and the potential disruption which this would create. There was unanimity among the respondents that the industrial relations climate where union recognition is conceded in an established plant is worse than if this had been granted in advance under a pre-employment agreement. It is often "traumatic";[42] the transition from a non-union to a unionised status is never "cleanly made". What often occurs, and this point was reinforced by the case studies conducted, is that some employees seek to unionise while others wish to remain non-union. A number of potential problems arise. Employee loyalties become divided between the company and a union, between individual unions, or between an official union versus a staff association, with disagreements around which option should be chosen. Where unionisation occurs, it is usually accompanied by debate and rancour within the company, the "very stuff" of difficult industrial relations.[43] This potential disruption is a major negative of operating on a non-union basis.

Secondly, where union encroachment does occur, the union(s) involved are likely to take a strong line to mark out their new territory. This has potential, in the short run at least, for conflicts to develop over both the scope and the substance of the bargaining relationship. With no previous history, an entire industrial relations structure has to be built "from the ground up in a climate of hostility".[44] With the encroachment of a union into a previously non-union plant it was said to take three to five years to regain the ground lost and recreate a good working climate.[45] As Aiken et al. noted:

> In the first chaotic days of the union, when company officials seemed almost stunned and uncertain how to cope

with the union, departmental union committees of stewards throughout the plant proceeded to negotiate changes in job classifications and rates with their foremen. It took some time before more formal procedures were obtained and definite limitations were placed upon the secondary leadership.[46]

Managers have to learn to cope in a unionised environment. The new relationship is established on a trial-and-error basis with all the potential for friction which this entails. Subsequent to recognition being granted there is often a settling down period during which industrial relations is erratic and considerably worsened. Organisations which have stressed the view that they deal with employees directly, and that there is no necessity for a third party presence, find it extremely difficult to adjust to a unionised status.[47]

A final point is the threat to employment stability where a non-union status is reversed. Several multinational companies operate on a non-union basis as part of a worldwide strategy. A number of the respondents made the point that these companies would disinvest, or scale down future investment, if unionisation occurred. In some cases this is simply posturing. In others, it is a deeply held philosophy and would be followed through. While the effect of poor industrial relations within unionised plants may also have consequences for job stability, the conversion to a unionised status is a very visible failing of a major policy tenet. The concession of union recognition is often seen as a failure of the local management team and their competence becomes questionable to corporate executives. It was said to take several years to shift the debris of a failed union avoidance policy, both in rebuilding relationships with employees and re-establishing credibility with the parent company.[48]

The Possibility of Multi-Union Encroachment

A further disadvantage of a non-union operation is the possibility of multi-union encroachment, and the subsequent difficulty of managing a plant where a number of unions are recognised. For example, where unions recruit from within the same grade, competition between them may be on the basis of militancy with all the potential for conflict escalation which this implies (the train drivers' disputes in CIE provide a good example of this in recent times). Respondents highlighted a number of instances where the relationship between unions within the same company were "uneasy". The time taken in dealing with a number of unions was a further negative which has to be taken into account by companies contemplating the non-union mode of operation.

The Conversion to a Unionised Status: Disadvantages for Individual Managers

The disadvantages for companies operating on a non-union basis under the heading of union encroachment can also be understood at the micro level, for example, in relation to the consequences for individual managers. For the human resources manager, in particular, worry and sleepless nights may be synonymous with operating on a non-union basis. Pressure on personnel executives is greater in the non-union sector and concern not to start a slide towards unionisation was stated to be a constant source of worry.[49] To paraphrase a well known quote, "uneasy is the head that wears the non-union crown". In my experience the personnel manager's job is less secure in the event of a recognition drive at a non-union plant (which the companies directly equate with poor performance). This puts these managers in an unenviable position as the factors which lead to unionisation are often outside their immediate control, for example, redundancy. It's not idle speculation. Several human resources managers have actually been dismissed due to union encroachment at plants where they worked.

However, the lack of job security should not be overemphasised. Maintenance of the non-union status is more often an extra burden of *worry* for personnel managers rather than being a direct threat to job security.

THE THIRD DISADVANTAGE: DEVELOPING COMMITMENT TO HUMAN RESOURCE MANAGEMENT

The third disadvantage for companies operating on a non-union basis is the core difficulty of ensuring that line managers take the personnel aspect of their role seriously and devote sufficient energy and attention to it. One personnel respondent remarked that it would "break your heart" trying to educate managers to cope with a non-union environment. Most of the respondents supported the point that non-union companies have to work particularly hard to develop a managerial value system that places sufficient emphasis on employee relations. Part of the challenge here is that managers recruited from the unionised sector often have little prior exposure to the positive employee relations policies which characterise the non-union sector. Such managers have to be trained (and indoctrinated) to cope with this difference in philosophy. Yet training alone will not ensure commitment if the necessary organisational focus and support is absent.

Organisations Seldom Measure Managers on the Employee Relations Aspect of Their Role

Ensuring that the employee relations aspect of each manager's role is emphasised and measured is a key factor in developing managerial commitment. For personnel staff (both in non-union and unionised environments) a constant task is to reinforce to line managers that their functional role and their employee relations role are mutually dependent. Yet successful employee relations strategies are not the sole preserve of the personnel function. The better managed non-union companies reinforce this theme at the chief executive and corporate level. In this way effective people management practices become part of the culture pursued by all managers. In the non-union plants visited, a number of the company founders were stated to be personally "committed to people" and this value system had permeated the organisations (the axiom "an organisation is the shadow of its leader" captures this point well). In contrast, within organisations where employee relations activity is not recognised or valued, it is often seen to conflict with day-to-day operational goals.

A very real dilemma for companies is that the maintenance of production levels is a visible, quantifiable, short-term goal while the maintenance of a proactive human relations strategy is a longer-term strategy which is not easy to measure, nor easily identifiable with specific actions. For example, at one client company we began with great intentions and a huge investment of management time in visualising a positive and productive culture. However "technical" issues during start-up and a pending Federal Drug Administration (FDA) audit put huge pressure on the executive team. They "took their eye off the ball" and the plant unionised in its fourth year of operation. Some management teams believe that you can invest a lot of time up-front in the "soft stuff" and then "get on with running the business". They believe that employee relations works like the digestion system in a large snake, that is, it only needs three "big" meals a year. In my experience the "non-union snake" needs to be fed little and often. Otherwise the organisation begins to miss the small cues which can avalanche into a recognition drive. The interesting point here is that it is possible to "do nothing" in the short term — often without any visible downside — but the "amber light" eventually comes on. Non-union companies who wish to maintain their status ignore this warning light at their peril. The economic cost of "rectifying" an established union drive can amount to ten times the cost of prevention. It simply does not make sense to ignore this area.

Industrial Relations is More Visible than Employee Relations

A sub-feature of the problem faced in developing managerial commitment to employee relations is that there is often little "mileage" in such efforts. As a consequence, politically astute managers will seek out areas of higher visibility in which to expend their efforts. The problem may be particularly acute in the non-union sector as within unionised companies an impressive array of structures often exist to give recognition to work completed. The number of official grievances raised/resolved, collective bargaining negotiations, visits to the Labour Court and so on all visibly highlight time spent in this area. Conversely, "employee relations" tends to be covert and can amount to a sequence of "non-events", for example, problems resolved so low in the grievance processing chain that they are not even recorded as problems. An analogy can be made here with preventative maintenance programmes. An engineer who goes on a call out at 5.00 am on Sunday morning may get more credit than one who schedules effective preventative maintenance programmes and works regular hours. Organisations need to be sensitive to those areas which, although they do not easily lend themselves to quantification, are nonetheless important. Employee relations in a non-union environment provides a classic example.

Organisations Often Have a Short-term Perspective on Employee Relations Issues

A second problem often faced within organisations is a lack of longer-term perspective. Few organisations have a well-defined concept or goal with regard to employee relations. Admittedly, given the vagueness surrounding some personnel themes (for example, "a positive organisational climate"), this can be difficult.

Yet organisations surmount similar difficulties with regard to financial planning (uncertainty in sales, currency valuations and so on) underpinning the point that the absence of strategic planning in employee relations follows more from a lack of focus rather than from any insurmountable difficulties.

The absence of a strategic employee relations focus probably relates to the training/background of individual managers. The education and training of senior management within disciplines like accountancy and engineering (which historically have predominated in the senior management ranks) provides a quantification bias. This may, in part, explain the discomfort felt when "softer" areas like strategic planning in human resource management or other social science issues are raised.[50] While it is difficult to generalise on this point, several years' practical experience has left me with little doubt of the reluctance (and even a non-acceptance) of strategic thinking with regard to employee relations issues in the unionised sector. In Ireland, the consulting "market" for reactive (problem solving) employee relations issues is 50 times the size of the market for engagement/participation (proactive) strategies. Management consultant graffiti (if such a thing existed) would read, "Reactivity Rules OK".

The fundamental reason for the absence of strategic employee relations planning in the unionised sector can be traced back to the view of employees as an expendable factor of production. Under the traditional model of industrial relations, organisations view human resource management as a fire-fighting or peace-keeping activity. The goals of personnel departments, where made explicit, are most often framed in the negative, that is, the absence of industrial conflict rather than on the human resource potential which can be unleashed when the correct motivational conditions exist. None of the unionised organisations visited during the research had invested any degree of time in longer-term strategic planning in this area. All were consumed in resolving immediate tactical issues (wage negotiations, particular changes and so on) rather than longer-term strategic ones ("How can we improve productivity in the next five years?"; "What type of organisation culture do we want to develop?"). In general, the time invested in any particular area will mirror the value or worth of that particular resource to the organisation. As employees are seen as a positive resource within the non-union sector, more time and effort is invested in managing employee relations issues. It's that simple. On the ground evidence supports this. Several of the non-union companies visited were acutely aware of the benefits of strategic employee relations planning and had invested a good degree of time in establishing goals and mapping out strategic action plans to achieve them. A number of companies had built measures on employee satisfaction levels into the line managers' objectives and stitched them into the salary review process in the same way that other technical objectives were set, overcoming the "invisibility" problem. In short, those organisations which had successfully maintained a non-union status over a sustained period have managed to maintain a balance between the twin objectives of productivity and effective people management.

Technical and Employee Relations Specialists: The Development of Dual-Role Managers

A key goal for many non-union companies is to build a management team that has dual competence in both the technical and employee relations aspects of their role. This is achieved by developing relationship skills for managers from technical disciplines (through both formal training and supervisory job assignments) and by reinforcing the value of such skills within the organisation through the reward (pay and promotions) systems. In the non-union sector managers are seldom successful (in career terms) unless they are "good with people". Some employees who are excellent "technically" actually leave these organisations, frustrated by a lack of career progress due to their lack of people management ability.[51] Several of the personnel respondents within the non-union sector cited examples where managers who were not perceived as competent in this area were transferred to roles with a predominantly technical rather than a supervisory focus. While some degree of interpersonal skills are necessary in all organisations, they are typically more highly valued within the non-union sector. Where change is a constant feature, huge demands are placed on managers to keep pace with technical innovations and improvements. It ranks as one of the great achievements of non-union companies in the high tech sector that they have managed to keep in touch with a rapidly changing technical environment while maintaining the demanding commitment to employee relations which is necessary to maintain non-union status.

Developing Managerial Commitment in Non-Union Companies: Structural Solutions

Along with measuring and reinforcing the value of "people skills", some companies have introduced particular structures to help line managers take ownership of employee relations. One example is a pre-determined communications plan which commits managers to holding briefing sessions on a scheduled basis with their subordinates. In this way a core company tenet — communications with employees — is not left to the discretion of individual managers but is given support through centralised planning (often some form of "cascade communications"). Many of the non-union companies have adopted this particular method (in some a specific employee designated to the communications area prepares general presentation material, relieving the line managers of this task). Local issues are then addressed on a more informal basis after the "main" presentation is given. Thus commitment to communications is not simply given lip service but is reinforced throughout the organisation.

For example, one company had a particular difficulty in getting managers to complete performance appraisals/salary reviews on time. These were constantly overdue with managers complaining that they had too little time to administer them and employees complaining that their salary increases were often delayed. It also tied up a good degree of personnel time. The company decided to bring all review dates into line on March 1 (previously they had been completed on employees' anniversary start date). This allowed the personnel department to put pressure on all managers during February and reviews were subsequently cleared by the second or third week in March of each year.[52] The central point here is not the relevance, or otherwise, of a particular initiative. Where a company wishes to maintain a successful employee relations policy, line management commitment towards achieving it is vital. Providing the necessary organisational support is a key ingredient to ensuring that "it happens". Overall, a striking finding which emerged from the research was the quantum difference between unionised and non-union companies in the focus devoted to effective human resource management. The best-managed non-union organisations took the time and effort to map out "goalposts" and detailed actions, ensuring a practical application of their philosophies (visions need landing gears as well as wings). While conscious of the time involved, the companies accepted this as part of the price to be paid for maintaining a non-union status.

THE FOURTH DISADVANTAGE: INCREASED ADMINISTRATION BURDEN

The fourth disadvantage for companies operating on a non-union basis is the increased administration burden which this imposes. While not as fundamental as the points made earlier, the extra administration workload nevertheless needs to be recognised. Operating on a non-union basis produces a greater administration workload in two ways. Firstly, payment systems in the non-union sector generally encompass a merit element to reflect individual employee performance (in line with the philosophy that employees are individuals and should be rewarded for their particular contribution). Regardless of the sophistication of the particular appraisal system used, these are *always* time-consuming. An employee's past performance has to be noted and recorded, discussed at a performance interview and target goals set for the future. This significant time commitment directly increases in relation to the number of people employed. It usually also involves some degree of personnel time in the distribution of appraisal forms and dealing with queries and grievances which arise from the process. In contrast, performance appraisal systems seldom feature in unionised companies (outside of the initial probationary period), as wage increases are typically paid "across the board".[53]

Appraisal systems have a further disadvantage in that they lead to a complex range of individual pay rates. Depending on the particular system in place, this can impose a tough administration burden. The "extra admin" can be appreciated when contrasted with the payment systems in place within unionised companies, which is typically a standard rate paid for particular jobs or grades which do not reflect individual performance. Further, rates are normally adjusted in line with national wage rounds or local agreements which are seldom of less than 12 months' duration. The administration burden for unionised companies is therefore significantly lessened because of the different philosophy on pay between the two sectors.

While the administration burden is recognised, it is accepted on the basis that this allows the companies to formally review performance, at least annually, with employees and also to adjust pay rates in line with performance levels rather than general wage movements. In the unionised sector the lower administration burden is traded off against these reviews taking place. It is only in the context that such appraisals are not deemed necessary that this area can be labelled as a disadvantage for the non-union companies.

FIGURE 10: ADVANTAGES/DISADVANTAGES FOR COMPANIES OPERATING ON A NON-UNION BASIS	
Advantages	
Flexibility of labour	• Maximum mobility of labour. • Less demarcation between jobs. • Changes in products/processes can be accommodated very quickly.
Direct communications/problem solving with employees	• Strong identity with company goals. • Upwards communication: Employees used as a resource. • Supervisory role bolstered.
Acceptance of authority	• Positive climate/working environment. • Loyalty directed towards the company. • Acceptance of managerial legitimacy. • No countervailing power of a union. • Levels of conflict likely to be lower.
Disadvantages	
Cost	• Large HR staff required. • Higher rates of pay/conditions.
Stability	• Possibility of multi-union encroachment. • Negative implications for future investment/poor perception of management group if unionisation occurs. • Fears of job security for personnel staff.
Managerial commitment	• Amount of managerial time spent on employee relations. • Managers need particularly good interpersonal skills. • Difficulty of developing managerial commitment to employee relations.
Administration	• Performance appraisals for individuals. • Wide diversity of wage rates. • Number of yearly wage adjustments.

Endnotes

---

[1] Quinn, Cornelius. *Maintaining Non-Union Status*. C.B.I. Publishing, Boston, Massachusetts 1982: 27.

[2] Foulkes, Fred K. *Personnel Policies in Large Non-Union Companies*. Prentice Hall, New Jersey 1980: 183.

[3] Vickers, Peter. Personnel Director, Nissan Motor Manufacturing (UK). From *Nissan: The Thinking behind the Agreement*. Personnel Department Institute of Personnel Management, London, August 1985: 19

[4] It should not be assumed that such behaviour is irrational. Most instances of job demarcation are based less on "bloody mindedness" than on an attempt to protect job security. The non-union companies may be able to dilute such practices through their stance on maintaining job security. This allows employees to operate on a flexible basis without feeling the threat of insecurity, a point covered in some detail later.

[5] Personnel Executive: Company J. Points made during interview with author.

[6] Personnel Executive: Company H. Points made during interview with author.

[7] "Trade Union Officials B and E". Points made during interview with author.

[8] "Trade Union Official C". Points made during interview with author.

[9] "Trade Union Official A". Points made during interview with author.

[10] "Trade Union Official F". Points made during interview with author.

[11] Extract from a company/union agreement. The clause is fairly typical.

[12] Mooney, Paul. "The Development of Pre-Employment Agreements in Irish Industrial Relations". Unpublished postgraduate dissertation submitted in fulfilment of a Diploma in Industrial Relations, Trinity College Dublin, 1984.

[13] Personnel Manager: Company J. Points made during interview with author.

[14] Toner, Bill. "Union or Non-Union-Employee Relations Strategies in the Republic of Ireland". Unpublished Ph.D. Thesis, London School of Busi-

ness; Roche, W.K. and Toner, T. "Human Resource Management and Industrial Relations: Substitution, Dualism and Partnership" in W.K. Roche, K. Monks and J. Walsh (eds). *Human Resource Management Strategies: Policy andPractice in Ireland*, Dublin, Oak Tree Press.

[15] Personnel Manager: Company 1. Points made during interview with author.

[16] Martin, Peter and Nicholls, John. *Creating a Committed Workforce*. Institute of Personnel Management, London 1987: 47.

[17] Personnel Manager: Company H. Points made during interview with author.

[18] "Industrial Relations Expert D". Points made during interview with author.

[19] Martin, Peter and Nicholls, John. *Creating a Committed Workforce*. Institute of Personnel Management, London 1987: 47.

[20] Powell, John. "Why am I Afraid to Tell You Who I Am?". Argus Communications, Illinois, 1969: 103.

[21] Bain, George Sayers. *The Growth of White-Collar Unionism*. Oxford University Press, London, 1970: 138.

[22] Flanders, Alan (ed.). *Collective Bargaining: Selected Readings*. Penguin, Harmondsworth, UK, 1969.

[23] "Industrial Relations Expert A". Points made during interview with author.

[24] Personnel Executive: Company H. Points made during interview with author.

[25] "Industrial Relations Expert D". Points made during interview with author.

[26] Brown, J.A.C. *The Social Psychology of Industry*, Penguin, UK, 1954.

[27] The concept of "good" industrial relations is used as a shorthand method to denote those points already touched upon (e.g. organisational flexibility, open communications, authority acceptance, lack of conflict etc.). One of the central dilemmas in discussing the "unionised" versus "non-union" sector are the differences which exist *within* each sector. Some of the generalisations made will not apply to particular organisations.

[28] Hawkins, Kevin. *The Management of Industrial Relations*. Penguin, UK, 1979: 132.

[29] Purcell, John. *Good Industrial Relations: Theory and Practice*, McMillan, London 1981: 6; Gardner, J. "Practical Personnel and Industrial Relations Management". From Pollock, Hugh (ed.) *Reform of Industrial Relations*, O'Brien Press, Dublin, 1982: 30.

[30] Shafto, Tony. "The Growth of Shop Steward Managerial Functions". From Thurley, K. and S. Wood (eds.), *Industrial Relations and Management Strategies*, Cambridge University Press, Cambridge, 1983: 52.

[31] Hyman, Richard. *Industrial Relations: A Marxist Introduction*. Macmillan, London, 1975: 89.

[32] "Trade Union Official E". Points made during interview with author.

[33] Fogarty, R., Davy, G. and McCarthy, P. "Final Report of the Commission on Industrial in the Electricity Supply Board" PRL. 553. Stationery Office, Dublin. 1969:29.

[34] "IDA Executive A". Points made during interview with author.

[35] The most widely publicised example of this in Ireland occurred during the maintenance dispute in 1969 when companies who were not directly involved in the dispute were picketed by the craft unions. Another high profile case was the Dunnes Stores dispute where employees refused to handle South African goods. This was a political issue, outside of the immediate company's resolve without damaging its competitiveness vis a vis other supermarket groups.

[36] "Industrial Relations Expert D". Points made during interview with author.

[37] "Trade Union Officials A and F". Points made during interview with author.

[38] Usually at, or better than, the 75th percentile point for the marketplace; of the five non-union companies surveyed four had this as their stated pay philosophy. The other company said that they maintained rates at an "above average" level.

[39] "Industrial Relations Expert D". Points made during interview with author.

[40] Foulkes, Fred K. "Large Non-Unionised Employers". From Jack Stieber et.al. (eds.) *U.S. Industrial Relations 1950-1980: A Critical Assessment*, Madison, Wisc., IRRA, 1981: 59.

[41] The terms personnel and human resources are used interchangeably. The higher ratio of personnel staff needs to be traded off against the normal "downtime" associated with industrial relations work completed by shop stewards which represents an invisible cost to unionised companies.

[42] Personnel Executive: Company I. Points made during interview with author.

[43] "Industrial Relations Expert D". Points made during interview with author.

[44] Personnel Manager: Company E. Points made during interview with author.

[45] Personnel Manager: Company H. Points made during interview with author.

[46] Aiken, Michael, Ferman, Louis A. and Sheppard, Harold L. *Economic Failure, Alienation and Extremism*. University of Michigan Press, Ann Arbor, 1968.

[47] "Industrial Relations Expert C". Points made during interview with author.

[48] Personnel Manager: Company F. Points made during interview with author.

[49] "Industrial Relations Expert C". Points made during interview with author.

[50] De Bono, Edward. *Lateral Thinking for Management*. McGraw Hill (UK) 1971: 80.

[51] Personnel Executive: Company D. Points made during interview with author.

[52] Personnel Manager: Company E. Points made during interview with author.

[53] In a wage/benefit survey conducted by the author (27 unionised companies) only one of the companies visited had any form of performance appraisal system for hourly paid employees (after completion of the

probationary period). While some of the companies argued that the unions would not accept these, the general impression left was that the companies did not have the personnel expertise or staffing levels to adequately manage such a system. Performance reviews, if incorrectly handled, can also be a source of grievances. Because of the sensitivity of the area, most companies prefer to forgo the supposed benefits of feedback and goal-setting with employees to avoid the more tangible administration burden and conflict potential which such systems generate.

7

Advantages/Disadvantages for Employees Operating on a Non-Union Basis

A CENTRAL QUESTION WHICH NEEDS to be addressed is the consequences for employees of operating on a non-union basis. In order to examine this an advantage/disadvantages listing has also been compiled for employees. Essentially the listing can be grouped under two headings: (a) those factors which result from the policies pursued by the non-union companies, and (b) those which follow from non-membership of a trade union. To some extent this is a false construct as some advantages have to be traded off against particular disadvantages. The points are considered in isolation initially in order to construct a simplified model. In a later section an attempt will be made to come to a reasoned conclusion on whether there is a net advantage or disadvantage for employees who work in the non-union sector.

First Advantage: Higher Wages/ Better Conditions of Employment

The first advantage for employees operating in the non-union sector[1] are the extra wages/benefits enjoyed. The majority of employees have an instrumental attitude to trade unionism, that is, if they can get more money through operating on a non-union basis they will accept it.[2] As noted earlier, the trade union officials argued that most of the non-union companies only pay "marginally" above the rates established in unionised plants. Yet while the degree of advantage was disputed, the fact that higher relative wages/conditions are paid in the non-union sector was accepted. A sub-element of the pay question was that reward systems in the non-union sector generally recognise the effort and performance of individual employees. This was said to be "fairer" as the principle of equity (that is, reward = performance) as distinct from equality ("across the board") increases applied. However, this may be a double-edged sword, as some employees benefit at the expense of those who are less efficient. Historically the function of trade unions had been to establish a levelling mechanism, pulling high fliers down and raising poor performers up. Unions thus bring about an "averaging effect".[3] It follows that in relation to pay for performance, it is not possible to speak globally about the benefits of operating on a non-union basis. Account needs to be taken of the situation of individual employees.

Promotion based on merit rather than seniority is an additional point, argued on the basis of equitable reward (an obvious advantage to organisations by virtue of the fact that it allows them to promote stronger performers). It can equally be held that promotion based on merit disadvantages employees with longer service and leaves them open to subjective ratings of performance which is based on personality or "fit".

Benefits in the Non-union Sector are Often Extended to Employees' Families

Many of the non-union companies take a wider view of the employment relationship through extending benefits/entitlements beyond the individual employee to the family. Areas such as drug/medicine subsidies which apply to the family and attendance at social functions were cited. The involvement of family members can be "quite exceptional" in the non-union sector[4] and copperfastens the view of non-union employees as being "special". Within a number of the non-union companies there was a strong emphasis on family involvement through "open days", off-site dinners which include partners and so on. Yet the very existence of the "extended employee" concept, to paraphrase from sociology, was distasteful to several of the trade union respondents interviewed who expressed general unease that Irish workers would be so gullible. These were seen as loosely disguised efforts to buy the support of employees' families. Such methods were equated with "singing the company song" and were said to be alien to the Irish culture.[5] However, in seeking to promote identity with employees and their families there may be a cultural barrier beyond which companies cannot overstep in the Irish environment. The extremes of worker/company identity (sometimes referred to as the "Japanese Model") did not feature at any of the non-union plants visited. Indeed, there was a definite contrast on this point between plants visited in the United States and those in Ireland. The example below may make this point clearer.

"G.E. is Me"

At one non-union plant in Ohio, employees of the General Electric Company often wore T-shirts bearing the emblem "G.E. is Me", seemingly without any self-consciousness and outwardly with some degree of pride. Conversely, at an Irish G.E. plant (unionised) a benefits function was organised to coincide with the end of a cost improvement drive. Employees who submitted an accepted cost improvement idea were invited with their partners to a social night out held in Dublin Zoo. As each couple arrived they were issued with a sports-type bag with the company logo and name clearly printed on the outside. There was an almost unanimous decry of the issue of such "prizes" which several employees later returned. The general feeling was that they did not want to be

used as an unpaid advertising vehicle for the company. As relationships at the plant were relatively good prior to this incident,
there is no reason to believe that the response was inspired
through some other grievance. It simply highlights a cultural difference in the Irish environment, a safeguard against what might
be considered "company identity excesses" taking place. While it
is difficult to be definitive on this point, there may be an element
in the Irish "psyche" which guards against this.[6]

Key differences of approach within the trade union respondent group emerged on this question. While some, as noted
above, were sceptical of the company's motives in involving family members, others made the point that many of the conditions of
employment (and the overall concept of employee relations) in
the non-union sector represent targets which the unions aspire to
in other organisations.[7] The paradox is that the type of employment relationship which many unions espouse as bringing about
a lowering of industrial conflict may, when installed, decrease the
perceived relevance of the union role to employees. Overall, the
strengthening of the company/employee bond posed a real dilemma for trade union officials. Some welcomed greater efforts
being made in the area of positive employee relations. With other
officials it was somewhat uncertain whether the identification of
employee with the companies, of itself, was being criticised or
whether the exclusion of trade unions from the employment relationship provoked some of the antagonism displayed.

Unions Argue that Employee Relations in the Non-Union Sector is "Paternalistic"

Several of the union respondents made the point that employee
relations in the non-union sector was paternalistic. The Oxford
English Dictionary defines paternalism as, "fatherly, limiting
freedom of the subject by well-meant regulations".[8]

The argument ran that while employees in the non-union sector may receive marginally better conditions of employment they do so at the expense of their personal freedom. Better terms and conditions of employment are traded off against involvement in collective bargaining. "Real" participation was alien to the non-union companies who believe in the "divine right to manage".[9] Overall, the non-union companies were seen to have a benign paternalistic approach to ensure that workers were kept in check, much as you might purchase a Mars bar to keep an unruly child quiet. In terms of consulting with employees on important matters, it "simply does not arise".[10] The outward show of commitment (and some minor substantive concessions) masks the true motive of avoiding loss of power to a union. In rejecting the paternalism charge levelled by the unions, a number of personnel respondents stated that employees are more interested in actual conditions of employment than in any labels which can be attached to them.

Overall scepticism was expressed on the point that employees view their relationship with a company as anything other than a wage/effort bargain. While the paternalism charge implies a different conceptual understanding of the relationship, employees' interests, in the main, focus on pay/conditions and job security. Non-union companies make strong efforts to meet employees' needs in these core areas. If this can be dubbed paternalism there seems little doubt that the non-union companies stand convicted on this charge. Yet this causes zero dilemma for the employees and remains a somewhat philosophical point. Indeed, it was argued that the only people who do not like the word paternalism are "trade union activists and intellectuals".[11] In what is essentially a political argument, the same actions can be labelled in completely different ways. If companies exercise responsibility toward their employees by providing safe work conditions and good wages, this can be labelled as paternalism *or* a strong commitment to people management.

The argument for paying attention to people management issues was made on the basis of business pragmatism. One respondent stated that his company did not apologise for their interest in
employees as "it works".[12] An analogy can be made here with an
address given by the author Tom Peters (of *In Search of Excellence*
fame) to the Irish Management Institute Conference at Killarney.
Speaking of a marketing conference at which he had participated
in the US, Peters stated that only a small number of speakers had
actually thanked their customers. Many of the other speakers labelled this "pat on the back marketing". It turned out that the
speakers who had mentioned customers were from IBM, the
moral being that "pat on the back marketing" translates into business success. In the non-union sector a strong value is placed on
attending to employee needs. While this could equally be termed
"pat on the back personnel management", the excellent climate
and relationships which exist within these companies contribute
to their financial success.[13]

THE SECOND ADVANTAGE: PROBLEM RESOLUTION

A major and continuing goal of the organisation is to
maintain a positive union-free environment. We strive to
create throughout our organisation an atmosphere which
gives recognition to each individual's needs, concerns and
problems. Our belief is that the interests of each employee
and the overall organisation are best served dealing with
people directly rather than through a third party. The
employees at [company name] have chosen to remain
union-free. It is not necessary that you be a member of a
union to receive fair treatment in this business.[14]

The fact that companies are more alert to resolving personal
problems was stated as the second benefit for employees in
the non-union sector. Non-union companies demonstrate sensitiv-

ity to employee relations, partly to maintain a union-free environment but also by reference to the holistic view of employees under the high commitment model detailed earlier. Numerous personnel techniques and practices have evolved to support this philosophy. Thus, all other things being equal, employees in the non-union sector have a better chance of having personal issues dealt with "speedily and fairly".[15] A counter argument proposed was that individuals have much less chance of getting issues satisfactorily resolved due to the absence of a countervailing force. While it was accepted that issues may be addressed "speedily", this is partly to camouflage the absence of a trade union. In practice it may mean that employees simply accept solutions which are imposed by their employer. There is often little alternative as pursuit of issues may label an individual as "militant", with negative implications for their future career, merit pay increases and so on.[16] While this could also apply to individuals in the unionised sector where employees can also be labelled as militant, the possibility of blatant discrimination is lessened. The supposed benefit of problem resolution in the non-union sector goes to the very heart of this debate. The relationship between an individual company and an employee is seen by some to be fundamentally unequal with unions helping to redress this imbalance. The positive benefits to employees therefore cannot be considered in a vacuum without reference to the losses incurred as a result.

The Unequal Relationship between Individual Employees and Employers

> Collective Bargaining to the non-union companies is like the crucifix to Dracula.[17]

The notion that employees in the non-union sector have a greater opportunity to have personal issues resolved was rejected by the trade union officials on the basis that this ignores the underlying power relationship between employer and employed in the capitalist system. The "classic" argument for the development and growth of trade unions is their so-called power equalisation function. As the relationship between individual employees and a company are unequal, the superior economic power of the employer can only be countered where employees combine together in trade unions. Simply because people may be unaware of (or choose to ignore) the power argument does not diminish the fact that "it is there".[18]

Not surprisingly, the personnel group held a different view. While the issue of power inequality may historically have been a factor in the employment relationship, the gap between "manager and managed" has been continually eroded. The educational achievements of many employees are at a higher level than at any previous time in the state's history. Employees were said to be both articulate and acutely aware of their rights which forces companies to treat them as other than "production oriented monkeys".[19] Authoritarian practices (which the power equalisation argument implies) would simply not be accepted by many younger employees. As Margolies argues:

> Young people, in particular, increasingly only accept authority when it is earned. Relationships are based on respect rather than structure. There is increasing emphasis on co-operation and less on a top down command approach. [20]

The changing educational profile of employees has meant that employment practices have changed and the employment relationship is not as unequal as before. The raft of labour legislation passed in recent years has further "levelled" the playing field. The final point is that it is not in the interest of non-union companies to demonstrate that there is a power imbalance as they need to continually underscore the point that employees do not need the negotiating strength of a trade union. The most tangible way for companies to do this is to be alert and responsive to the needs of employees.

Power is an Academic Notion: Employees are Interested in Pay and Conditions

The notion that power inequality represents a disadvantage for employees operating on a non-union basis was essentially rejected by the human resources respondents. Power only makes sense when it translates into substantive benefits or working conditions. As non-union companies score high on both counts, the notion of a power imbalance in the workplace is relegated to academic debate. While it can be argued that unionisation directly translates into greater worker control and democracy in the workplace, the limitations of the collective bargaining process must also be recognised. Negotiations usually range across well boundaried "areas" between company and union teams and the limitations of this arena should be recognised. One of the union officials argued that "the tragedy of ignorance is its complacency"[21] (that is, that employees are simply not aware of the benefits of membership unless they had experienced them). This point is not supported by the research evidence. Upwards of 50 per cent of employees in the non-union companies visited were previously unionised and had first-hand experience of the benefits of unionisation but chose to forego them.

The central theme running through the answers of the human resources respondents was the belief that, given a management philosophy which is people-orientated, unions are unnecessary. The non-union companies offer relative job security and competitive remuneration. In addition, because of the continuing threat of union encroachment, they do not attempt to maximise their power advantage. The vast majority of employees were said to "work for a living". Provided that the work itself was reasonably interesting, the management perceived as fair and the employment package competitive, most employees have little interest in pursuing the wider question on the power distribution in a capitalist society. Thus the "losses" associated with operating on a non-union basis largely depend on how much value employees place on having an independent voice.[22]

THE THIRD ADVANTAGE:
NON-PAYMENT OF SUBSCRIPTIONS

In addition to the benefits which follow from company policies in the non-union sector, a number of advantages follow from non-membership of a trade union. The fact that individuals do not have to pay union subscriptions is the first and most obvious benefit. While this is sometimes mentioned as a "throwaway" point, the monetary sum involved is not inconsiderable. At the time of writing weekly subscriptions for the largest general union (SIPTU) are about €6.00. This gives an annual subscription cost of something in the order of €300.00, net of tax. If we assume that an individual pays income tax at the tax band rate of 20 per cent and build in PRSI contributions, this means that each member has to earn approximately €400 to pay the annual subscription, a fact that is not lost on the membership.

THE FOURTH ADVANTAGE:
LESS FEAR OF WAGE LOSSES DUE TO STRIKES

The fourth stated benefit for employees in the non-union sector also related to income: the decreased risk of strikes and subsequent wage losses which would result. Income continuity was said to be a specific benefit of operating on a non-union basis as the incidence of strikes/industrial action is much lower in this sector. Coupled with the non-payment of union subscriptions this provides a monetary benefit to non-union employees. In reality, of course, strikes in the unionised sector do not simply represent a loss but must be seen in the context of the benefits achieved as a result of any industrial action taken. However, as the non-union companies keep a close link with marketplace developments in the unionised sector, employees in the non-union sector usually maintain their relative position (in industrial relations-speak this was historically termed a "free rider" position). Despite philosophical opposition which can be levelled against the achievement of gains at the expense of commitment by others, the reality is that employees in the non-union sector maintain their relative position without the income loss associated with industrial action.

THE FIFTH ADVANTAGE: NO COMPULSION TO JOIN A TRADE UNION

The final benefit for employees operating on a non-union basis was that they do not have to join a trade union. This was said to particularly benefit those employees who are not "joiners". One respondent suggested that a degree of antagonism exists towards closed shop arrangements, particularly among younger employees. As Ross argued:

> As an institution expands in strength and status, it outgrows its formal purpose. It experiences its own needs, develops its own ambitions and faces its own problems. These become differentiated from the needs, ambitions and problems of its rank and file. Trade unionism is no exception. It is the beginning of wisdom in the study of industrial relations to understand that the union as an organisation, is not identical with its members, as individuals.[23]

Underlying this point was the notion that unions were often unrepresentative of employees' views. Unions were said to comprise "10 per cent activists, 80 per cent who sit on the fence and 10 per cent who are pro-company". The shop stewards normally came from the activists group and did not represent the views of the majority.[24] General criticism of union policy and methodology with regard to employee servicing was raised by several of the human resource managers interviewed. While this was undoubtedly true in cases, the assertion that shop stewards were always militants was rejected by such an august body as the Donovan Commission in its landmark study of industrial relations in the UK.[25] The notion of shop stewards as "troublemakers" finds little support in the industrial relations research literature. They were more often part of the conflict diffusion rather than conflict generation process. However, there is little doubt that some proportion of employees would prefer to address issues on an individual basis rather than being subordinated to general union policy, and operating on a non-union basis provides a benefit to *this* group.

Once again the supposed benefit needs to be judged in the context of the inherent disadvantage which operating on a non-union basis poses. Not all issues of concern can be addressed on an individual basis. Where changes are being introduced which effect all or a number of employees, it is perfectly rational to express this view collectively. While this, de facto, does occur in the non-union sector, their collective voice cannot be harnessed with the same degree of cohesion which trade union organisation allows. The argument that an advantage exists for employees in not belonging to a trade union ignores the positive influence of collective strength. To achieve collective strength, by definition, employees have to surrender some of their individualism. As Hyman argues:

> In short, it is only through the power over its members which is vested in the trade union that it is able to exert power for them. [26]

In a similar vein, Allen notes:

The end of trade union activity is to protect and improve the general living standards and not to provide workers with an exercise in self government. [27]

As with most of the other areas touched upon under this heading, the supposed benefit which results from the non-compulsion to join a trade union cannot be considered in isolation.

*   *   *

A number of disadvantages apply to employees in the non-union sector. An attempt to capture the "big issues" under this heading is detailed below.

THE FIRST DISADVANTAGE: LACK OF JOB SECURITY

Several respondents made the point that job security in the non-union sector was weakened. In the event of a company deciding to cease trading, either wholly or in part, employees would be unable to exercise any degree of power or influence over the decision. While the point on the possible level of influence was accepted, the premise of the question was rejected by the human resource managers. Job security was seen to be solely related to the "health" of a company's trading position and the philosophy around the maintenance of employment levels. A unionised or non-union status was seen to be of little consequence. While it was acknowledged that fears on job security are a feature within the multinational sector generally, the argument that security is lessened in the non-union sector was rejected. Thus a core area of vulnerability of operating on a non-union basis is, when analysed, "not really a weakness of substance".[28] Supporting this point, another respondent stated that unions have no influence on job security; "customer service protects jobs, not unions".[29] This contention is borne out by the experiences of employees in the unionised sector. Layoffs, short time working and redundancies have become commonplace again in recent years in the post-Celtic Tiger economy. In the main, union membership has made little difference. In fact, unionisation itself may have contributed to job losses. The dispute within the Irish Press Group over the introduction of new technology closed down the paper and it did not re-open.

While issue can be taken against the content of *what* was said, there was a genuine belief within the human resource group that no significant disadvantage exists in relation to job security for non-union employees. Indeed, the argument was put forward that job security was actually superior. The advantages a non-union company can realise by offering secure employment, while difficult to quantify, were stated to be "very real". Removing the fear of job loss provides greater loyalty to an organisation, less resistance to technological change and better overall employee relations, factors which contribute to higher productivity.[30] Because non-union companies are more attuned to employee relations they recognise the benefits of providing job security and use the myriad of techniques detailed elsewhere to ensure it.

Does Unionisation Provide a Form of Job Insurance?

Not surprisingly, most of the trade union respondents rejected the above view. The highest percentage of employees who join unions were said to do so for job security reasons as unions are seen to resist layoffs and job losses. The major disadvantage for employees operating on a non-union basis was that they had no "insurance" against dismissal or redundancy. While individuals did not necessarily want to "collect" on the insurance, that is, be threatened with redundancy to test the level of service, unionisation acted as a safety net. Substantial numbers of employees in the non-union companies were said to be secret card-carrying members because of fears of redundancy or dismissal.

Part of the reasoning here can be attributed to the "poor press" which the multinationals receive, a suspicion that foreign firms "up and go", that is, when the tax advantage position ceases the companies will move to some other tax haven.[31] Well publicised closedowns reinforce the notion of instability in the multinational sector. Many companies maintain production facilities in a number of countries and multinationals can simply re-route work to other plants based on economic expediency. One union official, stating that he should not support this view (because members are supposed to be ideologically committed), argued that employees join unions on the same basis as they insure their cars, to cater for an eventuality "somewhere down the line".[32] Supporting this, another official made the point that unionisation is a very cheap insurance policy.[33] The core point— that interest in unionisation is often linked with fears on job security — finds good support within the research literature. As Curtin notes:

> Next to dissatisfaction with salaries the most frequent cited
> cause of union interest among employees is concern with
> job security.[34]

Yet while it is accepted that fears on job security may lead to an interest in unionisation, this does not address the central question of whether unionisation can actually protect against redundancies. This question on the relative job security levels between the two sectors is central to any advantage/disadvantage analysis for employees. Within the overall debate several sub-points emerged. Firstly, a distinction may need to be made between partial and total company closedowns. Secondly, account needs to be taken of the relative job security between groups of non-union employees and individuals within this sector. Finally, the effect of unionisation on complimentary areas (in particular the level of redundancy settlements achieved) needs to be considered.

Distinguishing between Partial and Total Company Closedowns in the Non-Union Sector

The argument can be made that non-union companies are more sensitive to (and thus try to avoid) partial redundancies, being aware of the unionisation potential among remaining employees where this occurs. To overcome this, a number of techniques are used by these companies to stabilise employment. These include hiring freezes, reliance on attrition or natural wastage, use of temporary or former employees for specified periods of time, inventory build-ups, use of sub-contractors, voluntary leaves of absence, vacation banking, short-time working, overtime working to meet temporary fluctuations in demand and early retirements. In return for these measures employees had to be willing to do different jobs, to be re-trained and move as necessary in exchange for the relative job security provided.[35] Thus the need to maintain a non-union status, in effect, guards against partial plant closedowns. In contrast, where business conditions dictate a total plant closedown the same constraints may not apply. The non-union companies can virtually leave overnight due to the lack of effective opposition.[36] A distinction was therefore made between partial redundancies (against which non-union employees may have relative job security) and total plant closedowns (which leave them exposed to the arbitrary decision of the employer). While this view has the benefit of outward logic, the question arises whether there is any firm evidence to support it.

In my experience there is no evidence to support the supposed "non-union exposure" in relation to total plant closedowns. While some people "try to make a summer out of one swallow" this is not supported by the research.[37] Closing down operations without regard to the impact on employees would imply that the concern shown for employees was purely a "front" to keep them non-union. Such a thin veneer of concern would not hold up over time. The fact that most companies maintain a non-union status, of itself, provides de facto recognition that the stance is genuine. Further, the record of several unionised companies in relation to total plant closedowns lends little support to the argument that unions protect against this. There are a number of examples of unionised companies who ceased operations seemingly with little regard for the social consequences of this decision and without much evidence of effective opposition. Overall, the distinction between total and partial redundancies, while interesting, does not stack up.

Job Security within the Non-Union Sector: Distinguishing between Individuals and Groups

There was a reasonable consensus that at the collective level a company's philosophy and trading position determined job security. However, at the level of the individual employee a high degree of "hire and fire" was stated to exist.[38] While the non-union companies would not suggest to employees, en bloc, that unionisation would influence the company to locate elsewhere, this may be presented in micro form highlighting the personal implications for individuals. A general communication on this issue might be counterproductive (pushing employees to unionise for "insurance" reasons). However, creating fear at the level of the individual employee was said to be a potent weapon in the armoury of non-union companies.[39] Several of the union officials put forward the view that while employees remain unorganised they are more open to arbitrary dismissal. However, there was no consensus on this point. Some of the respondents felt that it is unlikely that the non-union companies have a "worse" dismissals record and argued that there was no evidence to support it.[40] Others suggested that the non-union companies may have a *better* record in this area as tighter recruitment policies and more sophisticated personnel systems (for example, probation monitoring) lessen the likelihood of dismissals. As dismissals, particularly those involving a popular employee, are an Achille's Heel for non-union companies, they tend to be particularly cautious in this area. The need to maintain credibility with other employees, the ever present threat of unionisation and the company's overall personnel philosophy lessen the likelihood for authoritarian practices.[41] While the hypothetical point that individual employees in the non-union sector are more open to arbitrary dismissal was accepted, this does not happen in practice.[42]

One possible way to quantify this point was to review the dismissals records in the non-union companies visited. If it could be shown that they had a higher level of dismissals vis a vis the unionised companies (based on comparable headcount figures), this might support the point that job security is lessened for individuals. A lack of statistical data at the companies visited made a quantifiable judgement impossible, and the statistics published by the Employment Appeals Tribunal do not identify unionised and non-union companies. Even if such data were available it would still suffer from two fundamental weaknesses. Firstly, as the total proportion of unionised versus non-union employments is difficult to quantify, it would not be possible to establish definitively the levels of dismissals within each respective sector. Secondly, the likelihood is that a "unionised" bias would emerge from the data as many cases brought to the Tribunal are dependant upon trade union support. It is unlikely that the structures and functions of the Employment Appeals Tribunal are widely known or understood outside of a fairly limited circle (mainly legal and industrial relations).[43]

In summary, quantification of the point that individuals in the non-union sector are more open to arbitrary dismissal has to remain open ended. The absence of data makes it impossible to either prove or disprove this point. Yet while a theoretical possibility exists that job security for individual employees is lessened, it is unlikely to be a factor of significance. It ignores the fact that the non-union companies must continually convince the general body of employees that it is in their best interests to remain non-union. Decisions which reinforce the notion that employees need "protection" are resisted for this very reason. The rigour of the Unfair Dismissals Act imposes further limitations on a company's unilateral decision-making power in this area. Yet whatever the actuality, employees' perception may be that job security is lessened in the non-union sector. Without a formal negotiation process there is no tangible evidence of any "battle for job".[44] While the local management team may resist redundancies imposed by a parent company, the fact that such resistance is covert (and limited in terms of "muscle") may mean that such protection seems marginal to employees.[45] It follows that non-union companies have to make particular efforts to overcome the *perception* that job security is lessened by the absence of a trade union. Fears on the question of job security (as much as actual redundancies) were a core feature of the union drives studied as part of this research. In several case histories, such fears were the central driving factor in the push for union recognition. A vital part therefore of any job security policy is open communication with employees, avoiding generating unnecessary fear. Companies who are silent on their policy (despite the fact that they may actively support job security) inadvertently cause fear among employees and leave themselves open to union encroachment.

Can Better Redundancy Settlement Terms Be Achieved by Trade Union Members?

While unionisation has little impact on job protection, membership may provide a subsidiary benefit where job losses do occur. In the event of redundancy unions may be able to achieve better settlement terms as employees have more negotiating power. In the event of plant closures non-union employees "have no one to argue their case".[46] In the unionised sector the evidence suggests that companies tend to pay "well above the statutory".[47] In a non-union situation companies are not under the same pressure to pay high settlement terms and the "inevitable" consequence of this was that lower settlement figures are achieved.

The argument put forward was that regardless of how sincere companies have been on the issue of employee welfare, once the employment relationship has come to an end the focus reverts solely to the business, that is, cessation at the lowest possible cost. Companies may feel they've discharged their responsibilities to employees and simply pay statutory entitlements when they leave. While the level of redundancy settlements is, of itself, an important point, a sub-issue raised is the overall cost of redundancy payments which may covertly influence job security. High severance payments may deter a decision to rationalise due to cost considerations. The fact that severance pay (one official described it as "a sharing in the saving of taking people off the payroll") may be costly could dissuade some companies from ceasing operations as "money talks" to the multinationals.[48] Thus union membership may indirectly provide job security through the negative disincentive of a higher withdrawal cost.

It is a clever argument but almost impossible to prove or disprove. Despite the costs involved the evidence suggests that multinational companies will disinvest in Ireland. There are numerous examples where the supposed high cost of redundancies did not deter unionised companies from ceasing operations. Yet the point is interesting in that it begs the question as to how many unionised multinational companies now operating in Ireland would have ceased to do so (or scaled down their operations) if the cost had been lower (for example, statutory minimum). While impossible to quantify, it has the benefit of outward logic. If better settlement terms can be achieved by trade union members, this would seem to represent a genuine loss to employees in the non-union sector. This loss may be compounded by the fact that higher severance payments may actually dissuade companies from disinvestment, thereby providing a degree of job security.

THE SECOND DISADVANTAGE: IGNORANCE OF LABOUR LEGISLATION AND CONDITIONS IN OTHER EMPLOYMENTS

The second stated disadvantage for non-union employees could broadly be labelled as "ignorance" — both of employment legislation and conditions which prevail in other companies. Non-union status was therefore seen to disadvantage employees as it lessens their power vis-à-vis the employer in the information area.[49]

Lack of information was said to translate into two tangible losses for employees. Firstly, non-union companies can simply ignore the law because individual workers will seldom have any in-depth knowledge of it. As legislation plays an increasingly important role in the employment relationship, companies were said to want to remain non-union in order to "flout their obligations".[50] The second point raised was that employees do not have access to information on which to judge conditions of employment. Individual employees are seldom aware of the full range of benefits and conditions within other employments and it is difficult to get comprehensive information of this nature. Trade union membership gives access to such information either through work completed directly by the union official or through union research facilities. Such information provides negotiations leverage, which is lost to employees in the non-union sector. While the first issue raised would seem to represent a legitimate loss to non-unionised employees, the lack of information on benefits is a more marginal point. Given that the companies keep a sophisticated link with the marketplace to maintain their relative position, employees are unlikely to be substantially disadvantaged in this area. Further, while employees may not have access to detailed salary information, in my experience they can access this information informally (through family contacts and so on) and often have a surprisingly accurate picture of the marketplace.

THE THIRD DISADVANTAGE: DECREASE IN
CONTROL OVER WORKING LIFE

Even where employees have access to it, having information without the corresponding power to affect change may be of little value.[51] An example was given to support this point. At one manufacturing company visited, several toxic chemicals were used in the process. A particular incident which involved a large spillage and the subsequent dispersion of radioactive material was related. This was considered so serious by the company that they stripped down the entire laboratory to the point that even floorboards were removed on the basis that they might be contaminated. When employees working in the area asked that they receive a full medical check-up and a report on their health status they were initially refused. After considerable pressure from employees (through the union) the medical check was eventually conceded. This story was related as being "fairly typical" of the problems faced by trade unions in pursuing issues for members. The core point was that even where employees are unionised it can be difficult to resolve issues. Where they operate on a non-union basis they were said to have "little hope" of having such issues satisfactorily addressed.[52]

Another example related to a friend of a union official who worked in a non-union company and had to complete overtime against his wishes. In the unionised sector this supposedly would not be tolerated as general union policy dictates that overtime is worked on a voluntary basis.[53] Because the individual concerned was operating on a non-union basis he had to accept compulsory overtime, a loss of personal freedom.[54] A significant degree of control, in this case the option not to work overtime, was removed from the level of individual choice. An increase in workplace control is therefore a primary benefit of achieving trade union recognition. As Hyman argues:

> A trade union is, first and foremost, an agency and medium of power. Its central purpose is to permit workers to collectively take control over their conditions of employment which they cannot hope to possess as individuals; and to do so largely by compelling the employer to take account, in policy and decision making, of interests and priorities contrary to his own.[55]

Posing a number of rhetorical questions, one official asked if employees are unfairly dismissed whether the companies would fight their case and provide free legal aid against themselves? In the event of redundancy, would companies challenge their own settlement terms? In relation to safety, would a company challenge itself on the use of a dangerous substance? There was said to be a conflict within industry between capital and labour, each being a separate entity and needing an independent organisation to protect its separate interests.[56] Another official made the point that society, in general, is responsive to pressure groups. The most effective pressure group structure for employees was to band together in a trade union.[57] Real freedom, defined as the ability to participate in the introduction of change or to veto particular management actions which ran counter to the interests of members, was sacrificed by employees in the non-union sector.[58]

While the weight of evidence would seem to support the point that employees in the non-union sector suffer a decrease in workplace control, this must be seen in the context of the general limitations of trade union power. As detailed elsewhere, union power is normally restricted to the negative right to veto. It seldom encompasses the positive right to participate except to the extent that it can limit managerial prerogative in certain defined areas. An understanding of this is crucial to any debate on the losses associated with non-union status. A realistic assessment of the loss of control for employees in the non-union sector should only take account of the actual losses, that is, those areas where trade unions have in fact managed to extend control, rather than some hy-

pothetical loss. Once again a distinction needs to be made between the "upper" and "lower" tier non-union sectors described
earlier. In the sophisticated upper-tier non-union companies, a
range of practices are in place to ensure that employees are given
"voice".

While the loss of the countervailing power of the unions is a
reality, the limitations of what can be achieved in the unionised
sector must also be recognised. Most of the trade union respondents fully supported the concept of the "right of manage", albeit
on a fair basis, as being necessary for a company's ongoing successful operation. For example, one official made the point that he
always told new members that a union could "protect them from
slavery but not from work". Undoubtedly employees operating
on a non-union basis sacrifice the "safety net" or insurance which
unions provide, but this has to be weighed against the positive
gains detailed earlier. As with many of the areas touched on, the
loss in essence becomes a trade off.

THE FOURTH DISADVANTAGE: THE LOSS OF
SPECIALISED NEGOTIATION SKILLS

A long with the power of acting collectively, trade union membership also provides the benefit of negotiation specialisation. The loss of access to this represents a further downside for
employees in the non-union sector. One official made the point
that the amateur "will never be a professional". While an individual may win "the odd victory" they will generally not have the
skills to deal with professional company negotiators on an ongoing basis. Full-time officials develop their negotiations skills
through formal training and as a result of the vast exposure to collective bargaining which they receive through normal working.
As companies were said to treat individuals based on their "ability to negotiate",[59] this loss of specialisation constitutes a fourth
disadvantage for employees operating on a non-union basis.

THE FIFTH DISADVANTAGE: A GENERAL
DECLINE IN UNION POWER

As described earlier, a fully-fledged non-union policy can be understood as an effort to effect "union substitution". The companies identified the type of benefits and services that employees associate with union membership and put these "voluntarily" in place. The point was made that this would not be the case if a general decline in union power occurred. The presence of unions "waiting in the wings" forces non-union companies to provide pay and conditions which are at least comparable to the unionised sector. If the power of unions decreased, the pressure on the non-union companies to keep pace with (or marginally ahead of) the unionised sector would diminish. The undermining of the formal trade union structure may therefore, in the longer term, represent a loss to all employees.

Employees in the non-union companies were seen to be enjoying the benefits of trade unionism at one remove, thus undermining the structure of trade unionism indirectly by encouraging the spread of "non-union" companies.[60] Individual employees tend not to take this macro view, partly because the issue is not immediate (and therefore may not be recognised) and partly because such employees were said to pursue a philosophy of "me féin".[61] In practice it is very difficult for an individual employee to equate working on a non-union basis with a general decline in the power of trade unions as the link is extremely tenuous. It suggests a political awareness on the part of employees that is not widespread, and employs a moralistic argument that unionised employers are somewhat less concerned about themselves and more interested in the "general good" (an interesting point but not something often encountered!). However, these points do not fundamentally detract from the central argument that the development of the non-union sector may undermine the union movement which, in the longer term, may result in a "stalling" or even a reversal of the trend toward enhanced employee benefits and conditions at work.

In summary, a number of distinct advantages/disadvantages were seen to apply to employees in the non-union sector. These are captured in Figure 11.

FIGURE 11: ADVANTAGES/DISADVANTAGES FOR EMPLOYEES WORKING ON A NON-UNION BASIS	
Advantages	**Disadvantages**
• Higher wage/benefits levels. • Benefits extended to families • Reward system recognises good performance. • Promotion based on merit rather than seniority. • Personal grievances/issues resolved speedily. • No payment of union subscriptions. • Less fear of wage losses due to strikes. • Employment is not conditional on union membership. • No subordination to union policy	• Lack of insurance against dismissals or redundancy. • Lower redundancy settlements. • Ignorance of legislation/ conditions in other employments. • Decrease in control over working life. • Loss of negotiation specialisation. • General decline in trade union power may "pull down" wage/benefit increases.

Endnotes

[1] The "upper tier" non-union sector associated with the multinationals provides the focus here. Employees in the "lower tier" (small domestic employments) non-union sector are likely to be disadvantaged under this heading.

[2] "Trade Union Official B". Points made during interview with author.

³ "Industrial Relations Expert C". Points made during interview with author.

⁴ "Industrial Relations Expert D". Points made during interview with author.

⁵ "Trade Union Official B". Points made during interview with author.

⁶ Personnel Manager: Company F. Points made during interview with author.

⁷ "Trade Union Official F". Points made during interview with author.

⁸ Sykes, J.B. (ed.). *The Concise Oxford Dictionary*. Sixth Edition. Oxford University Press, 1976.

⁹ "Trade Union Official E". Points made during interview with author.

¹⁰ "Trade Union Official D". Points made during interview with author.

¹¹ "Industrial Relations Expert A". Points made during interview with author.

¹² Personnel Manager: Company I. Points made during interview with author.

¹³ Personnel Manager: Company I. Points made during interview with author.

¹⁴ Undated extract from Multi-National Company Employee Handbook.

¹⁵ "Industrial Relations Expert D". Points made during interview with author.

¹⁶ "Trade Union Official B". Points made during interview with author.

¹⁷ ""Trade Union Official A". Points made during interview with author.

¹⁸ "Trade Union Official B". Points made during interview with author.

¹⁹ Personnel Manager: Company I.

²⁰ Margolies, Richard. "The Changing Face of Work and Management". A One Day Seminar run at the Irish management Institute on 14 June 1985. *Irish Institute of Training and Development News*, July, 1985.

²¹ "Trade Union Official B". Points made during interview with author.

²² "Industrial Relations Expert C". Points made during interview with author

[23] Ross, A.M. *Trade Union Wage Policy*. University of California Press, Berkelely, 1948: 23.

[24] Personnel Manager: Company I. Points made during interview with author.

[25] Donovan, Lord. (Chairman) *Report of the Royal Commission on Trade Unions and Employers Associations*. HMSO, London, 1968.

[26] Hyman, Richard. *Industrial Relations: A Marxist Introduction*. Macmillan, London, 1975: 65.

[27] Allen, V.L. *Power in Trade Unions*. Clowes and Sons, London, 1954: 15.

[28] "Industrial Relations Expert D". Points made during interview with author.

[29] Personnel Executive: Company I. Points made during interview with author.

[30] Miljus J., Professor of Organisational Behaviour, Ohio State University, 1986, in conversation with the author.

[31] "Trade Union Official C". Points made during interview with author.

[32] "Trade Union Official F". Points made during interview with author.

[33] "Trade Union Official E". Points made during interview with author.

[34] Curtin, Edward, R. "White-Collar Unionisation Studies". Personnel Policy No. 220-A Research Report, New York, The National Industrial Conference Board, 1970.

[35] Personnel Manager: Company H. Points made during interview with author.

[36] "Industrial Relations Expert C". Points made during interview with author.

[37] "Industrial Relations Expert D". Points made during interview with author.

[38] "Trade Union Official D". Points made during interview with author.

[39] "Trade Union Official B". Points made during interview with author.

[40] "Industrial Relations Expert A". Points made during interview with author.

[41] "Industrial Relations Expert C". Points made during interview with author.

[42] "Industrial Relations Expert D". Points made during interview with author.

[43] As access to this information is almost a pre-requisite to pursuing an unfair dismissals case, the likelihood is that there would be a substantial bias in the data in respect of unionised employees. Even where the existence of the Tribunal is known it is a daunting task for an individual to take on a case "single handed". While legal counsel can be sought and may substitute for the role of a full-time official, the cost of this would act as a disincentive for many individuals.

[44] "Trade Union Official C". Points made during interview with author.

[45] "Industrial Relations Expert C". Points made during interview with author.

[46] "Trade Union Official C". Points made during interview with author.

[47] "Industrial Relations Expert C". Points made during interview with author.

[48] "Trade Union Official A". Points made during interview with author.

[49] "Trade Union Official E". Points made during interview with author.

[50] "Trade Union Official E". Points made during interview with author.

[51] "Trade Union Official E". Points made during interview with author.

[52] "Trade Union Official E". Points made during interview with author.

[53] Practises within the unionised sector differ in this regard. An analysis of 34 company/union agreements conducted by the author showed approximately a 50/50 split on this point of "mandatory overtime".

[54] "Trade Union Official B". Points made during interview with author.

[55] Hyman, Richard. *Industrial Relations: A Marxist Introduction.* Macmillan, London, 1975.

[56] "Trade Union Official E". Points made during interview with author.

[57] "Industrial Relations Expert C". Points made during interview with author.

[58] "Trade Union Official D". Points made during interview with author.

[59] "Trade Union Official F". Points made during interview with author.

[60] "Trade Union Officials E and F". Points made during interview with author.

[61] "Trade Union Official B". Points made during interview with author.

8

COMPARING HUMAN RESOURCE PRACTICES IN UNION AND NON-UNION SECTORS

A CENTRAL THEME STRESSED EARLIER is that the industrial relations system is undergoing a period of transition. One element of this is the development of high commitment work systems which have fundamentally changed the concept of the employment relationship. Given the correct conditions, employees are seen to yield tremendous motivational energy to organisations. If this analysis is correct, the philosophical change noted should translate into actual differences in personnel policies between unionised (traditional model) and non-union (high commitment model) companies. In order to test this hypothesis, a range of personnel practices in the companies visited were reviewed. It was assumed, a priori, that the level of sophistication would be greater in the non-union sector for two reasons. Firstly, the companies operate from a fundamentally different conception of the role of employees, with personnel policy being seen as an integrated part of general business policy rather than an adjunct of hire and fire practices. As Patterson argued, "Personnel strategy should act as a booster rocket to business strategy".[1] Secondly, in order to maintain a union-free status, companies must continually work at diffusing the perception that a trade union could negotiate better benefits, conditions or treatment for employees than those already in place. While there were a range of "drill down" possibilities, the areas selected for analysis were (a) recruitment/selection, (b) the degree of contact between management and employees, (c) salary and benefits, (d) grievance/discipline procedures, (e) training/development, (f) internal promotions, (g) communications structures and (h) job security.

THE RECRUITMENT PROCESS IN THE NON-UNION SECTOR

As a general point, the screening and selection process is more rigorous in the non-union sector, where companies put significantly more time and energy into recruitment.[2] There was also general agreement that the selection process in the unionised sector could be improved significantly, with some companies' practices being labelled as "appalling".[3] Indeed, general studies of recruitment, particularly in relation to manual jobs, report the widespread use of informal procedures which can be described as haphazard and casual. The criteria established are often implicit and unrelated to job performance with considerable reliance on "gut feel" and instinct.[4] Interestingly, as unions are committed to accepting all new recruits into membership (under the terms of pre-employment agreements this is normally the case), the absence of effective screening also becomes, in time, a problem for them.[5]

Tighter Selection Screens Out "Militants"[6]

In attempting to explain the higher degree of professionalism in the non-union sector in terms of recruitment practises, one argument put forward was that the extra efforts expended are simply designed to screen potential militants. During an address given by Gene Amdahl (the founder of the non-union company Amdahl) to a group of engineers, he supposedly stated that companies should use rigid screening procedures to ensure that employees had no background of trade unionism.[7] Potential employees were asked if they were, or had been, members of a union; active union members would not be selected for employment.[8] Despite these assertions, there is no evidence that a "blacklist" (in the sense of a centralised listing of people which is distributed between employers) exists. However, companies have become quite conscientious in carrying out telephone reference checks. If candidates have been poor performers or have had a strong union involvement in previous jobs, they are less likely to be employed in the non-union sector. Within the industrial relations system (given the relatively small size of the country), contacts become established between personnel practitioners. Where individual employees come to be dubbed "militant", this information would likely become available to companies through reference checking.

Ensuring Trade Union "Virginity": Recruiting School Leavers

One tactic which can be used to reduce the number of employees who have a unionised background is to positively discriminate in favour of school leavers (an industrial application of the Jesuitical philosophy, "give me the boy and I'll give you the man"). One of the non-union companies visited[9] is well known in personnel circles for its bias in this regard. The company places no prerequisite on skills, preferring to train employees in-house as a trade-off against the fact that such recruits have no prior trade union orientation.

There was mixed opinion among respondents with regard to the practicality of this policy. While there may be some benefits in recruiting school leavers, a number of possible disadvantages are also clear. Firstly, younger people are not conditioned to the discipline of factory life and may experience difficulty in adjusting. Secondly, because many younger people are single they are less likely to have family/mortgage commitments. They were thus seen to be less "stable" with the likelihood that labour turnover, in particular, would be higher. Thirdly, extra costs in training would normally have to be incurred as school leavers have few industrial skills. Finally, and this was the major objection raised, younger people were said to be more likely to suffer from career frustration if they do not get promoted quickly. Many have the "false expectations of youth", as one respondent described it, and companies who exclusively recruit school leavers may be storing up future discontentment. On the plus side, younger people were said to learn skills quickly and are generally more adaptable to change, along with the point noted that they do not have the same exposure to trade unions. However, most of the personnel respondents felt that a mixed age group gave better overall industrial relations stability and that the negative factors outlined outweighed any supposed gain from "having a factory full of acne cases". On the basis of this research the notion that companies in the non-union sector show a positive bias in favour of school leavers remains unproven.

Selection and Recruitment Impose Considerable Time Demands

The fact that effective selection is a hugely time-consuming activity probably best explains why it receives inadequate attention in the unionised sector. Job advertising, vetting application forms, conducting interviews, reference and medical checking all amount to a tremendous drain on available resources. The lead time on recruitment where all of these steps are taken can be several weeks for entry level jobs ranging up to several months for more senior positions. Line managers do not always appreciate this. Depending on the planning horizon at particular companies, this can be exacerbated with job openings expected to be filled within tight time constraints. This is particularly the case in relation to start-ups. Incoming multinationals seldom recruit their workforce over an extended time period. Unlike traditional industry, recruitment in a start-up is not simply the addition of extra employees as the business expands but often the establishment of a fully fledged workforce to meet an existing product demand. It is not unusual for multinational companies to have hiring targets of over 100 employees per annum.[10] This level of activity places a huge strain on human resources staff and adequate resourcing is essential if the recruitment task is to be tackled professionally and systematically. Where such resources are not in place, the effectiveness of the selection process is reduced significantly.

Poor resources invested in the recruitment process denotes a lack of understanding of the tremendous financial investment in individual employees over the total period of employment. For example, if it is assumed that the total cost of employment for one individual is €30,000 per annum, this equates to a cost of €600,000 (or its inflationary equivalent) over a period of 20 years. If a similar investment decision was made in any other area of business (for example, in buying a new piece of equipment) a huge amount of time and research effort would be invested before the decision to purchase. Few organisations appreciate the negative cost implications of a poor recruitment decision which, in part, explains the lack of attention given to this area. Within companies where the line management functions have significantly more clout than the personnel function (traditional model), it is unlikely that work associated with personnel (for example, recruitment) will be given the necessary time, effort or commitment to ensure that it is carried out professionally. In the non-union sector where the extra staffing resources are available, better recruitment decisions are a positive outcome.

Interview Follow Up: Reference Checking

The purpose of an interview is to try to determine (usually in a relatively short period) an individual's likely future job performance. This is a notoriously difficult and subjective task; predicting future job behaviour is an inexact science. The non-union compa-

nies visited had built a number of "steps" into the selection process to limit its subjectivity. A notable example is conducting systematic reference checks. The single best indicator of a potential
employee's future behaviour is their *past* behaviour. While this is
not a foolproof guide (as individual behaviour is not static and
will likely be conditioned by the new environment), it is the most
predictive measure of an unknown candidate.[11] Where reference
checks are carried out to supplement interviewing, companies can
significantly reduce the margin of error in recruitment decisions.

All of the non-union companies visited conducted reference
checks with previous employers. These were normally completed
over the phone using a standard protocol, with little reliance being placed on written references (one respondent remarked that
he had "never yet seen a poor written reference".[12] Previous employers (or school authorities where candidates had no previous
work experience) were contacted and the applicant's work record
(performance, timekeeping, attendance, attitude and so on)
checked. Some of the companies, as a policy, made two telephone
reference calls. This tight system of reference checking represents
an understanding of the limitations of selection interviewing.
While telephone reference checking is time consuming, non-union
companies are prepared to invest the necessary time and have the
resources to do this, increasing the likelihood of a better selection
decision.

New Employees are Closely Monitored during the Probation Period

Along with their more rigorous selection procedures, non-union
companies typically have a much better monitoring system for
new employees. This normally involves several performance and
"attitude" assessments being carried out throughout the probation period. Emphasising this, one of the union officials stated that
if new employees were a "quarter wrong" during their probation-

ary period the non-union companies dismiss them.[13] However, tight monitoring of probationary periods may also feature in the unionised sector. Most pre-employment agreements contain clauses similar to that outlined below:

PROBATION CLAUSE IN A UNION/MANAGEMENT AGREEMENT

"Employees will serve a (6) month probationary period before confirmation of employment. Throughout the probation period each employee's work standard conduct and suitability will be continually assessed. The company may, at it absolute discretion, terminate employment without giving a reason any time during the probation period should it find an employee's work standard, conduct or suitability to be unsatisfactory and no grievance or complaint may be filed by the Union concerning such action. Absences in excess of two weeks will be deducted in computing the actual employment."

Such clauses allow companies a degree of flexibility, a form of "selection breathing space". Yet in many cases, the unionised companies were said to put up a façade of selectivity and control but did not follow through. Once people were employed there was a virtual collapse of the monitoring system. This point was neatly captured by a local saying in Cork about Dunlops which ran "once you get your leg in there you're right".[14] It follows that a procedurally tight probation monitoring system only works when coupled with a system of monitoring and control which is actively managed. Recruitment is a highly subjective process and errors of judgement are often made. While the unionised companies are not prevented from running a tight probationary process, the fact that less emphasis in general is placed on personnel issues means that this area is not rigorously pursued. Tighter probation monitoring in the non-union sector is partly explained by the possibility of union encroachment but also follows from their sophistication in the personnel area generally and the extra HR staffing levels.

Overall a clear finding which emerged from the research was that the time devoted to recruitment/probation monitoring was markedly superior in the non-union sector. Stressing the importance of this, one human resource manager remarked that there are three important variables in effective employee relations, "recruitment, recruitment and recruitment".[15]

THE HIGH DEGREE OF MANAGEMENT CONTACT WITH EMPLOYEES IN NON-UNION COMPANIES

Underlying many of the specific personnel policies employed in the non-union sector was an attempt to develop employee identity with the organisation. Continuous contact between managers and employees helps copperfasten this. A number of structures had evolved to facilitate interaction between the two groups. For example, a striking difference which emerged between the unionised and the non-union companies visited was the amount of managerial time spent on the shop floor. The term "Management by Wandering Around" (MBWA) has become something of a catch-phrase. MBWA refers to the stated practice in Hewlett Packard and elsewhere that managers should spend a fixed proportion of their time on the shop floor. Such policies help to improve communications between the workforce and the management team, lessening the likelihood of a "them and us" climate developing which in turn supports the maintenance of a non-union status. The point was continually driven home that union drives most often come from *within* a plant. Some companies were stated to be so busy watching the union that they "forget to manage their own people".[16] In several of the non-union companies visited it was a stated part of the managerial brief to spend a proportion of working time on the shop floor. While none of the companies attempted to quantify it, the important point is that this particular objective was completely absent within the unionised companies benchmarked.

As with most of the personnel policies reviewed, closeness to the workforce was pursued for business rather than altruistic reasons. A continuous presence on the shop floor, while creating the perception that "somebody cares", also provides the significant benefit of a two-way communications link in which ideas from employees become available to the management team. Closeness to the problems encountered by employees is essential for any manager who wishes to make an effective contribution. A number of the respondents in the non-union sector expressed distaste for the "ivory tower" concept of management, where managers were seen to be aloof. Two of the human resource respondents, quite independently of each other, stated that such was their company's commitment to this area that individual managers had been taken to task for not complying with the policy of spending time "away from the office".[17] In contrast, some of the unionised companies visited had developed what could be described as an internal class system, with shop floor employees being ranked almost as "untouchable".[18] This can partly be explained by class divisions where managers and shop floor employees, who often come from different socio-economic levels, have little common identity or interests other than sharing the same employer. Yet keeping a "distance" from shop floor employees may actually be reinforced at some unionised companies in order to maintain "respect".[19] Through conditioning, and because aloofness is seen by some companies as a method to maintain status, strongly demarcated divisions between managers and employees are not uncommon (albeit this particular aspect of working life seems to be in general decline). Closeness to the workforce in the non-union companies visited was reinforced by the use of first names with employees. At some of the companies, managers wore open neck shirts without ties (over the past couple of years dress codes have become more relaxed generally in all sectors). While this may seem trivial it points to a movement away from traditional values, that is, less reliance on the traditional authority relationship of which "formal dress" and the use of surnames have been support features.

Closeness to the Workforce: An Environmental Solution

The notion of closeness to the workforce in a software sense also had a "hardware" element. In four of the five non-union companies visited the front line personnel office (employee relations manager-type positions) was actually located on the shop floor in order to facilitate employees "dropping in" to discuss problems on their way to the canteen and so on. In some of the plants all interface offices — job grades where employees need to spend a significant amount of their time with production personnel (for example, cost accountants) — were also located on the shop floor in an attempt to overcome the traditional geographical distance between blue and white collar employees. Here, specific efforts were made to overcome the traditional demarcation lines between manual and white collar workers. Where these distinctions can be blurred the possibility of a "front office superiority complex" is lessened.[20] In contrast, in many of the unionised plants the front offices could be dubbed "Mahogany Row" by virtue of the distance in space and physical surroundings separating the two groups.

As a further aid to promoting in-company communications, several of the non-union companies had specifically designed open plan offices — a sort of "no door" policy. The companies used wall partitioning with acoustic panels which was effective in reducing noise levels and in maintaining confidentiality (the two most often stated objections to open plan offices). Only very senior management levels had full "closed" offices on the basis that issues of confidentiality (disciplinary matters, finance policy and so on) would often be discussed.[21] In one non-union company visited where the offices are not open plan, large windows were inserted in all offices (subsequent to the initial construction) to help produce a climate of openness at the plant which was "missing".[22] These initiatives represent a direct physical attempt to improve communications and managerial closeness to employees. The fact that several of the non-union companies had actively considered communications with employees when planning the layout of their facilities provides further evidence of the divergent human resource management philosophy vis a vis the unionised sector. Examples outside of Ireland include the installation of huge escalators in the Hong Kong Shanghai Bank in an effort to encourage "open communication" (as people do not "talk" in elevators). The billion-dollar Chrysler headquarters in the US employed the same design principle for exactly the same reason.

None of the non-union companies had segregated dining facilities, albeit this particular distinction is becoming an outmoded practice across the entire industrialised sector. Interestingly, one practice which seemed somewhat at variance with the trend related to clocking in procedures. While some of the respondents made the point that single status (the same conditions for all employees) was a necessary ingredient of a successful union avoidance programme (for example, all employees clock in or no employees clock in), there was no consensus on this. Three of the non-union companies had grouped employees into differing categories with blue collar employees clocking in while white collar employees did not. Despite this distinction they had still managed to remain non-union. A general attempt to remove barriers (rather than an exact need to apply single status on each individual condition of employment) seems to be the requirement in maintaining non-union status.

Management Participation in Social Events

Another area in which management contact with employees occurs is through participation in social activities outside of normal working hours. Here again the non-union companies ranked higher than comparable unionised companies. While none of the non-union companies visited made compulsory attendance at social activities part of their managers' job specifications, it was an unwritten social rule that this should occur. In an organisation where people management skills are highly rated there is a link between social skills and promotion. If the culture of an organisation values the ability to relate to employees, managers who lack this "connect" skill may be overlooked in internal promotion decisions.

SALARY/BENEFITS POLICIES IN THE NON-UNION SECTOR

There was a consensus across the union/management divide that employees in the non-union sector enjoy high wage/salary levels and good relative conditions of employment. For example, four of the five non-union companies visited had a stated salary and benefit philosophy to maintain their rates of pay at the 75th percentile point or better in a comparable marketplace, while the fifth kept salary benefit levels "above average". This finding on salary/benefit levels in the non-union sector mirrors that found by Toner in conducting complimentary research in this area.[23] While it is difficult to quantify precisely the positioning of the non-union companies vis a vis unionised companies, figures between five and ten per cent were mentioned by a number of respondents (that is, basic rates of pay/benefits in the non-union sector were judged to be approximately five to ten per cent higher than those in comparable unionised employments). However, it must be stressed that this figure is a "guesstimate".[24]

The central point is that salary and benefit levels tend to be higher in the non-union sector, a finding which is supported by international research.[25] One respondent stated that he treated the various salary philosophies with a "grain of salt". As the companies tended to keep their wage data secret it is very difficult to quantify exactly what they are paying or indeed what the workforce were actually doing. Although some job titles (for example, general operative) are standard throughout industry, the actual work performed can be quite different between companies. While the non-union companies wish to portray the image that they are "high payers", gross pay was said to often disguise shift premiums, bonus payments and various other benefits when the basic rate "is often fairly tight".[26] While there was strong support for the point that the non-union companies pay good wages and conditions in relative terms, many unionised companies also rank well in this area. For example, in the Insurance industry, Irish Life & Permanent (unionised) was said to have "the best employment conditions in Ireland".[27] The intent therefore is not to create the impression that the non-union companies can easily be differentiated from unionised companies on the basis of pay/conditions as there is a good degree of overlap between the two sectors on this point.

The Rationale for Paying Higher Wages/Benefits in the Non-Union Sector

Several of the trade union respondents put forward the view that the high wage/benefit policies are pursued for union avoidance purposes. As the non-union companies currently pay rates which are in excess of the unionised sector (and assuming that there is some mechanism for these to be adjusted on a continuing basis), the rationale for union membership is, in part, removed and the maintenance of a non-union status "bought".[28] Yet while competitive salary and benefits is indeed a central pillar in the maintenance of a non-union status, high pay and conditions would not withstand union encroachment without the other support factors detailed. This point provides an overall rider to any discussion on the effect of pay levels on union avoidance. However, the potential impact of *inadequate* benefits levels should not be underestimated. Improperly managed or under-funded policies can provide an "Achille's Heel" for non-union companies, creating the perception that a union could make substantive gains for employees. In recognition of this, the non-union companies visited displayed a high degree of market sensitivity to wage and benefits rates.

Sensitivity to Wage/Benefit Rate Movements: The Use of Market Intelligence

Without doubt the non-union companies are highly sensitive to wage/benefit rates as a potential unionisation threat. They invest significant time and incur substantial costs in compiling wage and benefits data. The companies visited keep a sophisticated link with the marketplace to ensure their position is maintained, normally by selecting a group of comparable companies against which wage/benefit rates are matched. The "basket" of companies is determined on the basis of industry and company size (it makes little sense comparing the job rates in a small retail company with those in a large multinational manufacturing corporation). The non-union companies usually complete at least one physical survey each year of the companies. Although time consuming, it was felt this was valuable both in terms of gathering wage/benefits statistics and in allowing personnel staff to talk to their counterparts in other companies. Some of the companies completed more than one survey per annum and most themselves participated in surveys conducted by other companies. As the usual practice is that participating companies receive copies of completed surveys this, in effect, gave some of the companies up to six sets of survey data each year against which conditions could be tracked. Overall, the time and effort devoted to gathering this information provides another clear example of the sophistication of the non-union companies.

Critical to the successful maintenance of a non-union status is the ability to convince employees that they are doing at least as well as unionised employees. Managing the wage rates/benefits of a workforce is less a science than the art of convincing people on an ongoing basis that they are receiving an equitable reward for their services. At some of the companies visited the policy of maintaining rates of pay ahead of the unionised sector was stated quite openly to employees as a specific union avoidance mechanism. One personnel executive explained that his particular company communicate to employees that they can have excellent pay and conditions, above the union rate, or they can have a union but that "they can't have both".[29]

GRIEVANCE PROCEDURES: THE VALUE OF "OPEN DOOR" POLICIES

An obvious distinction can be made between grievance procedures in the unionised and non-union sectors, that is, the absence of representational structures in the non-union sector. One argument put forward was that non-union companies are actually "better" at resolving grievances, despite the absence of representation ("if anyone blows their nose the management are down to ask them if it's okay").[30] In research conducted by Toner grievance procedures were considered satisfactory by 76 per cent of non-union employees as against 48 per cent of unionised employees, which does not support the notion that the non-union companies exploit the lack of representation.[31]

In practice "open door" policies, supposedly a key element in the grievance procedures of non-union plants, are seldom used for the purpose of resolving grievances. Where employees cannot resolve a problem with their immediate superior, they tend to discuss this with someone in the human resource department, rather than go to some other member of management. Some employees are "not disposed to go and knock on the boss's door". In time such individuals were said to gather confidence in the system which increases usage.[32] An alternative explanation to account for the low usage of the "open door" is fear of retaliation if employ-

ees go "around" their immediate superior. Most take the safer option of taking unresolved problems to the personnel department,
a finding supported by research conduced in the US.[33] A central
difficulty in the operation of an "open door" policy, therefore, relates to the supervisor or manager bypassed who may resent criticism which comes to them indirectly, possibly interpreting this as
an "exposure" of their inability to senior management. As Foulkes
notes:

> If employees are fearful that management or their
> supervisor will retaliate or "get them" because they filed a
> complaint, they may be extremely reluctant to bypass their
> supervisor and use the formal procedure.[34]

In the companies visited where the open door policy was stated to
be used frequently it tended to be for less contentious reasons, for
example, seeking information. It seems likely that frequency of
use and the nature of issues raised under an open door policy is
dependant on the culture within particular organisations. Where
supervisors or managers feel that a grievance procedure is a
method of controlling them (as distinct from a problem solving
mechanism for employees), this may lead to subtle attempts to
sabotage the procedure through slow responses or attempts to
stifle grievances.[35] In a unionised company an employee would
have continuing recourse to the shop steward or the wider union
organisation which would provide a negative incentive against
this occurring. While employees in the non-union sector would
also have continuing recourse to the open door policy one won-
ders if they would not, over time, be seen as partly the cause of
their own problems. Discrimination which is blatant is easy to
challenge; that which is indirect is more difficult to oppose. One
union official felt that employees who continually used this structure may leave themselves open to dismissal, colourfully brand-
ing this aspect of human resources as the "open gate" policy.[36] In
contrast, within organisations where a genuine pluralism of inter-

ests is accepted, the presence of an open door policy may provide a useful additional problem solving mechanism for employees.

DISCIPLINARY PROCEDURES IN THE NON-UNION SECTOR

While grievance procedures are an important aspect of personnel policy, the area of discipline may be even more sensitive. Employees who have received a disciplinary action, regardless of the merits of individual cases, will likely have a negative response towards a company, at least in the short term. Disciplinary issues therefore need to be handled extremely sensitively.

In practice, disciplinary procedures across the unionised/non-union divide followed the "standard" route (verbal warning, first written warning, final written warning, suspension/dismissal). It would be difficult to argue, on the basis of the formal procedures reviewed, that employees in the non-union sector are exposed to harsher disciplinary measures that those who enjoy the "protection" of a union. Yet despite the fact that the procedures are similar in both sectors, the non-union companies were criticised by a number of the trade union respondents on their *method* of operating them. In the absence of a trade union, "there is no one to challenge the company or defend the individual". Procedural arrangements are supposedly continually violated with the non-union companies acting as "judge and jury" in their own case[37] (despite the criticisms voiced, no specific evidence was offered to support this). Further, as disciplinary issues constitute a potential weakness in the maintenance of a non-union status (poorly handled cases highlight to employees the *need* for third party protection), companies are unlikely to utilise their power advantage unreasonably. This raises an intriguing hypothesis with regard to the non-union sector. While union membership supposedly provides protection against unilateral management control, employees in the non-union sector may enjoy a greater degree of latitude with regard to work rules. The unionisation potential of grievances is recognised and such companies tread "softly softly".

Supporting this, Toner related a conversation held with an employee in a non-union plant who remarked that "it is impossible to get sacked from here".[38] Possibly more than any other single area, discipline issues starkly highlight the lack of a representational structure. Poorly handled disciplinary issues may convince employees of the need to protect their interests under the umbrella of a union. A "blind eye" policy has less likelihood of creating a negative response and the non-union companies are often lenient on disciplinary issues to protect their status, trading off the "sins of the few" against the greater good of maintaining non-union status. In relation to actual disciplinary actions, non-union companies need to convince the remaining employees that they are not taking an overly hard line, that is (a) they have done everything possible to sort the problem out and (b) when a disciplinary action does take place there are "no surprises". Because the non-union companies are sensitive to both of these points, when corrective action does on occasion become necessary the attitude of the remaining workforce was said to be "it's about fucking time".[39] A further reason put forward to support the "reduced sentences" hypothesis, was that non-union companies do not need to be as careful about setting precedent and can treat each situation on a case by case basis, lessening pressure to uphold a "tough line" policy as a protection against future occurrences.[40]

Several respondents rejected the notion of soft-pedalling. In general a more regimented order of workplace rules was said to exist in the non-union sector. For example, at one of the largest non-union companies visited there had been a drive to reduce absenteeism and a number of employees with poor records were dismissed. This was offered as "proof" that the non-union companies implement disciplinary action when it becomes necessary. However, such examples are inconclusive. The level of absenteeism, the length of time prior to action taking place and the remedial work attempted in the interim period all dictate whether companies are "soft-pedalling", rather than the final response viewed in isolation. The suggestion that the non-union companies may be somewhat lax in the enforcement of discipline was given credence by a further factor uncovered during the research. When the human resources respondents were asked to quantify the number of dismissals which had taken place they could only point to isolated examples and the levels seemed extremely low by general industry standards. It was put to the respondents that this, de facto, provided evidence that they did not rigidly enforce disciplinary procedures. This viewpoint was rejected on a number of grounds. The human resources executive in one company suggested that non-union companies had a better than average track record in recruitment and do not need to pursue as many disciplinary cases as companies which pay less attention to this area. The personnel manager in another felt that due to the positive group norm which existed in the non-union companies, employees did not "swing the lead" because of peer group pressure. There was therefore less emphasis on, or need for, formal disciplinary procedures.

While it was not possible to come to any definitive conclusions, the impression remains that non-union companies do not fully enforce disciplinary procedures. Whether this is primarily due to efforts to maintain non-union status is difficult to determine. A possible explanation may be provided in distinguishing between punitive and corrective disciplinary actions, that is, between actions which have as their end focus the "right to manage" and those which attempt to resolve particular problems. The non-union companies were said to place a greater reliance on counselling, to "bring the employee around".[41] Rather than placing an over-reliance on formal procedures (punitive focus) the non-union companies seem to make greater efforts to resolve issues (corrective focus) which may be misinterpreted as soft-pedalling.

TRAINING AND DEVELOPMENT POLICIES

The area of training and development provides a further differentiation between the unionised and non-union sectors. Training provides tangible evidence of the pro-people philosophy of a company. The depth of commitment to this area in the non-union sector was shown by the number of internal staff dedicated to training, the extensive use of external consultants and the significant costs incurred. Non-union companies take training very seriously which supports the broader point that significant differences exist in relation to how people are managed between the two sectors.

Training Methods: "Sit by Nellie" versus Formal Programmes

The vast majority of training for hourly paid employees in the unionised companies visited was completed as part of the normal work routine. Several disadvantages are inherent in this method. Training is composed of three distinct elements: skills, knowledge and attitude. Training which is solely completed "on the job" is biased towards imparting skills but is usually deficient in the other areas noted, leading to a focus on how a job is done rather than why it is done in a particular way. While on the job training (commonly termed "sit by Nellie") is widely recognised as being deficient in this regard, few companies make a conscious effort or are willing to incur the additional costs to supplement this with other methods, for example, classroom instruction or formal on-the-job training where the outcome is measured against predetermined production or behavioural objectives. With a heavy emphasis on training, the non-union companies "put their money where their mouth is". Slogans like "people are our most important asset" are glib and empty phrases in many organisations. The amount spent on training (which ranged up to five per cent of payroll costs in the non-union sector) provided tangible evidence of the belief that employees really do bring something special to the party. The fact that training in the non-union companies visited was run through an amalgam of direct instruction and indirect methods (classroom instruction, plant tours outside of the immediate work area and so on) provided tangible evidence of the commitment to people and to the professionalism in the personnel area.[42]

Active attention and commitment to training supports the central thesis that non-union companies view employees as a core resource. Effective training and development policies help to maximise people's contribution and brings the "pro-people" philosophy to life. Training and development policies in the non-union sector also link into broader personnel strategy in a number of ways. While the purpose of training is usually stated as enabling employees to reach the standard of an experienced worker in the shortest possible time, a broader understanding of their job is also given to employees which provides better identity with the company. Training programmes which create a bond between a company and its employees (enculturalisation) spill over into a positive industrial relations climate. Professionalism in the training area thus indirectly supports the maintenance of a non-union status, creating a stronger employee/company identity bond.

Supervisors: The "Shock Troops" of Non-Unionism

The non-union companies visited were all well aware of the importance of front-line managers. This group plays a hugely important role in the maintenance of non-union status. All of the non-union companies visited trained these managers in the "basics" (communications, performance management, planning, motivation and so on), and several of the more sophisticated ones added an additional "layer of non-union expertise" on top of the foundation training. (Examples of some non-union training materials are detailed in Appendix C).

INTERNAL PROMOTIONS POLICIES
IN THE NON-UNION SECTOR

One of the central ways in which non-union companies emphasise their commitment to employees is through a positive bias in favour of internal candidates in promotion decisions. It is a particularly visible way to underscore the point that a company has a strong commitment to its people. Where individuals identify their career path with a particular company, this can be a strongly influential factor on behaviour. The success motive provides a method by which a company can influence (and control) those employees with career aspirations.

While none of the companies visited gave a carte blanche guarantee that they would always promote internally, the non-union companies were unanimous in expressing a positive bias towards existing employees when filling vacant positions. All of the respondents made the point that internal recruitment was seen by employees as a positive aspect of their conditions of employment. Internal promotions have a further benefit in allowing positions to be filled speedily and more objectively than outside hiring (all external candidates look good at interview). Three companies qualified this point, stating that it was somewhat dependent on the level of people required. At lower skill levels in the organisation it is easier to recruit internally because there is less pressure from a training perspective. At higher levels, the skills may have been brought in as the training "lead time" may be too long or the cost of training too high.

Internal Promotions Need to be Carefully Managed

Despite the potential benefits, internal promotions need to be carefully managed to avoid several potential pitfalls. Normally positions advertised solicit a number of internal candidates. With only one eventual "winner" this leaves a number of unsuccessful candidates and managing the dissatisfaction which this creates is difficult. Performance appraisal data and job selection "reasons" are often subjective and it is not always possible to give accurate feedback as to *why* individuals were rejected in preference to some other candidate. Some people do not respond to negative feedback or may simply be unable to change particular traits. Where individual candidates continually seek to be promoted without success this can, over time, cause a considerable degree of frustration, a feeling that they are "trapped".[43] Thus internal promotions are a double-edged sword with regard to their effect on employee relations. While outwardly it may appear that such a policy helps to develop a positive industrial relations climate, it needs sensitive handling to ensure this is the actual outcome.

A further disadvantage cited was the fact that a policy of internal promotion can lead to an inbred view of the organisation. One of the non-union companies in the research was described as being "incestuous" by virtue of the fact that they never hire from outside the company, except for entry level employees.[44] Companies therefore may lose the benefit of bringing fresh talent and perspective into the organisation through a too rigid focus on internal hires. While internal promotion policies have to be carefully managed, all other things being equal they help to contribute to a positive workplace climate. A central finding emerging from the research was that the non-union companies were much stronger in their support for internal promotions than the unionised companies visited.

COMMUNICATIONS POLICIES/STRUCTURES

Attempting to quantify communications structures or to measure their effectiveness at individual plants is a notoriously difficult task. Indeed, the perceived effectiveness of communications is heavily influenced by the overall quality of the management/employee relationship and cannot be viewed in isolation. Notwithstanding this, the formal communications system can supplement the primary relationship and a number of "best practices" can be detailed. Four specific areas were reviewed: (a) responsibility for communications, (b) communication around new technology/process introduction, (c) disclosure of company results and (d) prevalence of staff committees or associations in the non-union sector.

Responsibility for Communications in the Non-Union Sector

The commitment of the non-union companies to effective communications has already been touched on. Formal responsibility for the process is typically well defined and measured (in all cases it was assigned to a named individual or department). In three of the five companies, overall responsibility for communications, in the sense of ensuring that this occurred rather than it being carried out directly, lay with the human resource department. In the two remaining companies, responsibility lay with the line management group on a department-by-department basis. In better managed companies, communications is not seen to "just happen" but is planned in advance. Three of the five companies visited had formalised the communications process (that is, issued a formal schedule for communication events). While a sequence of communication events was not centrally planned in the two remaining companies, it formed part of each functional manager's job objectives and was appraised as part of their overall performance. In other words, it was not left to chance.

It was continually stressed by respondents that communications is a key factor in an effective policy of human resource management. Various systems had evolved at the plants to give this substance. At all of the non-union plants the primary communications vehicle were regular department meetings on the basis that employees are most concerned with issues relevant to their particular area. In addition to the departmental meetings a number of other structures were utilised. For example, at one company a "communications exchange" was held on a biannual basis. The underlying rationale was that a company should not presuppose what employees want to know. In order to solicit specific information, employees submit anonymous questions on pre-printed forms placed strategically throughout the plant. The senior manager within the department to which the question is addressed subsequently meets with the individual or work groups and responds to the points raised.

A common method used throughout the non-union sector was "skip level" meetings where the managing director meets with employees directly on a programmed basis. This provides the opportunity for all employees to meet with the senior plant executive, at least annually. The other two frequently used methods were (a) "cascade" communications, information prepared centrally but delivered locally, often with add-on local issues and (b) state-of-the-nation addresses usually run by the managing director, sometimes supplemented by visiting executives. In addition to the above, ad hoc communications were also held when events at the plant overtook the planned communications sessions. One theme stressed at a number of plants visited was that employees also have a responsibility for keeping themselves informed. They were encouraged to speak to section managers in areas where they had a particular interest or wanted to find out specific information by using the "open door" policy. While there was some divergence between the companies around the particular methods employed, a high commitment to the communications process existed at all of the non-union plants visited.[45]

New Technology/Process Changes: Informing Employees in Advance

The second area reviewed under the communications heading was the introduction of new technology and process changes. As change often underlies industrial relations problems in the unionised sector, investigating this area would provide an insight into how the non-union companies surmount potential problems. What emerged was that communications on both the introduction of new technology and process changes was an ongoing feature at the non-union plants. It is not coincidental that respondents from this sector made the point that both of these areas were fully accepted by employees, highlighting the connection between the level of advance communications with employees and their acceptance of particular changes. Where communications take place with regard to specific changes, this allows the mutuality argument ("here's how this change benefits all of us . . .") to be reinforced. Where communications efforts are not made, or are made reactively in response to employee grievances, companies often find themselves in the position of having to justify particular actions. Companies in the non-union sector operate closer to what is generally termed the "Eastern Model" of decision making where more time is taken in the planning (and consultation) stages of a decision. Once this process is complete it normally requires less implementation time. Those who argue that the degree of communication/consultation in the non-union sector is overly time consuming (an objection raised by some of the personnel respondents in the unionised sector) may be focusing on one part of the time equation only.

In the non-union companies visited specific efforts were made to keep employees informed both of changes being made and their underlying rationale, a huge task given the rate of change and the size of the workforces. An example of this occurred in one company at the time the research was in progress. An automated materials handling system was introduced to the warehouse section of the plant. Employees had not only been kept informed of this from inception, but had also been involved in the *design* of the system. This was undertaken both for the purpose of communication and on the basis that the materials personnel (hourly paid employees) could make a significant contribution to this decision.

Therein lay a glimpse of the philosophy of the non-union companies visited, with employees viewed as a valuable resource. This provides the core distinction between companies which operate under the high commitment model and those which do not. Support for this point is again provided by the research conducted by Toner where 57 per cent of employees in the non-union companies rated discussions on pending changes as "good" or "very good" compared with 25 per cent of unionised employees.[46]

Disclosure of Information on Company Results

The third area considered under the general heading of communications was the amount of information on company results/ profitability given to employees. Significantly, four of the five non-union companies visited were completely open with regard to production quotas, sales figures and profit and loss results. In the fifth company, although the profitability figures were not released, a good degree of openness existed in relation to production and sales results. In contrast, none of the unionised companies visited released these figures to employees (with the exception of one company where sales forecasts were communicated). A cynic might argue that the openness in the non-union sector could be viewed as simply an attempt to anticipate pending legislation, that is, companies are merely putting such information voluntarily into place instead of having this grafted on at a later date, for example, under the Information and Consultation Directive. However, the fact that none of the unionised companies visited supply this information to employees is significant as they will equally be affected by forthcoming legislation. Again, the difference in philosophy between the non-union (new model) and the unionised (traditional model) companies is highlighted. The openness in the non-union sector with regard to trading results is less an attempt to anticipate pending legislation than a view of employees as being capable of assimilating data and responsible

enough to withhold information which may damage competitiveness. The non-disclosure in the unionised sector reflects both an
underlying difference in philosophy and an attempt to limit the
collective bargaining opportunity for the unions (who would
likely use positive trading results as a basis for increased
wage/benefits claims).

Discussing the Reason for Being Non-Union: How "Open"?

In relation to the question on why the companies wanted to remain non-union there are three emerging communications "positions" which can be taken:

1. **In-Your-Face:** This is a very up-front statement about why the
   company does not wish to deal with unions. In Ireland, Ryanair probably provides the best example.

2. **Soft Sell:** A more low key approach with the need for unions
   in some organisations acknowledged but the advantages of
   remaining union-free in this company/industry highlighted.
   IBM is a good example here.

3. **Don't Ask, Don't Tell:** The non-union topic is undiscussible;
   managers are fearful and avoid it if possible.

In my consulting role I typically advise companies that the second
option is best and help them to develop a positive message
around this (see communications materials in Appendix B).

The Prevalence of Staff Committees/Associations in the Non-Union Sector

The final area reviewed under the general heading of communications was the prevalence of staff committees and associations. A
staff association can, in theory, provide a forum for communications between a company and employees and may also support
the maintenance of a non-union status, creating an impression
that an independent structure exists, diffusing the search for offi-

cial union membership. Given this supposed benefit, it could be expected that this structure would be commonly employed in the non-union sector.

Staff Associations Have Gone Out of Vogue

Staff associations have become much less common in recent years and those which are already in place continue to operate to "a very limited degree".[47] Two reasons explain this. Firstly, the notion of a staff association as a communications vehicle has largely been superseded by the changing emphasis, that is, the move to more direct communications under the new model of industrial relations. Rather than communicating through a representational structure, the growing trend is to talk to employees directly.[48] The trend towards more open communications and the development of a myriad of participation structures through which employees can voice ideas and concerns largely explains the fact that no "new" staff associations are being developed.[49] Secondly, despite the hypothesis that a staff association may help to maintain non-union status, the point was made that these may actually fuel the process of unionisation.

One respondent suggested that staff associations have gone out of "fashion" since the 1970s mainly because those which did exist tended to affiliate to official trade unions,[50] that is, the unions had "captured them".[51] A thin line exists between communications and negotiations. In practice it was said to be quite difficult to steer staff associations away from areas in which the "right to manage" would be challenged. Over time the role of employee representatives tended to move from their original brief (as a conduit for information) to one of a lobby group on behalf of employees. As it is unlikely that all issues raised in a staff association forum can be resolved satisfactorily, it is a relatively simple step from this to a search by employees for union recognition to increase their negotiations clout. One is reminded of Marx's phrase that in time, quantitative becomes qualitative.

A second point which emerged was that staff associations exist as a sort of "half-way house" between formal union recognition and operating on a completely non-union basis. The existence of a staff association was an implicit recognition that a company either does not have the resources, or the desire, to communicate with employees on an individual basis. Since management commitment to employee relations provides a cornerstone in any union avoidance policy, this, of itself, may represent a signal of "weakness" in the management resolve to remain non-union. Where this is the case the likelihood is that the power of the staff association will, over time, grow as that of management diminishes (an analogy can be drawn with management in a unionised company handing over its communications role to the unions). A third point made was that employees usually elect representatives to serve on a staff association. This process mirrors the election of shop stewards in a unionised environment and highlights the representational role of specific employees. It thus provides a stepping stone towards the conversion to full recognition. For all the above reasons many staff associations converted to full union membership which explains their decline in popularity over recent years. None of the non-union companies visited as part of this research had staff associations. In working with a range of non-union organisations over the last number of years, I have tried to dissuade them from establishing staff associations for all of the reasons outlined above. The impact of the EU Information and Consultation Directive has put a new spin on this (points explored in detail elsewhere). Interestingly, trade unions have traditionally taken a cynical view of staff associations, "viewing them as a poor apology for a real trade union and inhibiting collective solidarity".[52]

JOB SECURITY POLICIES IN THE NON-UNION SECTOR

One factor which clearly distinguished the non-union from the unionised companies visited were the job security policies employed. Employment stability was an important goal of the non-union companies studied, a finding supported by evidence from outside of Ireland. For example, IBM operates a full employment policy as part of their worldwide employee relations strategy. The company offers alternative employment to those employees whose jobs and skills are eliminated by economic or technological change.[53] While it is difficult to generalise, non-union companies are typically supportive of employment stability.[54] The consensus view was that the non-union companies operating in Ireland make strenuous efforts to provide job security for employees. Four of the five companies visited that had successfully managed to maintain their non-union status had never experienced redundancies during their period of operation in Ireland. While there are favourable environmental factors which contribute to the realisation of stable employment, the depth of conviction within the senior executive group to support this is a key explanatory factor. The advantages that a company can realise by offering full employment, though not always measurable, are very real. Removing the fear around job insecurity was seen to provide greater loyalty, less resistance to technological change and better employee relations — all of which contribute to higher productivity and business success.

One argument put forward by some of the trade union respondents was that the success of the non-union companies in maintaining employment levels must be viewed in relation to the growth rates in the high tech sector. It is relatively easy to maintain employment levels when an industry is experiencing high growth. The situation, if viewed over a longer period, may not be as positive.[55] The evidence does not support this view. For example, one non-union company visited had been in operation for 25 years without a layoff. It is extremely difficult for unions to argue that job security is less certain in a non-union environment where a company can highlight this kind of stability. Indeed, the argument that employment stability is explained by the growth within particular economic sectors is overly simplistic. Not all of the non-union companies visited have had a smooth order flow since commencing operations in Ireland but have typically maintained employment levels. This has been achieved by the companies taking a "swings and roundabouts" approach to redundancies. If a company can highlight a solid track record in the area of job security the attraction of a union on the basis of job protection will find little appeal among employees. However, a guarantee of job security is not a necessary or a sufficient condition for the maintenance of a non-union status. Several large companies which have experienced layoffs have remained non-union. In contrast, there have been cases of successful union drives among organisations which provide full job security. Tenured college professors, for example, have voted to join unions as have the majority of government employees, both of which enjoy absolute job security. Overall, however, there is little doubt that job security is a major component of a successful union avoidance policy in the multinational sector. In the three case studies conducted where union encroachment did occur, job insecurity was highlighted as the *primary factor* in relation to successful union drives.

Personnel Practices: Summary Points

Overall, a marked difference between the personnel policies employed in the unionised and non-union sectors was a finding which emerged from the research. Under almost every heading reviewed, the non-union companies rated higher than comparable unionised companies. The question remains, however, whether the primary underlying goal was to maintain a non-union status or to maximise human resources (albeit these are not mutually exclusive). The HR respondents suggested that the non-union companies have a different conception of the core worth of employees. People are seen as a positive resource to be utilised rather than a potential nuisance to be tranquillised. Central to this is a belief that business success and a satisfied and motivated work-force are dependant variables. To this end, great energy is devoted to providing equitable pay/conditions, to resolving employee prob-lems speedily, to keeping employees informed and, as far as possi-ble, to providing security of employment. While it was recognised that conflicts would arise on occasion, continuous efforts were made to stress the mutuality of the employment relationship and the fact that the parties could work through their differences with-out recourse to a third party. Sometimes, the policies in place to give effect to this philosophy were quite striking. In one company executives were obliged to leave meetings or cancel appointments, within reason, to resolve employee problems — such was the value placed on the maintenance of a strong relationship with employees.

Excellence in Employee Relations: The Telephone Company Experience

One union official related a colourful experience of a strong com-mitment to employee relations which he had witnessed while on a visit to the University of Wisconsin in the US. During his visit there was a large business convention in the city which had brought people from all around the world. Thousands attended and the effect for the communications provider (at that time, the largest telephone company in the world) was that the phones were "bouncing off the hooks day and night for seven days".[56] This put a tremendous strain on what was normally regarded as a small station. The union official happened to be in the exchange at the conclusion of the convention. All around the building large signs read "well done" and gave a statistical breakdown of the amount of calls handled during the week. In addition, a senior executive of the company had flown in from New York to address the staff and a small buffet was laid on in recognition of the diffi-cult work conditions. This was cited as an example of a large con-glomerate operating as a small family business. The official, in his

own words, was "astonished". He cited the example of a bus
driver taking a number 22 bus from Drimnagh and driving all the
way to Cabra across Dublin city at 5.30 pm, and asked to imagine
the level of frustration that this causes. At the end of the day
when the driver finishes his shift, no one says to him "well done".
The more likely response from his superiors is "what fucking kept
you?"[57] While the analogy is poor (in equating a normal work routine with an abnormal one), the central thrust of the point is accepted. Many companies do not, at least outwardly, appear to be
interested in the problems faced by employees or to recognise
above average performance. The telephone company example
where the management knew that employees had worked hard
and invested the time and energy to come down and say to them
"well done, we care" provides an illustration of a commitment to
employee relations which was characteristic of the general efforts
employed in the non-union companies visited.

The research conducted by Bill Toner referred to earlier specifically addressed the issue of satisfaction/dissatisfaction levels in
unionised and non-unionised companies in Ireland. His findings
highlighted that levels of job satisfaction (measured against a
range of criteria) are *superior* in the non-union sector. A key conclusion was that satisfaction/dissatisfaction levels are directly affected by employees day-to-day experience of work. Where a
company exercises fair supervision, pays good wages and has systems in place to encourage "employee voice", the supposed loss
of "insurance" implied in the absence of trade union membership
is not seen to be important.[58] In short, the need for the countervailing power of a trade union is a "political" perspective which is not
often shared by employees.

Progressive personnel policy, like many other areas of business (for example, quality), receives much lip service in the general business literature. However, the non-union companies ag-
gressively pursue it even to the point where it seems to make little
business sense (measured in narrow cost terms) to do so. For ex-

ample, when viewed on a cost basis, the employment of full-time personnel representatives on shift to handle personnel queries cannot be justified. Yet if the basis of evaluation is changed to "what will be most effective from a people management perspective", it makes perfect sense. In order to maximise the "whole", cost sacrifices sometimes need to be made in particular areas. It is not coincidental that both of the non-union companies visited which operated a shift cycle had personnel staff working on a shift rota basis. To the best of my knowledge, no unionised company operating in Ireland employs a similar practice. This acceptance of short-run cost factors provides a qualitative difference between the unionised (traditional model) and non-union (high commitment) companies visited. Throughout the research no magic formula or set of "silver bullet" techniques were discovered which, if brought into play, would achieve a positive industrial relations climate. The belief that employees are a key resource is more important than any specific policy employed. In practice, the non-union companies have a range of human resources practices in place. Some of these simply mirror "best practice" in other organisations. Some are specifically targeted at remaining non-union. A model which I've developed to help companies know "what to focus on" is outlined in Figure 12.

FIGURE 12: POSITIVE EMPLOYEE RELATIONS TOOLKIT: THE BUILDING BLOCKS

1. Recruitment	2. Induction Philosophy/Clear Stance o Unions	3. Safety/Physical Comfort
4. Training & Development	5. Employee Communications/ Voice (two way)	6. Job/Work Design (Tools, Team)
7. Salaries	8. Benefits/Non-monetary Compensation	9. Easy Access Employee Relations Structure (ER troops)
10. Job Security	11. Performance Management System (High & Low Perf.)	12 Sympathetic Grievance/Problem Solving Structures
13. Career/ Management Planning	14. Positive Community Relations Profile	15. Sports & Social Activities
16. Low Status Symbols (offices, cars, titles, etc.)	17. Fun/Hoopla (celebrating success)	18. Explicit Company Values/Noble Purpose
19. HR Function Role - Ombudsman	20. Senior Management Visibility (e.g. MBWA)	21. Employee Engagement Mechanisms (e.g. lean teams)

Above the Line: Visible to Staff

Waterline

22. Supervisory/ Management "Union-Free" Training	Positive ER Leadership from CEO and Senior Players	24. "Worst Case" Scenario Planning (e.g. strike plan)
25. Specific Training in Positive ER Philosophy for all managers	26. ER "Climate" Audit/Assessment Systems in Place	27. Solid Relationship with Local Suppliers

Below the Line: Invisible to Staff

Joint Ownership   *HR Ownership*   *Line Ownership*

Distinguishing between Primary Motivations to Remain Non-Union

In trying to reconcile the conflicting perspectives (for example, non-union companies are not pro-people, but anti-union) a distinction can possibly be made between two separate types of non-union companies. Companies with the goal of effective human resource management as their primary motivation have been described by one researcher as *philosophy-laden*. They have well thought out beliefs concerning the treatment of employees, their philosophy is usually stated in writing and was generally first articulated by the company's founder. The non-union status is less a goal than a result of the successful implementation of that philosophy. A core belief is that if management functions effectively, a union is not necessary. Proponents of the non-union mode of operation argue that this is the best way to mobilise employee commitment and loyalty.

In contrast, companies where the primary motivation is to remain non-union may be described as *doctrinaire*. For certain reasons, senior management has decided that a company (or some plants) are to be kept non-union and implement "union avoidance programmes" to achieve this.[59] The argument that operating on a non-union basis is "commercial" masks an underlying distrust of unions and a reluctance to have the managerial view open to challenge. It is therefore useful to think of the motivation to maintaining a non-union status as running along a continuum. This concept, as expressed by Foulkes[60] is outlined in Figure 13.

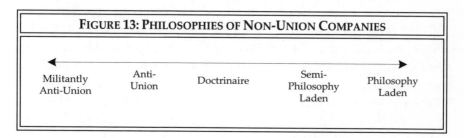

| FIGURE 13: PHILOSOPHIES OF NON-UNION COMPANIES |

Militantly Anti-Union   Anti-Union   Doctrinaire   Semi-Philosophy Laden   Philosophy Laden

Foulkes' work provides a useful distinction between companies within the non-union sector which, to some extent, makes it possible to accommodate both the trade union and the personnel managers' different responses to the questions around the core philosophy of the non-union companies operating in Ireland.

Some of the respondents felt that the non-union companies were anti-union by definition and raised the question of whether there was any merit in trying to distinguish between, what appears on the surface at least, a philosophical debate over "titles"[61] (one official described the attempt to differentiate between companies on this basis as "an exercise in hair splitting"[62]). Yet it is precisely such fine tuning which provides a comprehensive understanding of the differences *within* the non-union sector. The distinction made provides a more accurate analysis than treating all non-union companies as a homogenous group. Without such insight, analysis is relegated to the level of generalisations.

Endnotes

---

[1] Brian Patterson, then MD of Waterford Crystal, speaking at the Institute of Personnel Management Conference in Killarney.

[2] "Trade Union Official C" and "Industrial Relations Expert D". Points made during interview with author.

[3] "Industrial Relations Expert D". Points made during interview with author.

[4] Brooks, D. *Race and Labour in London Transport*, Oxford University Press, London, 1975; Courtney, G. "A Survey of Employers Recruitment Practices" Social and Community Planning Research. London, 1977; Blackburn, R.M. and Mann, M. *The Working Class in the Labour Market*. Cambridge University Press, Cambridge, 1979; Jenkins, R. "Managers, Recruitment Procedures and Black Workers" Working Papers on Ethnic Relations No. 18, University of Aston, SSRC Research Unit, 1982; Oliver, J.M. and Turton, J.R. "Is there a Shortage of Skilled Labour?" *British Journal of Industrial Relations* Vol. XX, No. 2. pp, 195–217, 1982.

[5] "Trade Union Official F". Points made during interview with author.

[6] It must be recognised that behaviour labelled as militant may simply be the rational pursuit of objectives, albeit contrary to the "establishment" view. The term is used here to denote the widely accepted understanding of the term which implies trade union or political activism or both.

[7] "Trade Union Official D". Points made during interview with author.

[8] "Trade Union Official E". Points made during interview with author.

[9] Company I.

[10] Based on my own experience and conversations held with personnel managers in the multi-national sector during this and previous research.

[11] Personnel Managers: Companies F, H, I. Points made during interview with author.

[12] Personnel Managers: Company I. Points made during interview with author.

[13] "Trade Union Official F". Points made during interview with author.

[14] "Trade Union Official A". Points made during interview with author.

[15] Frank O'Donoghue, then Personnel Manager, Bausch and Lomb, speaking to the Institute of Personnel Management (Waterford Branch) on the topic of "Employee Relations". In his time Frank ran a very "sophisticated" personnel department and Bausch and Lomb was one of the better managed unionised companies in Ireland (proving that it can be done).

[16] Personnel Executive: Company I. Points made during interview with author.

[17] Personnel Executive: Companies D, H. Points made during interview with author.

[18] Personnel Executive: Company E. Points made during interview with author.

[19] In recruitment interviewing over a number of years this point has been continually highlighted by numerous supervisory/managerial job candidates describing the most effective style of leadership.

[20] Personnel Executive: Company A. Points made during interview with author.

[21] There was mixed feeling throughout the group on this particular aspect of the non-union companies method of operation. An office brings not only privacy (for personal telephone calls etc.) but also status and territory. In the non-union companies which utilised open plan offices, people continued to mark out their patch with such bric a brac as family photographs, plants, posters etc. which is a common human territorial phenomenon. Some of the more progressive unionised companies have adopted this particular stance, e.g. Bank of Ireland overhauled its executive offices in 2002 and First Active took the same decision when it moved to new offices in Leopardstown, Co. Dublin.

[22] Personnel Manager: Company H. Points made during interview with author.

[23] Toner Bill. "The Unionisation and Productivity Debate: An Employee Opinion Survey in Ireland". Unpublished M.Sc. (Econ) Thesis. London School of Economics, 1984.

[24] A definitive analysis of this question would have required the construction of a salary survey with individual jobs sketched out in detail and "matched" between unionised and non-union companies. This was outside the scope of the research.

[25] Foulkes Fred, K. *Personnel Policies in Large Non-Union Companies*. Prentice Hall, New Jersey, 1980.

[26] "Industrial Relations Expert C". Points made during interview with author.

[27] "Trade Union Official C". Points made during interview with author.

[28] "Trade Union Official F". Points made during interview with author.

[29] Personnel Executive: Company D. Points made during interview with author.

[30] "Industrial Relations Expert A". Points made during interview with author.

[31] Toner, Bill. "The Unionisation and Productivity Debate: An Employee Opinion Survey in Ireland". Unpublished M.Sc. (Econ) Thesis. London School of Economics, 1984.

[32] "Industrial Relations Expert D". Points made during interview with author.

[33] Drost, Donald A. and O'Brien, Fabius P. "Are There Grievances Against Your Non-Union Grievance Procedure"? *Personnel Administrator*, January, 1983.

[34] Foulkes Fred, K. *Personnel Policies in Large Non-Union Companies.* Prentice Hall, New Jersey, 1980: 317.

[35] Drost, Donald A. and O'Brien, Fabius P. "Are There Grievances Against Your Non-Union Grievance Procedure"? *Personnel Administrator*, January, 1983.

[36] "Trade Union Official D". Points made during interview with author.

[37] "Trade Union Official E". Points made during interview with author.

[38] "Industrial Relations Expert A". Points made during interview with author.

[39] "Trade Union Official F". Points made during interview with author.

[40] Personnel Manager: Company F. Points made during interview with author.

[41] "Industrial Relations Expert C". Points made during interview with author.

[42] It would be incorrect to create the perception that all of the non-union companies have a very structured training process which is centrally driven. At one of the largest non-union companies in the country the internal phrase used is: "you own your own development" and employees are encouraged to be self-sufficient in this area (albeit, the company does provide financial support).

[43] Personnel Manager: Company F. Points made during interview with author.

[44] Personnel Executive: Company H. Points made during interview with author.

[45] At the time of writing the "big unknown" is the potential impact of the European Information and Consultation Directive. The non-union companies are certainly concerned about its "collective" structure. It remains

to be seen exactly what impact this will have on workplace communications.

[46] Toner, Bill. "The Unionisation and Productivity Debate: An Employee Opinion Survey in Ireland". Unpublished M.Sc. (Econ) Thesis. London School of Economics, 1984.

[47] "Industrial Relations Experts A and D". Points made during interview with author.

[48] "Trade Union Official C". Points made during interview with author.

[49] "Industrial Relations Expert C". Points made during interview with author.

[50] "Trade Union Official C". Points made during interview with author.

[51] "Trade Union Official B". Points made during interview with author.

[52] Gunnigle et al. *Industrial Relations in Ireland*. Dublin: Gill and Macmillan, 2004: 127.

[53] Peach, Len. "Employee Relations in I.B.M." *Employee Relations*, Vol. 5, No. 3, 1983: 17

[54] Foulkes Fred, K. *Personnel Policies in Large Non-Union Companies*. Prentice Hall, New Jersey, 1980: 317.

[55] "Trade Union Officials B and E". Points made during interview with author.

[56] "Trade Union Official F". Points made during interview with author.

[57] "Trade Union Official F". Points made during interview with author.

[58] Toner, Bill. "The Unionisation and Productivity Debate: An Employee Opinion Survey in Ireland". Unpublished M.Sc. (Econ) Thesis. London School of Economics, 1984.

[59] Foulkes Fred, K. *Personnel Policies in Large Non-Union Companies*. Prentice Hall, New Jersey, 1980:45.

[60] Ibid.

[61] "Trade Union Official B". Points made during interview with author.

[62] "Trade Union Official A". Points made during interview with author.

9

WHY DO PEOPLE JOIN TRADE UNIONS?

IN ORDER TO EMPIRICALLY ASSESS the reasons why Irish people join trade unions, three in-depth case studies were conducted as part of this research. These were based on companies which had commenced on a non-union basis but became unionised over time. A number of points emerged which suggest a degree of commonality in people's motives in seeking union membership. In all, eight areas have been identified which directly or indirectly led to union encroachment. From these a tentative hypothesis of the factors influencing unionisation in Ireland have been constructed.[1] It must be recognised that the quality of the management/employee relationship is hugely significant here. While the establishment of a list of "unionisation" factors is useful, whether these actually lead to a union drive will depend on the particular circumstances in each workplace. For example, it is overly simplistic to suggest that redundancy (the first factor noted) will always lead to a search for recognition or that a prior background of trade union involvement will always resurface. Similar events will have different outcomes in particular organisation contexts. To restate: the strength of the management/employee bond is the key determinant of the maintenance of a non-union status and this point provides an overall rider to the listing proposed.

The First Factor: Redundancy

In the three case histories studied where companies had experienced a union drive, redundancy was a primary factor in steering employees towards unionisation. Two points seem to be relevant here. Firstly, as highlighted earlier, "staff" employees have traditionally considered themselves to be closer to the company than the hourly paid workforce. Because of this it is usually assumed that companies have a greater loyalty towards maintaining staff employment levels in the event of a downturn in business. Redundancy breaks the psychological contract (expectation of job security) with employees. When expectations are unrecognised, denied or not fulfilled, people act as if something which has been promised to them has been withheld or denied.[2] When redundancies occur the myth of employee/management closeness evaporates with those involved typically speaking of feeling "let down" by the company.[3] In such circumstances, employees often opt to seek the protection of a union.

Job Security: A Psychological Contract with Employees

Offering job security in a contract of employment is significant for two reasons. Firstly, it points to an understanding of the relationship between employees and the company as something more than simple economics. Part of this relationship may be an unwritten expectation of security on the part of the employee as a quid pro quo for the maintenance of a non-union status. Where job losses occur, employees often look to a union for the personal protection which they felt was provided by their employer. While this may represent a misunderstanding or overestimation on the part of employees, redundancy is a primary driver of union recognition in Ireland.

A second issue relates to the personal insecurity which surrounds a redundancy situation which is almost always a traumatic experience for individuals. Loss of income and long-term security is compounded by the immediate loss of self-esteem, of becoming "status-less", unemployed. In a climate where employees feel "let down" by a company and personally vulnerable, unionisation provides a strong attraction to fill the vacuum. Further, while the events leading to a redundancy situation are usually outside the control of individual employees, joining a union is at least *something* which can be done and may relieve anxiety simply on the basis of "activity". The attraction of unionisation lies in the psychological protection afforded by a group and the possibility of countervailing power. In some cases it may even serve as a protest to the management team for allowing the situation to occur.[4] There is a dichotomy here in that non-union staff employees often have a lower "hit rate" during redundancies than unionised employees who work for the same company. This is because companies normally wish to protect the non-union status quo. If non-union employees were more vulnerable this would encourage greater levels of union penetration.

While the specific reasons will differ from case to case, there is little doubt that a strong link exists between threatened or actual job loss and union encroachment. It is not coincidental that the companies visited that had successfully managed to maintain a non-union status place an extremely high value on job security. It raises the question whether companies should address their policies on this, up front, with employees. Within the non-union sector, there are two separate "approaches" to this:

- **"Don't mention the war"**: some companies feel that even mentioning job security can lead to fears. While every effort is made to maintain employment levels, this is done behind closed doors and not openly discussed.

- **"Put it on the table"**: some of the non-union companies are quite overt in detailing (a) their efforts to maintain job security and (b) the policies they would pursue in the event of a business downturn. Their belief is that "non-discussion" will not make this fear go away and it is best to be up front about the reality. I typically suggest to a company that they address this issue overtly — letting employees know that they will do everything in their power to provide employment security — even detailing the actual steps which would be taken in the event of a downturn in business.

It is generally more difficult to maintain a non-union status in an organisation which has big "swings" in the need for labour. In some companies a huge "rush to recruit" followed by outplacement programmes for large groups of staff make it very difficult to maintain a "we are all in this together" view.

THE SECOND FACTOR: INFLUENCE OF INDIVIDUALS

The second factor (in order of importance in the case histories studied) was the influence of individual employees. In the cases reviewed, individual employees were closely associated with the union drives and acted as catalysts for union encroachment. These individuals were considered "strong" personalities, which points to a tentative conclusion that a drive for unionisation is most often associated with an employee(s) who has a relatively high standing.

Despite the fact that individual employees were seen as primary actors in the drives toward unionisation, it is difficult to state categorically that *their* influence led to union encroachment.[5] The placing of "blame" for a union drive on an individual employee by the management team may indicate a simplistic analysis in response to a complex social phenomenon. Most movements have identifiable leaders but their influence needs to be carefully weighed alongside a range of other factors. The identification of union drives with particular individuals provides the additional benefit of removing the "blame" from the management team, partly absolving them from the results of their own actions or incompetence. For both of these reasons some degree of scepticism must be maintained around this point.

THE THIRD FACTOR: PREVIOUS UNION BACKGROUND

The third most important point in relation to union encroachment concerns the background of the individuals involved and, specifically, whether they had previously been union members. A unionised background usually results from a promotion from the unionised ranks or through membership in previous employment(s). My personal belief is that where non-union employees have previously been union members they are more likely to unionise than if unionisation is being contemplated for the first time. It can be argued that union membership poses a dilemma for individuals in terms of loyalty (where the company is opposed to unionisation) or status (where unionisation is equated with a working class response inappropriate to the resolution of "staff" grievances). Where employees have previously been unionised this "dilemma" may already have been resolved. In simple terms, membership is easier to contemplate the second time around.

This finding impacts both a company's recruitment and internal promotion policies. On the first point companies who wish to maintain a non-union status must ensure that they adequately screen potential recruits through a thorough system of reference checking. While it would be unrealistic to expect all candidates to have a union-free background, the *level* of involvement is taken as a key indicator here. The assumption is often made that previous trade union involvement, particularly in an official capacity (shop steward, branch committee member and so on), is likely to be re-activated in the "new" job.[6] Without doubt, this is a controversial point and may seen by some as discriminatory. Nevertheless, for companies tasked with maintaining a non-union operation, the previous background of individuals is important data to be assessed.

In relation to internal promotions (where the hourly paid workforce is unionised), continual upgrades to the staff ranks may mean that, over time, a group of staff employees become established to whom unionisation poses no philosophical dilemma. Companies must weigh this factor (and that of bringing fresh talent into the organisation) against the positive benefit of providing internal promotion opportunities.

THE FOURTH FACTOR: GROUP STRUCTURES

There should be little surprise in the finding that the existence of cohesive groups is influential in the process of union encroachment. This research bears out the widely held contention that where a number of employees are involved in similar work, a group consciousness develops which provides a foundation for the encroachment of trade unions.[7] Indeed, the central rationale for trade unionism — support through unity — has most relevance and appeal where broadly similar issues are at stake. The opposite also seems true. Where there is a strong emphasis on individual contribution and the structures to support it (for example, merit payments to individuals), unionisation is less likely.

In the case histories studied, the union drives came from within the foreman/supervisory groups (although groups in general, for example, technicians, are vulnerable to unionisation). While it may be impossible to avoid the development of such groups in a large workforce, the knowledge that unionisation often springs from "groups" provides some forewarning. Supporting this point, union avoidance strategies at a couple of non union companies attempted to identify vulnerable groups which were most likely to unionise. This information was sourced through various "intelligence" systems which monitored the ongoing organisation climate (attitude surveys, scheduled communications meetings of various types and so on). Various "early warning systems" and risk assessment criteria were also in use. In some cases this was ad hoc, in others it was elevated to quite a science (see, for example, the early-warning diagnostic tool in Appendix A).

THE FIFTH FACTOR: LOWER ORGANISATION LEVEL

All other things being equal, lower ranking employees (in or- ganisational hierarchy terms) are more likely to seek to un- ionise than more senior employees for a number of reasons.

Firstly, rates of pay and conditions are generally better as an individual moves up the organisation hierarchy. It follows that there may be less of a need for a union within the higher grades on the basis of having achieved better salary levels/conditions of employment. However, this of itself, does not explain the ration- ale for unionisation. In recent years the unionisation of relatively highly paid groups of employees, for example, airline pilots, points to factors other than pay levels as determinants of mem- bership growth. Further, pay is a relative issue. The absolute amount is usually less important than its comparability with oth- ers and the perception of self-worth of the job holder.

Possibly a better explanation is that employees at higher levels in an organisation often have a different experience of working life. Senior employees typically have greater involvement in (and identity with) company goals. Discretion in work flow, the ab- sence of close supervision and more interesting work may com- bine to produce a significantly different experience of work for these employees. Both the nature of the work performed and the efforts made by companies to involve them mean that senior em- ployees are often ideologically closer to "management" and may be dissuaded from union membership through "philosophy diffu- sion". While fears in relation to promotions, future career oppor- tunities and so on may partly account for the decision to remain non-union, no evidence emerged from the research to support this.

However organisational level cannot simply be equated with position within the formal hierarchy. Some categories of employees are defined on the organisational chart as part of the management team (for example, team leaders) while in reality they often carry out narrowly defined functions with little decision-making authority or involvement in policy formation. If the perception is created that their needs are not being adequately catered for, they may gravitate towards a trade union to promote their interests. Thus a subtle but important distinction can be made here. Position or level within an organisation is important in steering employees towards or away from unions on the basis of the significantly different "experiences" of work which normally feature at different organisation levels.

The final point under the heading of organisation level relates to the general perception of union membership. Senior managerial and professional employees may distance themselves from unions on the basis of "elitism". As unions traditionally have been closely associated with a blue collar, working class image, membership may imply an identity of interest with such groups. In Burn's judgement the union approach to white collar workers has generally been misdirected:

> It is an approach that is primarily class-conscious rather than career-conscious, one dedicated to fighting the company and opposing the management rather than improving relations and co-operating with management to improve conditions of work for the worker. Too often the philosophy has been to proletarianise the white collar worker; to ask and induce him to accept the methods and mental outlook of workers in the mass production, maintenance and craft occupations, even though his problems, interests and goals are not common and coterminus with those of shop workers.[8]

The "image" of unions is still a conditioning factor for some professional/managerial employees who have little exposure to the union movement. One HR respondent made the point that most professional employees feel that it is only hourly paid workers who unionise and that it is "somewhat degrading" to join a union.[9] Supporting this, another felt that the unions generally overplay their working class image. Young people, who may have secured their first job in industry and are positively looking forward to a career, do not want to hear that they are "downtrodden".[10]

Where a lack of understanding or even bias against unions exists, it obviously poses a recruitment barrier. However, this barrier can be successfully overcome. For example, the ASTMS was able to overcome this by reversing the notion that union membership implied a working class status. The recruitment of "high status" groups such as university lecturers, scientists and management grades across all industries lent a new respectability to union membership, moving it away from the "cloth cap" image. The very title of the union reinforced this by incorporation of the word "association" rather than "union". As one report noted:

> Substantial inroads into the service sector, white collar occupations and areas where women are concentrated will likely only take place by the presence of unions that have special portfolios and are seen as being "like us" and not like the stereotype of the labour movement generally.[11]

It is more than coincidental that in the companies visited where union encroachment occurred, employees opted to seek recognition with a union which was *not* already recognised (the supervisors did not want to belong to the same union as the group whom they "managed"). Where status differentials already exist within a company between grades of employees it is not surprising that employees themselves attempt to uphold these in relation to membership of voluntary organisations (the ideal of a wider working class solidarity is probably not foremost in the minds of potential white collar union members).

THE SIXTH FACTOR: LOOKING FOR A "NEW" UNION

In the cases studied, staff employees opted to affiliate to union(s) outside of those already recognised for the hourly paid workforce. As noted earlier, this process could simply be classed as elitism or "snobbishness", the seeking of association with a higher status group. While this may provide part of the rationale for the choices exercised, it is certainly no more a condemnation of it than where it occurs in society generally. Seeking association with a union identified with particular categories of employees is no different to striving to belong to any "elite" group (club, school, neighbourhood and so on). However, it is unlikely that elitism provides the full explanation for the finding. An additional factor is that an outside union may have more promise as potential members cannot test the service until they have "purchased" it. The argument that members can simply leave the union if the services provided do not meet expectations is inherently weak. Unlike membership of other voluntary organizations, de-unionisation, in the sense of employees relinquishing membership en bloc, does not occur in Ireland. While employees may disagree with policy or even opt to transfer to another union, once the threshold is crossed it is a bridge seldom re-crossed.

Focusing on Issues Relevant to the Membership

It follows that where a union is trying to achieve membership growth the marketing of its image will be a significantly influential factor in its success. Where an attempt is made to recruit staff employees, unions should not be seen primarily as "blue collar" or working class organisations — an inappropriate image, in status terms, for the target group. As Hyman argues:

> Trade unions are not class organisations, uniting all those who work for a living; workers combine along narrower lines of common identification and common interests.[12]

Focusing on issues relevant to a particular grouping is likely to be a more fruitful use of resources than a general recruitment campaign. For example, one ASTMS recruitment campaign was directed at the threat of job insecurity which supposedly featured prominently within the white collar, non-union sector. The slogan: "The Board And I Have Decided That We Do Not like The Colour Of Your Eyes" (a fictitious letter from management to the workforce reinforcing the notion of insecurity through arbitrary, selective dismissal) was adopted. This type of targeted recruitment is more effective than, for example, the distribution of standard leaflets which supposedly have mass appeal across all groups. "Know your audience" is therefore wise counsel to a union seeking membership growth, both in terms of highlighting the issues which are relevant to the group and understanding their political (radicalism/conservatism) profile. Unions should appreciate that the felt need for a union may well be instrumental rather than ideological,[13] a point supported by the general research literature. A classic example uncovered during this research related to ASTMS who organised the staff in Udaras na Gaeltachta. They proved acceptable to the membership as they were the only union which could guarantee a complete service in the Irish language, despite the fact that they are an English-based union.[14] It is this attention to detail, dovetailing services to meet the real or perceived needs of groups of members, which separates vibrant unions from those which remain stagnant in membership growth terms.

THE SEVENTH FACTOR: PARTLY UNIONISED WORKFORCE

A number of respondents made the point that it is more diffi-cult for a union to gain recognition in a totally non-union company than in one that is partially unionised. Managing a un-ionised and a non-unionised group side-by-side is fraught with difficulties. In a partially unionised company there are normally a number of internal allies who support the case for extending rec-ognition either openly as activists, or covertly through the provi-sion of information — a "major asset" to a union seeking to ex-tend recognition.[15] The non-union group can also be influenced toward joining on the basis of maintaining relativities. Where a unionised group makes tangible gains in benefits or conditions of employment (or is seen to have more organisational voice), the question of "who represents us" is often raised. Even where com-panies automatically extend negotiated benefits, the group "set-ting the pace" is seen to have more clout. For example, if 10 per cent is given to staff following union negotiations this can create the perception that future increases for the non-union group will be limited by the skill of the union negotiators. Conversely, pay-ing the 10 per cent "up front" to the non-union group gives the unions a firm starting base for their negotiations and highlights, in advance, the company's likely settlement position.

Managing the relativity of pay and benefits between the two groups is not the sole problem for companies with this structure. The ritual of wage negotiations may itself signal to non-union staff that a company is paying "more attention" to the unionised workforce. Increases in wages or benefits along with challenges to management decisions serve to highlight the fact that unionised groups often have more control over their working environment.

Several other points can be put forward to support the conten-tion that union encroachment is more likely in a partially union-ised company. Firstly, many of the wholly non-union companies support their status by the claim that they do not wish to involve a "third party" in the employment relationship. In a partially un-ionised company, where unionisation is already conceded to some employees, this particular argument cannot be used. Secondly, the fact that the companies already have experience of trade unions may lessen the "fear" of encroachment (albeit this point could work in reverse if the current relationship is adversarial). Thirdly, for multinational companies in particular, union encroachment may be more acceptable to the parent company where recognition has already been conceded to some grades and the structures in place (negotiations expertise and so on) to deal with this. Finally, many companies that operate on a non-union basis as part of a world-wide co-ordinated strategy have a wealth of expertise in managing this status and are likely to put time, effort and resources into developing a positive employee relations culture. Given all of the above, it is more difficult to maintain a non-union status with staff employees where the hourly paid workforce is unionised. The corollary is also true: it is likely to be easier for unions to achieve membership growth within a company where unionisation is al-ready in place than to "pioneer" a non-union company.

THE EIGHTH FACTOR: SHIFT WORK

In all of the plants where shift work was a feature, rostered em-ployees were seen as pro-union. Two possible reasons may be advanced here.[16] Firstly, shift work is perceived as being socially disadvantageous by most employees. While most manage to adapt their lifestyle and some may even prefer it (often those who can pursue a specialist interest during mid-week), the available research evidence suggests that the majority of employees prefer day work if this is a viable option.

> Research has shown that while some individuals prefer to work at night, a substantial number of people find that

their separation from the community pattern of living can
be unacceptable as a regular thing. [17]

Premium pay supposedly compensates for the unsociability of
shift work. However, this typically becomes an accepted part of
the remuneration package and, over time, is taken for granted
(like the old joke, "at the end of the money there is always a bit of
month left over"). It can be argued that shift workers become increasingly disgruntled with their working pattern. As this usually
cannot be changed, they address issues which are more open to
discussion. Shift work by its nature, then, has increased potential
for creating employee dissatisfaction which in turn can act as an
environmental factor in the search for union recognition. My own
experience in working with shift workers in numerous client companies is that an unconscious belief develops that "the management team do not care about us" ("we get all of the left-over crap
food which the day workers wouldn't eat", "I can't get time off to
go to my brother's wedding next Saturday" and so on).

Secondly, depending on the particular shift cycle and management commitment to the area, poor communication is often a
feature of shift working. This results from the fact that there is
normally little (sometimes zero) management presence outside of
core working hours. Employees who work outside "normal"
hours are often not informed of major business events and come
to rely on the grapevine for information. Unless specific efforts are
made to address this it can lead to a communication vacuum, a
feeling that "nobody knows", which may be negatively interpreted as "nobody cares". Where shift work is a feature, companies need to make particular efforts to ensure good communications in order to sustain a non-union environment. One official,
agreeing that shift work helps in the unionisation process, reinforced the point made earlier that trade unionism cannot be imposed on workers but must "be driven from within". In order for

this to occur a union consciousness must develop. Shift work helps by differentiating shift employees from other groups.[18]

A summary of the points, in order of priority, which led to union encroachment in the case studies conducted are outlined in Figure 14. While they do not constitute an exhaustive list[19] of factors which lead to membership growth, they highlight possible "Achilles' Heels" for companies wishing to maintain a non-union status.

FIGURE 14: FACTORS LEADING TO UNION ENCROACHMENT	
1. Redundancy	5. Organisational Level
2. Influence of Individuals	6. Search for a "New" Union
3. Previous Union Background	7. Partly Unionised Workforce
4. Group Structures	8. Shift Working

Endnotes

[1] Because of the small sample size, this listing is tentative, offering a basis for further research in the area rather than definitive conclusions Since the initial research was conducted, I have been directly involved in an additional eight cases of attempted union recognition (some successful, some unsuccessful) This later experience is incorporated into the findings presented.

[2] Levinson, C.R. *International Trade Unionism*. Allen and Unwin, London, 1972.

[3] Personnel Manager: Company B. Points made during interview with author.

[4] The question is raised whether a union would want or even attempt to protect jobs in these particular circumstances. Unions generally do not wish to organise members about to be made redundant as they constitute a financial liability. No examples are known to the author where a union recruited members when the decision to make these redundant had already been taken. While it can be argued that unions generally

protect jobs (for example by challenging companies on such areas as the introduction of labour shedding technology, re-investment, profitability in the total group rather than a particular plant, etc.) this refers more to the ongoing role of an established union. The general consensus within the respondent group was that union power to protect jobs, particularly in the multi-national sector, is limited. Where a decision to shed labour has already been taken, unions can do little more than ensure that re-dundancy remuneration is on par with settlements reached elsewhere.

[5] During the research it was not possible to speak directly to the individuals concerned; motivations attributed were based on the views of the personnel representatives interviewed. Hence the need to be somewhat tentative in this area.

[6] A study published in 1975 showed that 58% of union activists had previously held a union post (Hillary et al., 1975: 125). This gives some research credibility to the argument that prior exposure to union membership is likely to resurface (at least in the case of activists).

[7] Lockwood, David. *The Black-Coated Worker*. Allen and Unwin, London 1958: 17; Bain, George and Sayers, Elsheikh, F. "An Inter-industry Analysis of Unionization in Britain". *British Journal of Industrial Relations* Vol. XVII pp 137/157, 1979: 142.

[8] Burns, Robert K. "Unionization of the White Collar Worker". From Joseph Shister (Ed.) *Readings in Labor Economics and Industrial Relations*, 2nd edition, Lippincott, Chicago, 1956: 51.

[9] Personnel Executive: Company A. Points made during interview with author.

[10] Personnel Executive: Company I. Points made during interview with author.

[11] McKersie, Robert, Katz, Harry, Kochan, Thomas and Piroe, Michael. "Is a New Industrial Relations System Emerging?" From Thomas A. Kochan (ed.) *Challenges and Choices Facing American Labor* op. cit. 1985: 341.

[12] Hyman, Richard. *Industrial Relations: A Marxist Introduction*. Macmillan, London, 1975: 35/6.

[13] "Trade Union Official F". Points made during interview with author.

[14] "Industrial Relations Expert C". Points made during interview with author.

[15] "Trade Union Official E". Points made during interview with author.

[16] It could also be argued that due to physiological changes in the body's chemistry (due to disturbed sleeping and eating patterns) shift workers are in some way more likely to unionise (see, for example, McCarthy: 1981); as this point was outside the scope of the current research it is not pursued.

[17] Mann F. C., Mott D.E., Loughlin O.E. and Warwich D.P. *Shift Work: The Social, Psychological and Physical Consequences,* University of Michigan Press, Ann Arbor, 1965.

[18] "Trade Union Official D". Points made during interview with author

[19] A number of other factors have been shown to be influential in trade union growth patterns which have not been explored in the current study. For example, several studies have demonstrated that the size of establishments is a particularly important determinant of unionisation (Bain et al., 1979; Elsheikh et al., 1980; Hirsch, 1982).

10

How Unionisation Occurs

A N IMPLICIT ASSUMPTION IN MANY of the recruitment methods currently employed is that unions can significantly influence potential members in their decision to join. For example, it was suggested by several of the trade union respondents that the unions should become more "proactive" in launching membership drives as a solution to falling membership levels. Some unions have already done this. My understanding is that sometime during 2003 SIPTU appointed a senior official as "National Secretary" (the equivalent of a "marketing manager" in a trading organisation). The rationale is easy to understand. Full-time trade union officials typically operate a dual mandate: (a) They provide services to the existing membership and (b) they attempt to capture new members. Inevitably, a tension develops between both roles ("it's difficult to remember your objective is to drain the swamp when the crocodiles are biting your arse"). In practice, the operational (servicing) agenda often explodes to fill the available time and "strategy issues" get pushed to the bottom of the in-tray. The response by SIPTU was the recognition that more strategic marketing efforts need to be made. Yet a central question remains as to how much influence the unions actually exercise over the decision to join. The answer to this question is vitally important in that it determines whether, in the face of declining membership levels, the unions can mount effective membership campaigns to offset losses.

Although some dissenting views were expressed, overall there was general agreement among respondents from both sides of the industrial divide that the decision to join a union is normally initiated by the potential members themselves rather than by unions. This view finds good support from the research literature:

> Unions and their leaders basically act as catalysts in the recruitment process. Before a group of workers can be successfully organised there must be some irritating condition resulting in a widespread feeling of dissatisfaction. Unions cannot create this antipathy, they can only discover where it exists, emphasise it, and try to convince the workers that it can be remedied by unionisation. Union recruitment is by its very nature largely a passive process.[1]

How Unionisation Occurs

In my experience the process of unionisation can be described as follows. The initial drive for membership is usually sparked off inside the workplace, a process largely outside the control of the unions. Several of the most potent issues have already been detailed but there can be other "very specific" issues, for example, a "regrading" exercise which is poorly implemented, the movement to week-end working or the non-payment of a national wage increase. In the majority of cases these "speed bump" issues are resolved internally and the tension "goes away" over a period of time. Most issues do not come to fruition in membership growth terms. However, if employees decide to pursue recognition the unions can, *at that stage*, exert a significant degree of influence on the particular union chosen. Given the complexity of the area and the fact that each situation is somewhat unique, it is not possible to be more specific on this (for example, to quantify the number or the seriousness of particular issues or even the timeframe). The overall process flow is outlined in Figure 15.

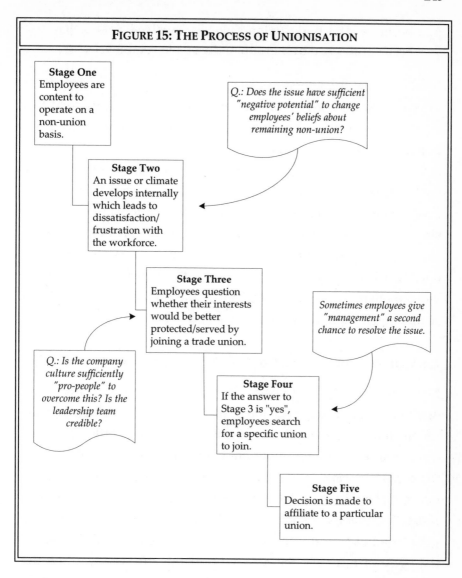

FIGURE 15: THE PROCESS OF UNIONISATION

Stage One
Employees are content to operate on a non-union basis.

Q.: Does the issue have sufficient "negative potential" to change employees' beliefs about remaining non-union?

Stage Two
An issue or climate develops internally which leads to dissatisfaction/ frustration with the workforce.

Stage Three
Employees question whether their interests would be better protected/served by joining a trade union.

Sometimes employees give "management" a second chance to resolve the issue.

Q.: Is the company culture sufficiently "pro-people" to overcome this? Is the leadership team credible?

Stage Four
If the answer to Stage 3 is "yes", employees search for a specific union to join.

Stage Five
Decision is made to affiliate to a particular union.

The unions only influence this process at the fourth stage, that is, after the decision to unionise has already been taken. This finding is completely consistent with other research completed in Ireland and the UK:

It is worth noting that in all of the cases examined, the initiative to unionise always came from within the

business. The trade union only get involved after it has
been approached by a group of dissatisfied employees.[2]

It follows that membership drives are unlikely to be successful if
directed toward a group of employees who have not reached this
stage. Employees have to answer the question "why do we need
to join a union?" (at an unconscious level my experience suggests
that employees ask the question, "will this company look after
me?"). It is only where union membership is seen to provide a
positive benefit, over and above existing conditions, that the decision to unionise is made.[3] Growth in union membership is therefore primarily determined by the particular work environment
over which the unions exercise very little influence. The counter
view, that employees opt for membership on the basis of an "irre-
sistible pitch from the unions", was said to be "ludicrous".[4]

Companies, Not Unions, Control the Unionisation Process

My own experience with companies who have granted union recognition (and those who have successfully maintained a non-
union status) supports the contention that there is little danger of
a successful "externally motivated" union drive. Union drives (or
to be more precise, drives which have any measure of success) can
normally be routed back to an internal issue which was allowed to
fester. The unions are not at the helm of membership growth, they
get carried along on a tide of in-house grievances and a substantial body of research exists to support this.[5] In a sense then the
term "union drive" is somewhat of a misnomer, implying as it
does that the unions initiate and lead the decision to affiliate. Re-
labelling the phenomenon "employee unionisation drives", while
unyieldy, more accurately reflects the reality of membership
growth.

   One old story, which supports this, referred to the former Ma-
rine Port and General Workers Union (MPGWU). At one point the
union, seriously concerned about the decline in membership lev-

els, launched a formal membership drive. To support it, an official was given leave of absence from normal duties for almost six months and conducted a campaign to recruit new members. Armed with promotional literature, he visited numerous factories and offices, encouraging non-union employees to join. The experiment was eventually discontinued due to its total lack of success; zero membership growth was achieved during the period. This example of a union committing both time and financial resources to recruitment without success reinforces the points made above. While the image of the particular union or the skills of the individual official may partly explain the lack of success, the fundamental reason is that unions do not recruit members, *they join themselves* when they perceive a need for unionisation.[6] Because of this, the more sophisticated non-union companies employ a range of "sensing mechanisms" to continually take the pulse of the organisation (see Appendix A).

Once Involved the Unions Take a Strong Stance on Achieving Recognition

The perception that unions are influential in the process of membership growth may, in part, be explained by union efforts to achieve recognition rights *after* they have been contacted by potential members. While the initial drive normally springs from an internal source, once a union engages in a recognition claim it can become a particularly intractable issue. This is in the nature of such disputes. Despite the supposed protection of the Unfair Dismissals Act (which specifically "protects" against dismissal on the grounds of unionisation) employees involved in the search for union recognition often feel "vulnerable to discrimination" by the employer. To "back out" of a recognition case was said to be a disaster for employees, especially those who were influential in the initial drive for recognition.[7]

Another factor is that recognition disputes, possibly more than any other single industrial relations issue, tend to have a particularly high profile. The union official involved is therefore likely to put a significant effort into this area on the basis of "visibility" and the likely impact on their personal reputation.[8] Within the industrial relations arena, few issues are so clearly won or lost as a recognition case.

Yet economics is an important consideration for the unions. It costs as much to negotiate a wage deal for ten as it does for 1,000 members, the difference being that 1,000 subscriptions will "support a full-time official, and a car, and an office".[9] An amusing anecdote was related during the research on this point. At one of the larger general unions (which shall remain nameless) visitors were stopped at the reception desk by the hall porter. If they announced that they wanted to join the union they awere queried about the level of *potential* membership at their place of work. If their answer was "less than ten" they were told to visit the offices of "x" (an alternative union) "who look after such members".[10] This story, whether true or folklore, highlights the fact that a trade union is a business enterprise. Recruitment of small pockets of members may simply be uneconomical in terms of providing a full membership service with a consequent drain on resources. Unions were said to increasingly have to learn that they are commercial organisations and that "missionary zeal" can be taken too far. Indeed, formal rules on recruitment show that most unions are not simply "open houses". Some will not recruit people in dispute with their employer. In simple terms they do not consciously "take on trouble". The possibility also exists that new members may relinquish their status once the particular dispute has been rectified, that is, the threat of membership is used as leverage on a particular issue. Becoming a union member in these circumstances was said to be analogous to "trying to join the VHI as you feel yourself having a heart attack in Lower Abbey Street".[11] Because of this the unions are somewhat reluctant to become embroiled in recognition disputes. Unsuccessful disputes are both demoralising and costly.

The Acceptability of Union Officials as an Explanatory Factor in Membership Growth

A sub-feature of the status consciousness point noted earlier is that individual union officials need to be acceptable to groups of potential members. Employees relate better to union officials who understand and are perceived as able to represent their interests and who are "like us". Implicit in this is the notion that education levels between officials and members should be broadly equivalent. While this point should not be overstated, "it is there".[12] Some of the unions recognised this, at least implicitly. For example, the Federated Workers Union of Ireland (which amalgamated with the ITGWU to form SIPTU) was said to have pursued, over a number of years, a philosophy of recruiting a better educated and more articulate official. This contrasts with the more normal recruitment methodology where officials rise up the ranks of the union hierarchy (most often operating initially as unpaid shop stewards). The recruitment of more highly educated officials was supported for two reasons. Firstly, it would enable the officials to negotiate on complex technical points (for example, effects of wage rises on inflation) on an equal footing with the growing number of professionally trained human resource managers. Secondly, it was felt that officials may be more acceptable to some of the higher educated groups of members if they came from the same socio-economic groupings and had a similar educational background (versus the traditional categorisation of union officials as "male and stale"). However, this particular strategy partly backfired on the union as subsequently a large number of officials transferred to management positions where conditions of employment were generally better than those provided by the unions. An inherent problem in the recruitment, for example, of university graduates is the likelihood of poaching by companies who have direct contact with these officials.

However, the problem of poaching by companies is not solely connected to educational levels. Where pay, conditions and career structure are superior on the management side the "poacher turned gamekeeper" syndrome is likely to continue.[13] Despite the notion of a fundamental political division between the two sides of industry, the attractiveness of the "Queen's shilling" is likely to account for some experience transfers on an ongoing basis.[14]

ATTRACTING NEW MEMBERS:
UNION RECRUITMENT METHODS

Part of the research was directed towards uncovering and assessing the recruitment methods employed by unions. What emerged is that recruitment methods have changed little since the foundation of the union movement. A systematic approach is notable by its absence, with the use of uncoordinated, ad hoc methods being the norm.[15] In part this is due to the unions sensing that issues outside of their direct influence determine union growth. For example, the traditional view in Britain, largely associated with the work of George Bain,[16] is that an overall increase in union density is unlikely to result from the recruitment strategies or tactics of individual unions. Unemployment, inflation, workplace size and government policy are the key determinants of union density.[17] Yet while this may be so, the implications for individual unions are somewhat different. As one source notes:

> . . . the pattern of growth was never even between unions recruiting in similar circumstances. Unions differed according to whether or not the national or regional leadership made growth a priority.[18]

If the above is accepted, the strategies of individual unions can impact recruitment results. A range of the current recruitment methods employed are considered below in more detail.

Direct Contact with Individuals

The distribution of literature and direct contact with individuals still provides the cornerstone of recruitment efforts as it did over the last 100 years. Leaflets promoting union membership and the placing of stickers on cars are the "advertising" methods most often used by unions. These serve the equivalent role to "cold calling" in the sales area, in this case helping to extol the benefits of union membership. The earlier points made, that factors internal to an organisation are more potent in membership growth than union initiated efforts, are directly relevant here. Timing is thus all important in the success of this particular strategy.

One official related an interesting experience which underscores this point. During one recruitment drive he completed two "cold calls" on an insurance company in Dublin distributing union promotional literature and application forms to employees as they were leaving work. The first trial run was conducted in September with a similar exercise being completed the following May. There was no response from the potential members on either occasion. The following September, two clerical officials from the union completed a similar exercise which resulted in approximately 160 signed forms being returned, a major breakthrough. The official stated that, at that stage, he began to question his own competence having twice completed the exercise to no avail. Subsequently he discovered that there had been a major reorganisation within the company. Fears around the job security implications of this had driven the positive response.

This begs the question of whether there is any merit in distributing pro-union literature at a time other than when there is some circumstance within a company which has created a pro-union environment. The evidence suggests that the productiveness of this approach is, at best, marginal. Yet the efforts may not be completely wasted. What is probably the case is that the promotional literature influences potential members towards the selection of a *particular* union (on the same principle as "brand" advertising). In the example noted above, the earlier attempts may have both communicated the type of union services available (to potential members who may not be aware of them) and steered them toward this rather than some other union. The overall rider remains, however, that employees themselves largely determine the timing of unionisation. The ability to "take the pulse" within particular organisations at given points in time maximises the effectiveness of this particular strategy.

Union Sales Package is Outdated and Unsophisticated

Interestingly, few of the unions visited during this research use presentation aids (videos, PowerPoint slide shows, overhead projectors etc.) as part of their recruitment armoury. The sales package is definitely "old technology". I asked the officials why the unions did not upgrade their recruitment hardware and use more modern advertising techniques, similar to sellers of other services. Several reasons underlie the general reluctance to move away from traditional methods.

Firstly, union reluctance to make more use of the media/ advertising or high tech presentation aides for recruitment purposes can partly by explained by the fact that a trade union is seen as "an instrument of justice".[19] Given this, it is felt to be almost morally wrong to promote union services using sophisticated *sales* techniques. The debate on whether doctors and solicitors should advertise their services, and whether this might lead to a lowering of professional standards, provides a good analogy here. The notion continues to exist in some union circles that advertising represents an attempt to coerce people into doing something that they may not otherwise wish to do and may be ethically unacceptable. Yet competition between the unions for membership is a reality. The notion therefore that the use of different advertising methods to achieve membership growth would, of itself, lead to a lowering of standards, seems spurious. Possibly the underlying (unspoken) view was that given the cost of high tech recruitment methods, the larger unions would benefit at the expense of those unions less able to afford it (this point is supposition and was not explored in any detail). A sub-point under this heading was the fact that high tech advertising or promotional techniques are non-traditional and are resisted on this basis. Change, of itself, normally brings dissenters, and some of the older officials, schooled in a different environment, may not be totally comfortable with newer methods. For these reasons the unions have tended to shy away from upgrading their recruitment methodology and continue to use methods developed in an earlier era.

The second explanatory factor in the unions' reluctance to upgrade their advertising methods may be based on cost considerations. "Payback" from advertising activity is notoriously difficult to quantify. As it is not possible to calculate precisely the equation of membership gain per euro spent, proponents may find it difficult to justify advertising expenditure on a cost effective basis.

The Advancement/Promotion of Individual Grievances

One of the traditional methods used to promote union membership is through the "exploitation of grievances" with individual employees.[20] That the unions may actually promote grievances (as distinct from addressing ones that had already arisen) is not suggested here. In this, as in many of the other areas covered, the unions tend to play a reactive role. The initial contact is most often instigated by the individual employee(s) rather than the unions. "We never recruit members, they've recruited themselves when they ring up".[21]

Once a potential member has contacted a union about joining, an official would subsequently meet the person(s) involved and decide how best to pursue the particular campaign. If the decision is made to contact the general body of potential members the unions have to be somewhat subtle in their approach. Employees may have a reasonably good working relationship with their employer and the views expressed by the individual who made contact may not be representative.[22] Even where they are, contact with the union may reflect a concern over a specific issue rather than a more general level of dissatisfaction.[23] Union officials are normally skilled enough to understand that a single viewpoint does not provide a solid foundation on which to build a campaign.

When meeting an individual or a group to discuss such issues, the unions use an informal presentation package. A "talk" would normally be given by the official in a pub (or, occasionally, in a potential member's house). The major concern of individuals at this stage is that they do not wish to be identified as a catalyst in the drive for membership. Anonymity is protected in an informal "off the record" atmosphere where the unions attempt to build confidence in the services and protection which can be provided.[24] Employees with previous experience of trade unions can be influential in encouraging membership and can be used to good effect by giving testimony of previous union successes.[25]

Holding Meeting of Non-existent Union Branches

The setting up of meetings of non-existent union branches is a further tactic which is used to contact potential union members. For example, a notice would be distributed that a meeting of the (Company X) branch will take place on a particular date, creating the illusion that this does in fact exist.[26] A meeting set up publicly in this way would likely achieve more support for, as noted above, non-union employees generally wish to remain anonymous at this stage. This method avoids the clandestine atmosphere of meetings held in individuals' houses, and was said to have been used to good effect in the past.[27]

Direct Approaches to Companies: A Proactive Strategy for Union Growth

A further tactic open to the unions in attempting to secure recognition rights is through contacting companies directly.[28] Most incoming multinationals are contacted by one or a number of unions during their start-up phase, a process documented in earlier research on the development of pre-employment agreements.[29] The general approach was stated to be "soft sell", a discussion around the type of constructive relationship which could be established (in the case of a start-up) or for a meeting to decide terms and conditions for members already recruited (in an existing company).[30] To support their case, the unions normally state that a "substantial" number of employees have already joined and ask for a meeting to put forward points at issue. A tactic used by some companies (possibly to gain more information on the movement's leaders) is to ask the union for a listing of members to "prove" this, but this is always refused.

Companies (other than those which had already decided to concede recognition) typically refuse to meet with the union, in any capacity, feeling that this would give de facto recognition to the union's representational role.[31] However, the personnel respondents were divided in their response as to how they would handle this. While some stated that it would be more prudent to simply ignore the contact, others meet covertly with the union officials to explain their position. As many of the multinationals located in Ireland have unionised their workforces (blue collar employees), it might be implied from this that directly contacting companies has been a successful union growth strategy. This is overly simplistic. The reasoning underlying the unionisation of plants is multi-factorial and cannot be attributed to the fact that some companies were contacted directly by the unions. In reality, even if this did not occur, those companies would have contacted the unions, having already made the decision to co-opt a union presence. The question posed under this heading is whether a direct approach strategy has been successful in persuading companies who would otherwise have operated on a non-union basis to unionise their plants.

Of the five non-union companies visited, only two had been directly approached by the unions. SIPTU and a number of craft unions had contacted one company by letter during their start-up phase. The personnel manager met with the union officials and informed them that the company intended to operate on a non-union basis (approximately 20 employees have subsequently joined but the company does not recognise the union for bargaining purposes). SIPTU was also in contact with another company by letter at the start-up phase but the company refused to meet them. Direct contact with companies would seem then to be an ad hoc strategy rather than one which is universally used by the unions. As a tactic, direct contact with companies seems to be marginal in the process of securing recognition rights.

Covert Union Methods: The Use of "Sleepers" or "Union Plants"

One of the more colourful points which arose from the research was the concept of "sleepers" or "union plants" being used to effect membership growth.[32] These are employees in the non-union sector who supposedly pass information to the unions. As we have shown above, assessing the internal climate at particular companies is critically important in determining issues with "potential" and the correct timing for unionisation drives. It follows that such intelligence would be of significant benefit to the unions. However, the practical use of sleepers in Ireland was a hotly debated topic. Before this point is addressed in more detail a number of qualifying remarks on how sleepers operate (on the assumption that they do operate) need to be made.

Firstly, a sleeper is not in the employment of a union and does not receive either direct or indirect payment of any kind.[33] Neither are they directed into specific jobs (the confusion here possibly arising over the term "plants" which is used interchangeably with "sleepers"). The most usual way that sleepers come to the attention of the unions is through their having had prior contact/membership with a union either directly themselves or through family contacts. One official outlined the process as follows. A sleeper usually contacts a union with details on some issue or concern for employees within a particular organisation. The official contacted would highlight to the individual that if they wish to establish a union presence, particularly if they work within a totally non-union company, they will likely be up against a highly organised personnel department and operate in an environment where there will be "a premium on people to inform on them".[34] They are told to play a low key role, especially if they have not yet completed their probation period. Union fees are either waived completely or they are advised to "pay a few bob now and again". They are further told to talk only to people they could trust completely.[35]

Sleepers were said to play a covert role in organisations, operating as information moles. They would not directly lead a union drive and may themselves be the last people to join to keep their position secret.[36] The official quoted above claimed that at times several different unions run people in parallel in the same company without knowledge of each other and that unions sometimes "run them in tandem".[37] There was even a suggestion of a political dimension to the role of sleepers. The unions were said to have used these in the 1970s when the non-union sector was first becoming established. The individuals involved were supposedly allied to left wing, and particularly, Trotskyite groups.[38]

The Use of Sleepers: Myth or Reality?

A number of the respondents rejected the notion of sleepers out-
right, on the basis that they had not previously heard of the
method being employed. For example, an executive from the IDA
argued that there is no evidence to support their existence. However, even if sleepers are used by the unions, there is not likely to
be any great evidence of their operation. By implication, they tend
to work covertly and would not come to the notice of companies.
The argument that they do not exist because there is no direct
evidence of them is inherently weak. Another participant dismissed the concept as "pure fiction" on the basis that sleepers
would not get through the selection system. While there was said
to be some talk of sleepers, this is "more gossip than reality".[39]
This latter point assumes that the screening process is 100 per cent
effective which is questionable.

   One union official's response to the question of sleepers was
one of complete disbelief. Union officials who suggested that this
method was used were said to be reading "Our Boys" or "Kitty
the Hare". He stated that he would not mind putting a couple of
his sons in jobs "not even as sleepers".[40] This latter argument mis-
represents the notion of sleepers as earlier outlined. There was no
suggestion that the unions have the ability to "plant" employees
directly into companies; the relationship becomes established *after*
they have been employed. Yet this official's dissent highlights a
contradiction within the union group. The national group secretary of one major union strongly supported the point that sleepers
are used, while the branch official in Cork denied all knowledge
of it. While one possibility could be that he was simply feigning
disbelief in order to protect the method, I was left in no doubt that
he was completely unaware (and dismissive of the point) that
sleepers are used by the unions. This opens the possibility that
sleepers may be managed further up the union chain of command
than the branch officials. Another possible explanation is that

such methods are employed on an ad hoc basis where people contact a union, and that simply through lack of exposure particular
officials never become aware of their operation. Another senior
official, supporting the point that sleepers had been used to good
effect in the past, suggested that they are sometimes left dormant
(depending on the economic climate) but "can be reactivated
when things get better".[41]

The Effectiveness of Sleepers as a Recruitment Tactic

Overall, it is not possible to conclude definitely whether sleepers
are or are not used by the unions. However, the fact that the
method was detailed by several of the union respondents, independently of each other and without any prompting, would seem
to suggest that this method is employed on occasion. Further, several of the union respondents when questioned were quite prepared to elaborate on the methods employed to manage sleepers
(how the initial contact was made, maintained and so on). If it is
accepted that sleepers would indeed provide a useful mechanism
for the unions to gain an insight into the organisational climate at
particular workplaces, the weight of evidence would seem to suggest that this method is employed on occasion, albeit the number
of sleepers in place or their practical usefulness could not be determined.

Endnotes

---

[1] Bain George Sayers .*The Growth of White Collar Unionism*. Oxford University Press, London. 1970: 99.

[2] McGovern Patrick. "Trade Union Recognition — Five Case Studies",
IRN, 9 February 1989.

[3] Messick, D.M. "To Join or Not to Join: An Approach to the Unionization Decision", *Organizational Behaviour and Human Performance*, 9, 126–
132, 1973; Ferber et al: 1980.

⁴ "Trade Union Official D". Points made during interview with author.

⁵ Guest, David, and Dewe, Philip. "Why do Workers Belong to Trade Unions? A Social Psychological Study in the U.K. Electronics Industry". *British Journal of Industrial Relations,* Vol. XXVI, No. 2, July 1988: 78.

⁶ Miljus J., Professor of Organisational Behaviour, Ohio State University, Ohio, 1986, in conversation with the author.

⁷ "Industrial Relations Expert C". Points made during interview with author.

⁸ "Trade Union Official C". Points made during interview with author.

⁹ "Industrial Relations Expert C". However my experience is that unions normally invest substantial effort and resources in recognition disputes, even where it is unlikely that the financial return (in terms of potential subscriptions) would recoup their outlay.

¹⁰ "Industrial Relations Expert C". Points made during interview with author.

¹¹ "Industrial Relations Expert C". Points made during interview with author.

¹² "Industrial Relations Expert D". Points made during interview with author.

¹³ Interestingly IBEC also suffers in this regard, highlighting the fact that the direct experience of industrial relations (on either side of the industrial divide) may provide the core attraction to companies.

¹⁴ "Trade Union Official B". Points made during interview with author.

¹⁵ "Trade Union Official F". Points made during interview with author.

¹⁶ 1970: 90/100

¹⁷ Beaumont P.B. "Individual Union Success in Obtaining Recognition: Some British Evidence", *British Journal of Industrial Relations,* Vol. XXV, November, 1987: 323.

¹⁸ Undy R. *Change in Trade Unions: The Development of U.K Unions Since 1960.* Hutchinson, London, 1981: 162.

¹⁹ "Trade Union Official A". Points made during interview with author.

[20] "Industrial Relations Experts A and D". Points made during interview with author.

[21] "Trade Union Official C". Points made during interview with author.

[22] "Trade Union Official F". Points made during interview with author.

[23] "Industrial Relations Expert D". Points made during interview with author.

[24] "Trade Union Official F". Points made during interview with author.

[25] "Industrial Relations Expert D". Points made during interview with author.

[26] "Industrial Relations Expert A". Points made during interview with author.

[27] "Trade Union Official B". Points made during interview with author.

[28] "Industrial Relations Expert A" and "IDA Executive A". Points made during interview with author.

[29] Mooney, Paul. "The Development of Pre-Employment Agreements in Irish Industrial Relations" Unpublished postgraduate dissertation submitted for fulfilment of a Diploma in Industrial Relations, Trinity College Dublin, 1984.

[30] "Trade Union Official A". Points made during interview with author.

[31] "Trade Union Official A". Points made during interview with author.

[32] In the US this method is sometimes referred to as the "Trojan Horse Technique" (Lewis et al., 1978).

[33] "Trade Union Official F". Points made during interview with author.

[34] "Trade Union Official B". Points made during interview with author.

[35] "Trade Union Official B". Points made during interview with author.

[36] "Trade Union Official F". Points made during interview with author.

[37] "Trade Union Official B". Points made during interview with author.

[38] "Industrial Relations Expert A". Points made during interview with author.

[39] "Industrial Relations Expert D". Points made during interview with author.

[40] "Trade Union Official A". Points made during interview with author.

[41] "Trade Union Official F". Points made during interview with author.

11

How to Deal with a Union Recognition Drive

In order to understand how non-union companies deal with recognition attempts, it is necessary to understand the legal position on union membership in Ireland. In the first section below, a review of the current legal position on union membership is detailed along with a couple of significant recent changes. The second section takes a look at how companies have approached union recognition drives from a pragmatic industrial relations perspective.

The Irish Constitution Protects the Right to Join a Union[1]

The 1937 constitution, Bunreacht na hEireann, establishes certain rights and freedoms which, in the way they have been interpreted by the courts, have had a significant impact on Irish labour case law. Citizens who feel that their constitutional rights have been infringed may take an action in the courts to have these rights defended and vindicated. Where any conflict arises, the constitutional rights take precedence over statute law, underlining the importance attached to the constitution. Article 40 (6.1.111) of the constitution expressly establishes the right to form or join unions. In simple terms, every Irish person has a constitutional right to form or to join a trade union — if they wish to do so. However, there is no corresponding *obligation* on an employer to bargain with the union.

The Right to Join a Union Implies the Right "Not to Join"

Besides stated rights, the Supreme Court has ruled on a number of occasions that other personal rights are *implied* in the constitution. In particular, freedom of association established under Article 40 noted above has been judged to imply a freedom to dissociate. This has been confirmed in challenges to the constitutionality of certain types of closed shop arrangements. For example, in the *Educational Company of Ireland v. Fitzpatrick (1961 IR 345)* the interpretation of the "negative right" not to join a trade union was first stated. Without this counterbalancing "right not to join" ("disassociate"), the courts ruled that the right to join a union becomes, in effect, a compulsion to join. In this particular case it was held that Section 2 of the Trade Disputes Act 1906 did not protect the defendants, as their action (picketing) was designed to frustrate a "constitutional right" of workers to choose with whom they would associate.

This decision was reaffirmed in *Meskell v. CIE (1973) IR.* Coras Iompar Eireann (CIE) and four trade unions had entered into an agreement whereby it was agreed to terminate the contracts of employment for all employees. Employees were to be offered immediate re-employment on the same terms with an additional condition that each would join and continue in membership of a named trade union (that is, a "closed shop" was being established). Meskell, a CIE employee, objected to the new provision on principle and a subsequent action for damages against the organisation was successful. The Court held that his dismissal was in violation of his constitutional rights (that is, the implied right "not to join a trade union") and the agreement between the union and CIE was held to be a conspiracy.

Union Membership Cannot be "Imposed"

In a number of judgements, the decisions of the courts have therefore indicated a "moral" objection to compulsory union membership. Firstly, it is argued that freedom of association is stifled where an individual is faced with the unacceptable choice between joining a union and getting a job. This in effect is a Hobson's choice; freedom of association becomes in reality compulsory association. Secondly, the courts have interpreted the constitution in favour of the freedom of choice of the individual above that of the group.

These decisions touch on the central dilemma of closed shop arrangements. On the one hand, the constitutional guarantee of individual liberty, and on the other, its implications for union security arrangements. This situation may be partly attributed to the fact that Article 40 has been taken to imply a protection of two freedoms (the right to form or join associations and the negative right not to join) which are potentially mutually exclusive. Other questions remain unanswered. To date the rulings do not necessarily protect prospective employees who are required to join unions as a pre-condition of obtaining employment nor affect the legality of action, short of picketing, taken to encourage existing employees to join unions. Although the existence of the negative right of non-association has been made clear, the degree of protection has been left open (for example, if an employee was "sent to Coventry" for not joining a union, the remedy is unclear).

The Waiver of Constitutional Rights[2]

In theory, an employer may require a prospective employee to waive their constitutional rights as a condition of employment. Such a condition will not be unconstitutional where the law takes the view that there is no coercion or compulsion involved in the arrangement. A prospective employee is free to refuse the job offered. Many pre-employment agreements contained such clauses, for example, it was a condition of employment that new employees waive their constitutional rights by agreeing to become members of a named union with which the company had a "house agreement". If they later refused to join the union (or left the union), dismissal on these grounds would not breach their constitutional rights. However, it *could* be argued that an employee who took a job and agreed to join a union (or agreed to remain "non-union") because of economic deprivation, had not "voluntarily" waived their rights. Accepting this, dismissal of an employee who later ceased to be (or became) a union member may be open to challenge on these grounds.

The courts will not easily infer that an employee has waived his constitutional rights. However, in *Gr v. An Bord Uchtala (1980)*, the majority of the Supreme Court adjudicating on an adoption case decided that citizens can lawfully waive their constitutional rights, reaffirming the earlier decision in *Becton Dickensen v. Lee (1973) IR: 1*. O'Higgins CJ pointed out that in order for the waiver to be effective the citizen must have full knowledge of their rights and must give free consent. A basic legal principle is that ignorance of the law cannot be used as an excuse or defence. In this instance it would seem that employers must expressly point out to employees their rights with regard to freedom of association.

Laws, to be effective, must have general acceptance. The fact that the closed shop was historically accepted indicates a desire for this arrangement. Undoubtedly the practice sometimes results in a restriction of individual liberty. Non-unionists were sometimes coerced into membership and existing members forced to obey union rules by means of the threat of expulsion. In its pre-entry form, the practice could be used to deny workers the right to compete for particular jobs (for example, historically only existing members of a union could apply for a job as a printer which maintained the trade within particular families). Union security arrangements and simplified bargaining structures for the company made the closed shop an attractive arrangement for both parties and avoided the dangers of multi-unionism.

The Law and the "Non-Union" Issue

With regard to the broader issue of non-union companies maintaining this status, there has been somewhat of a "Mexican standoff". While individual members had a right to join a trade union, there was no legal compulsion on a company to recognise it. Companies took the view that what employees did "on their own time" was none of their business. While they would not "tell" employees to join or not to join a trade union, they equally held the view that employees could not dictate company policy with regard to forcing union recognition. Companies essentially took the view that neither party should dictate to the other what to do in relation to union membership. Where union drives occurred, companies could (and did) simply ignore the call to attend the Labour Relations Commission or the Labour Court. However, in recent times the legal landscape has changed.

NEW INDUSTRIAL RELATIONS LEGISLATION: A TWIN-TRACK OPTION

Two new pieces of legislation have been passed recently which have changed the landscape around trade union recognition. These are the IR Amendment Act 2001 and the IR (Miscellaneous Provisions) Act 2004.[3] Under the guise of "modernising" our industrial relations machinery, this legislation was designed to support trade unions seeking recognition, albeit it stops somewhat short of making this "mandatory" on employers. While the title "Miscellaneous Provisions Act" may seem innocuous, this is an extraordinary piece of legislation which actually overturns the existing industrial relations provisions.

Under the "old" legislation (Industrial Relations Acts of 1946, 1969 and 1990), trade unions seeking recognition followed a particular process. If progress could not be made directly with a company, the union concerned could refer the "recognition dispute" to the Labour Court under s.20 (1) of the Industrial Relations Act 1969. As we have seen earlier, invariably the Labour Court ruled in favour of recognition, but the company could ignore the ruling and this recommendation could not be enforced. A key weapon for the unions was strike action to "force" recognition. This was fully legal as long as the provisions of the Industrial Relations Act 1990 were observed (for example, specific notice periods had to be given). This was a "high stakes" strategy and for many years the unions sought legislative means to make recognition "compulsory", partly as a remedy for employees where their employer was hostile to unions and maintained this status through fear, and partly as a simple means to secure membership growth.

Why Was the Industrial Relations Act 2001 Passed?

Over time, the unions became disenchanted with the existing legislation, arguing that employers were "frustrating" its spirit by simply ignoring the procedures. When unions sent correspondence to non-union companies, they were often "ignored". If the case eventually made it to the Labour Court (the unions were able to refer this unilaterally), attendance by the company was voluntary. They could not be compelled to make a defence or even show up at the hearings. Despite several high profile disputes, including in some cases prolonged strike action, there was no obligation on an employer to recognise a trade union for collective bargaining purposes. The Ryanair dispute (March 1998), which was particularly high profile but ultimately unsuccessful from the unions' perspective, provides a good example of how companies with steel resolve could overcome any threat from the unions.

Under the newer legislation, an alternative route has been opened up for unions seeking to gain a foothold in organisations. It is not either/or — both options are now open to a union seeking recognition, in effect making it more difficult for organisations to maintain a non-union status.

The End of "Voluntarism"?

The Industrial Relations (Amendment) Act 2001 represented a radical movement away from the "voluntarist" system, giving the Labour Court the power to make binding determinations on pay and conditions regardless of the views of the parties to the hearing. The new legislation was offered as a quid pro quo to the union movement (a key "social partner") in order to get them to continue supporting national pay agreements. The unions had been pushing this particular button for years, hoping to put union recognition on a "statutory" footing (similar to what exists in the UK and the US).[4] Irish employers had always resisted this, chiefly on the basis that it could have a significantly detrimental effect on direct foreign investment. There is a well-established non-union industrial group in Ireland which needs to be "protected" with several of the non-union companies openly stating that they "will not do business" with unions even if this means relocating elsewhere. When the size of some of these employers is considered (for example, Intel has over 4,500 people on site in Leixlip), the government was under some pressure to find a compromise solution. The unions evidently made the point that this new legislation would not be used to "go after" good employers (for example, upper-tier multinationals), but would be used to target bottom-tier indigenous employers where pay and conditions significantly lagged behind the market. This tacit agreement was broken by the unions immediately, however, by targeting the multinational sector, for example, Amersham Health (G.E.) in Cork.

The procedures in the 2001 Industrial Relation Act were long-winded (there were 11 individual steps and the process could take up to 18 months). The unions' experience was that employers were able to frustrate this by long delays. The amended legislation made "procedural corrections" which put a definite timeframe around the procedures (indicative timeframe of 26 weeks, with the possibility of extending this to a maximum of 34 weeks). Indeed the speed at which the amended legislation was passed highlights the fact that the unions "have the ear" of government, a point reinforced earlier. It follows that the unions now have a "dual track" along which they can pursue recognition claims. It has led to an (almost) unbelievable scenario where a trade union can unilaterally bring an employer to the Labour Court by stating that it has a number of "members" in that employment (but does not have to offer any proof whatsoever). The terms and conditions of employment can then be legally imposed on the employer by the Labour Court (if they insist on continuing to operate "union-free"). The Irish state has now taken on the role of determining the terms and conditions of employment for non-union companies (at a time when unions represent fewer than 25 per cent of employees in the private sector). It is undemocratic nonsense.

A TYPICAL APPROACH FOR RECOGNITION FROM A UNION

The unions now have two different options, depending on which piece of legislation they want to use to pursue a recognition claim. The options are not mutually exclusive and the unions can pursue *both* avenues if they wish.

Typically, a company receives a letter from a trade union asking for a meeting to discuss issues on behalf of its members who are in employment. The number of members is never stated and the "issues" may be somewhat general, for example, "to discuss the terms and conditions of our members. Under the newer legislation, unions are obliged to state the "issues" which are in contention. However these can still be somewhat vague, such as:

- Failure to comply with national wage agreements (even though the company may have a different mechanism to adjust salaries)

- No pensions scheme in place

- Disciplinary procedure is out of line with the Labour Relations Commission's "best practice" model (specifically, the fact that it does not allow for trade union representation).[5]

The letter will either be written by the local full-time official or may come from head office.

Historically, a lot of the non-union companies would have ignored the letter, hoping that the threat would simply "go away" (that is, that the union would get distracted servicing their existing membership or would pursue "easier targets"). Typically the union would then send a second letter, again with an overall "positive tone" ("to seek ways in which we can be mutually supportive . . ."). Under the new legislation where a company continues to ignore the correspondence, the Labour Court may take the view that the company has been rude or discourteous to have ignored a "legitimate" approach.

How Should the Employer Respond?

The employer's response depends on which avenue the union has taken. If it's the "new" legislation, the advice now is to politely reply to the unions' letter, stating the company position on why it wishes to continue with a direct relationship with employees.

> "Thank you for your letter of September 10th. We recognise the rights of each individual to join organisations of their choice but are happy that our internal procedures are working well. Our recent survey shows that . . . etc.".

While it is unlikely that this will end the approach, it is "procedurally correct".

The Initial Labour Relations Commission Hearing

The employer may (in all likelihood, will) receive an invitation from the Labour Relations Commission suggesting a meeting to discuss the concerns raised by the union. Some employers refuse, arguing that meeting a union in any setting constitutes *de facto* recognition. There is no legal obligation to attend such a meeting. However, if the issue is subsequently referred to a full Labour Court hearing, "non-attendance" may damage the company's position (making it seem that they had "something to hide" or that their non-union status is simply a wish to maintain unilateral control).[6]

The current advice is to attend this meeting and to "set out the company's case" (why you wish to remain non-union). Apart from the "courtesy" argument detailed above, attendance at the LRC allows a company the opportunity to get feedback on the exact issues and to assess the depth of feeling around them. The advice is to "go and listen" and digest the complaints put forward in a non-aggressive manner.

It's a judgement call, however. Some companies take the view that any form of correspondence or attendance is a "sign of weakness" and they simply ignore the various approaches. It is possible under this heading to attend the Labour Relations Commission (Advisory Service) hearing but to refuse to engage in any meaningful way with the union (or even to sit in the same room as the union representatives). This stance is not as extreme as non-attendance and may preserve the employer position of not recognising the union.

The issue can be "resolved" at this juncture, if the employer concedes the points put forward by the union. For the purposes of our discussion, we will assume the employer continues to maintain the non-union stance and the recognition dispute continues.

What Typically Happens Next?

Smart employers return to the workplace and redouble the efforts to:

- Find out what the centrally important issues are.

- Work to resolve them, reinforcing the benefits of maintaining a union-free environment.

As with all recognition claims, the real drive comes from "inside the tent" and the employer needs to ensure they are doing everything possible to address any in-house issues which employers see as negative. From a procedural perspective (new legislative route) there is a "cooling-off" period at this point. Assuming that there is "no change" to the position outlined above, the issue will normally be referred on by the union for a full Labour Court hearing.

The Full Labour Court Hearing

As with any Labour Court hearing both sides complete written submissions in advance. Regardless of the "legislative avenue" which the union has taken, once again there is no legal obligation for a company to attend, but it is advisable to do so (both to show courtesy to the Court and to ensure that the company arguments are articulated and understood). It has to be recognised that the Labour Court has historically shown a consistent bias in favour of unionisation, regardless of the specific arguments made. However, a company should make their arguments to remain non-union as coherent as possible (and use whatever internal employee "evidence" is available).

Likely Outcomes from the Labour Court

There are two separate possibilities (depending on which "avenue" the union took to make the original case).

- **Old Legislation:** The Court will usually recommend that the company should recognise the union for bargaining purposes. This recommendation is not enforceable as it relies on the "voluntarist" nature of Irish industrial relations (albeit, the new legislation highlights that the industrial relations system is becoming more legalistic and may change in the future).

- **New Legislation:** The Court may make a "determination" (not a "recommendation") that the company deal with the union in relation to allowing individual representation, for example if some individual is going through the "disciplinary procedure" they can be accompanied by an individual of their choosing, including a trade union official. They can also make recommendations around current pay or conditions of employment which are ultimately enforceable through the Circuit Court.[7] However, a critically important point is that under the 2001 and 2004 Acts, the Labour Court *cannot* make a recommendation on the granting of recognition rights for a *group* of employees.[8]

After the Labour Court: What Happens Next? (New Legislation Route)[9]

The simplest "what happens next" is where a company accepts the ruling and puts the necessary procedures into place to put it into operation. A second possibility is where a company (which may have completely "ignored" the process to date or "gone along" but disagreed with the final outcome) decides not to progress the Labour Court ruling. In this case the union has the option of applying to the Circuit Court for an enforcement order. Interestingly, because the legislation is so new, there is no case law on this (but it is crystal clear that it can happen).

The twin-tracks open to the unions in pursuing recognition claims are detailed in Figure 15.

Figure 15: Dealing with Union Recognition Claims

The "Old" Legislation
(sec. 20, subsec. 1, Industrial Relations Acts, 1946, 1969, 1980. Duration: open-ended)

↓

Union writes to the company

↓

Company often ignored this or wrote a polite "not interested" reply.

↓

Union unilaterally refers the case to the Labour Relations Commission (LRC).

↓

Company often ignored this step or wrote a polite "not interestd" reply, refused to return phone calls, etc.

↓

Issue referred to the Labour Court by the union. Company "invited" to attend *(if it is s.20(1) 1969, the union must agree to be bound by the result, prior to a hearing).*

↓

Company often ignored this step or wrote a polite "not interested". Company often did not attend LC hearing.

↓

LC invariably issued a recommendation granting union recognition *(recommendation was binding on the unions but not on the company, but was almost always pro-union).*

↓

Company could either accept or ignore the recommendation.

↓

Unions would sometimes "escalate" the issue, e.g. withdrawal of labour to "force recognition". Some companies conceded, some held out.

The "New" Legislation
Industrial Relations Acts, 2001, 2004. Duration: 26-34 weeks from the time the LRC contacts the company.

↓

Union writes to the company about individual issues or "terms and conditions" (they are precluded from addressing recognition from groups of employees under this legislation).

↓

Company often ignored this or wrote a polite "not interested" reply.

↓

Union refers to the LRC (they must follow a prescribed format).

↓

Company can ignore or work with the Industrial Relations Officer (IRO).

↓

If not resolved, issued referred to full Labour Court hearing.

↓

LC makes a "determination" (note new language: this is not a "recommendation".

↓

Company can ignore, but . . .

↓

Unions can apply for a Circuit Court Enforcement Order (usually issued a couple of weeks later).

↓

Company must comply (the determination can be appealed to the High Court, but only on a point of law).

CHANGING LEGISLATION:
SUMMARY OF THE "BIG ISSUES"

Who is Targeted?

The "between-the-lines" agreement among the social partners was that the legislation was not designed to tackle the "sophisticated" non-union employers who already have good procedures in place, such as mechanisms to track the marketplace on pay and so on. It was designed to tackle the "back-street" employer who treats employees poorly and uses their non-union status as a way to achieve unilateral control.[10]

However, the unions are a "business" and there is little mileage in chasing "two potential members in a back lane panel beaters". The new legislation will have bolstered the trade unions by offering (a) multiple routes to address the recognition question and (b) the ability to "show progress" to potential members because of the defined timeframes (maintaining momentum is one of the key negatives for a union pursuing a union recognition case). It certainly can be argued that the threat of unionisation has increased for *all* non-union employers, despite the so-called "original intent" to target bottom-tier employers (there seems to be some "walking amnesia" now within the union movement on the original intent of this legislation). The new legislation represents a fundamental (and, in my view, mistaken) movement away from voluntarism which has served the country well for many years.

Most troubling in all of the above is the notion that non-union companies have an "impossible target" to maintain, that is, it is simply impossible to keep 100 per cent of staff 100 per cent happy. The so-called "right-to-bargain" legislation has now given trade unions a method to exploit this to essentially make it much more difficult for an employer to maintain a non-union status even if only a tiny percentage of employers are disaffected. It represents more a "cave-in" to union pressure rather than a serious attempt to overhaul the industrial relations system in Ireland.

Don't Lose Perspective

A number of labour lawyers who see this as a business develop-ment opportunity have over-hyped the extent of this "new threat". As always in this area, the best defence is a good offence. The way to avoid dealing with unions is to manage your people well in order that they don't feel the need to approach a union for fair treatment. If the question is, "would this company look after my interests", you need to ensure that the answer is "yes"! You need to manage this proactively and not wait to make your case to employees *after* you've been contacted by a union.

Review Current Procedures

In reviewing your current grievance procedures, you may have to allow an employee to be represented by a person of their choice (colleague, parish priest, solicitor, a trade union official, their mother!). You probably need to modify the language in your cur-rent procedures to read "can be represented by a fellow employee or by a person of their choice who is acting in a personal capac-ity". This would seem to be fully defensible under the new legisla-tion (if the Labour Court ruled otherwise you could appeal this on a "point of law" to the High Court). The second area of concern is around "market tracking" of salaries and ensuring that this proc-ess is transparent and rigorously benchmarked. Is this the case at the moment in your organisation?

One Best Response?

While the "do nothing" tactic is not wise under the new legislation, it may continue to be a realistic option if the union is using the old (1969) legislation route. Each case has to be decided on its merits and there is no "one-best-response" here. In several recognition disputes a variety of strategies have been successfully employed. There is no "one size fits all" under this heading.

You May Need Support

Companies often need external support when going through a recognition dispute. The principal components of this expertise are courses in the art of remaining non-union, expert legal advice, industrial psychologists who develop and implement surveys and climate testing and industrial relations specialists who guide employers step-by-step through organising campaigns. Not everyone welcomes the development of this new consulting expertise. As one union source commented:

> . . . we are seeing today the new psychological terrorists of . . . industry. Drawn from the ranks of lawyers, labour relations specialists and psychologists, their weapons are emotional intimidation and subversion of the law. Whenever and wherever working people seek to organise, this guerrilla army dressed in three piece suits stands ready to resist.[11]

ON THE GROUND: HOW DO NON-UNION COMPANIES DEAL WITH UNION RECOGNITION DRIVES?

Along with the legal considerations sketched above, there are five practical industrial relations responses to a union recognition drive:

1. Refuse to recognise the union's demands

2. Propose a problem-solving route

3. Set up an internal staff committee

4. Offer recognition for individuals

5. Concede recognition to the group.

Each of these options is explored below.

OPTION # 1: REFUSE TO RECOGNISE THE UNION'S DEMANDS

Under this heading companies write to the union stating that it is not company policy to deal with "third parties" and then communicate this to employees. In some companies, the staff is simply unaware of the strength of the management opposition to unionisation and back off once this becomes known (see earlier points on making your non-union status known in advance). Some companies use external political influences in an attempt to get the union to "back off" (for example, a local politician who has clout, contact with the IDA and so on). It may help if the company has something to trade in this regard (for example, additional jobs at the site or influence with another multi-national who is considering locating in the area). This is a subtle route which needs to be pursued carefully and it is very difficult to establish its impact.

Advantages

- It allows companies to get their message to staff and test the "strength of feeling" behind the union drive.

- The union's budget for recruitment may be limited and it could be difficult for them to sustain a recruitment initiative.

- External pressure *may* have some bearing.

Disadvantages

- It may provide the union with the argument that the company is "afraid" of them. (Companies often use this option in conjunction with doing something more constructive to address the specific concerns that exist internally).

- It is unlikely that the union will "leave it at that" and they often take a case under one or more avenues of the industrial relations legislation (see earlier points).

OPTION # 2: PROPOSE A "PROBLEM-SOLVING ROUTE"

If they are not already fully aware of the issues involved, an employer should work with employees to surface their concerns and put together a plan of action to address them. A key group here is the supervisors and companies need to enlist their support in developing an appropriate response.

Developing an Internal Communications Message

The best way to progress this is to develop an internal communications message which might run as follows:

- We are surprised at this turn of events and the depth of feeling.

- We are now aware that there is a genuine problem.

- We wish to explore the issue in more detail and have decided to progress it (either asked an independent expert to look at the issue or conduct a DIY investigation).

- The process undertaken will be as follows (detail the process, often some form of intervention which uses focus groups and semi-structured interviews).

- The "outcome" of the process will be made "open" to all parties to ensure transparency.

Identify Groups Associated with the Union Drive

During a union drive, it is normally possible to identify three "groups" of employees:

- A Group — *"What is the problem here?"* There is usually a lot of goodwill towards the company in this group. Concern is about growing the business to its full potential and protecting employment.

- B Group — *"There are significant issues here which need to be addressed."* There is also goodwill towards the company in

this group who wish to see it prosper but want the specific issues addressed.

- C Group — *"The war has started. Let's progress this as speedily as possible."* There is less goodwill towards the company
in this group. Some employees have little concern if a company survives or not and some see it as a very "temporary
home".

Sometimes companies decide to take a hard line on the issues involved. Alternatively, it is often possible to make concessions to
some individuals. Once the central issues are understood, the exact route forward can be chosen.

Advantages

- It sends a very clear message to the workforce of the company
intent/resolve.

- It highlights the fact that "we are listening". The immediate
response shows good faith that "something is being done".

- It may give "ammunition to the moderates" and allow time to
deal with the central issues.

- It is possible to highlight the benefits of maintaining the status
quo, for example, to keep the group on a non-union basis (if
the organisation can "prove the case" to the staff that unions
are unnecessary).

- If the organisation gets some concessions from staff (if these
are required) it can reduce the overall settlement cost.

Disadvantages

- Unfair dismissal legislation specifically forbids dismissal resulting from union activity and the likely redress is reinstate-
ment (that is, there is a legal and ethical limit to what can be
done and this should not be exceeded).

- It could potentially backfire. Any "threat" (even implied) may have the opposite effect. It can inflame the remaining group if the company tactics are seen to be illegitimate in any way.

- A union can use any over-the-top reaction as evidence that the remaining staff need the protection of a union.

- The union response will likely be that it is a management ploy to avoid the issue of unionisation and that it is a "whitewash" technique.

- Can be high cost if a lot of consulting time is used.

OPTION # 3: SET UP AN INTERNAL STAFF COMMITTEE

Some companies concede the point that the organisation has not managed staff concerns well to date. They offer a staff committee as a device to address staff concerns and ensure they have an ongoing "voice" (the hope sometimes is that the staff committee will disappear over time and this represents a short-term "tactic" rather than a genuine change of position on behalf of the company).

Advantages

- It can be easier to manage this internal structure.

- Depending on the workforce profile, it can dovetail with an in-built "snobbishness" that unions are a "blue collar" organisation.

Disadvantages

- It can lead to internal rivalries/friction about the best way forward.

- Staff committees sometimes convert into full recognition status (that is, it represents a diminution of the argument that the company deals with all employees "one-on-one").

- May go against parent company culture of negotiating with staff employees on an individual basis.

OPTION # 4: OFFER RECOGNITION FOR INDIVIDUALS

Some companies decide to concede recognition in "individual cases" but not for the group, for example, the concept of unionisation would be akin to an insurance policy for individual staff. The union has no role in advancing terms and conditions of employment for the group as a whole but would offer a "safety net" for individuals in the group.

Advantages

- It may take the sting out of the initial union drive.

- It offers a credible management response.

- It maximises company flexibility (in the sense that it avoids the "collective" countervailing power of a union).

Disadvantages

- It is unlikely to be immediately acceptable to the unions who may "continue the fight".

- It provides a "floor" of union recognition, which can later grow to full recognition status.

OPTION # 5: CONCEDE RECOGNITION TO THE GROUP

Some companies simply decide that they can no longer "hold out" and negotiate a new working agreement with the union.

Advantages

- It resolves the immediate recognition issue and is likely to be acceptable to staff.

- Anticipated union response: Full acceptance.

- For "unsophisticated" companies, it recognises a reality that the union threat is not likely to disappear and allows them to get on with "running the rest of their business".

Disadvantages

- May create a political problem for the plant with the parent company, for example, a slow down in future investment at the site.

- It makes it more difficult to communicate the company's stance on remaining non-union with the rest of the staff group.

- Individuals may refuse to join the union "on principle" and it can lead to internal frictions among employees.

Endnotes

---

[1] While there is a need to understand the legal position on union membership, there is no suggestion here that companies should travel the legal route: "For many employers and unions there is a great reluctance to resort to constitutional rights in industrial disputes. Thus we have the paradox that the Constitution is hugely important, yet rarely used. In addition to the general disadvantages of resorting to the law, there are additional reasons why employers and unions are reluctant to resort to appealing to constitutional rights. First, cases can involve enormous costs, far outstripping any benefit if one wins and involving the potential for huge losses if one loses. Second, such cases take many years to come to trial, which conflicts with the frequent need to resolve industrial disputes speedily. Finally, the outcome of cases can be quite uncertain, as demonstrated by the frequent reversal of High Court decisions by the Supreme Court and by the differing opinions expressed by Supreme Court judges when deciding cases".

[2] The legal status of pre-employment agreements has always been somewhat ambiguous. The right to associate guaranteed under article 40 of the constitution, has been interpreted to imply a negative right to dis-

sociate. It would seem that in almost all cases, the pre-entry closed shop is likely to be declared unconstitutional and the post entry closed shop similarly be declared unconstitutional if imposed on existing employees. Individuals may agree to join particular unions as part of their contract of employment. Even where a declaration is signed to the effect that this waives their constitutional rights with regard to freedom of association, it is still unclear whether this provision could be successfully challenged on the basis that the waiver had been "involuntarily" attained. The legality of such provisions has never been determined by an Irish court. Even if the waiver of constitutional rights with regard to freedom of association were declared unconstitutional, there is nothing to prevent companies and unions agreeing that a particular union would be the only one recognised for bargaining purposes. This in effect, would provide many of the benefits outlined for the closed shop as it currently operates albeit without the financial security for unions provided by compulsory membership.

[3] This is an interpretation of "what's happening" as a result of the new industrial relations legislation. It is not meant as a substitute for full legal or industrial relations advice should you be faced with an actual recognition claim or an approach by a trade union. You should also review the original legislation and familiarise yourself with the details of the procedures. Given the complexity and sheer volume of legislation, it is becoming increasingly difficult for human resource managers to avoid having some "formal legal training". (With 25 individual acts and 7 different enforcement bodies, there is now an "employment rights industry".)

[4] This had been "on the boil" for some years. The Irish Congress of Trade Unions (ICTU) put together a paper on this entitled "Recognition and the right to bargain" and IBEC also constructed a detailed position paper on the subject. Eventually a high level group of representatives from both sides of industry, senior civil servants and the IDA were given a brief to examine this issue under para.9.22 of Partnership 2000. The intent to *change* the system was clear in the working brief which stated that: "In order to assist employers, employees and unions, the industrial relations system and institutions would be modernised during the period of Partnership 2000". In the end the report stopped short of mandatory recognition of trade unions but did open up "another front" on which the union recognition battle can now be fought.

5 Individual representation: Where a company conducts an "investigation" into an employee (discipline issue), does the employee have a right to be accompanied by a person of their choice? My current understanding is that if a person is denied this "right", that the "procedure" will be seen to be unfair, even if the substantive case is proven. Interestingly, there are a number of codes of practice which have been agreed between ICTU and IBEC. With the movement towards a more legislative approach, these have become enforceable. All non-union companies should review these codes and ensure existing disputes resolution/after procedures are overhauled to meet the minimum standards set.

6 The thinking from within the Labour Court can be determined from some of the recent written judgements. For example, in the case of *Marble & Granite Supplies Ltd. v. Services Industrial Professional and Technical Union (SIPTU)* (CD/O3/525 Recommendation No. 17699) the court stated that whilst "they accepted that the procedures set out in the Code of Practice on Voluntary Dispute Resolution are, by definition, non binding on parties, they find it regrettable that the employer declined an invitation from the Labour Relations Commission to process the dispute through those procedures". While this may seem like a simple "ticking off", the Court may be less amenable to taking on board an employer's point of view if the employer has failed to use the disputes resolution machinery.

7 In some of the cases to date, the Labour Court has also stated that a company should pay "future" national agreements, effectually taking this decision out of the hands of the employer. To date, the Labour Court has dealt with 25+ cases under these procedures. It is worthwhile to source these cases through IBEC and review the actual wording. My understanding is that the Labour Court has been using "language" which is more in line with collective bargaining, for example, focusing on representation by a trade union official and excluding some other possibilities, colleague, solicitor etc. IBEC have made a strong case to the Court to ensure that all of the options in the new legislation (for example, representation by a colleague) are given equal billing.

8 The notion that the Labour Court could not make a recommendation on recognition under the new legislation was initially unclear. My understanding is that this only became clear following information discov-

ered under the freedom of information act — taken from the minutes of a meeting held on 11 March 1999.

9 New code of practice on victimisation: Interestingly, there is also a new code of practice on victimisation (which is, effectively, part of the new law). This deals with "deviant" behaviour (either by the company or by the unions) during a dispute. For example, if an employee expressed a view that they wished to join a union and this resulted in "adverse or unfavourable treatment", this person could take a case of victimisation to the Labour Court. Similarly, if a manager in a company was deemed to be victimised by the union, she/he could take a claim against the union. The type of issues which constitute victimisation are clearly laid out in the legislation. No cases have yet been taken under this legislation so it is difficult to be certain about how this will work in practice. The penalties are up to two years pay — quite a substantial remedy.

10 The "defining" case on this in recent times concerned Amersham Health in Cork, a company owned by General Electric. The company essentially made the case that "unions are unnecessary" there. "The Court saw no basis on which it could conclude that the terms and conditions in GE, when viewed in their totality, are out of line with acceptable standards" (*IRN News*, 2 December 2004).

11 Georgine, Robert A. "From Brass Knuckles to Briefcases: The Changing Art of Union Busting in America". Centre to Protect Worker's Rights. Washington, DC, 1979: 2.

12

HAVE TRADE UNIONS OUTLIVED THEIR USEFULNESS?

"Ten thousand times has the labour movement stumbled and bruised itself. We have been enjoined by the courts, assaulted by thugs, charged by the militia, traduced by the press, frowned upon in public opinion, and deceived by politicians. But not withstanding all this and all these, labour is today the most vital power this planet has ever known, and its historic mission is as certain of ultimate realisation as is the setting of the sun." — Eugene V. Debs[1]

THE PREDICTION THAT THE MISSION of the union is certain of ultimate realisation can now be questioned. The decline of intensive manufacturing, the increasing use of labour saving technology, the move towards non-traditional methods of workplace organisation and the emergence of innovative human resource policies have changed both the demographics of employment and the rationale for unionisation.

The non-union companies visited during this research argued that they provided the services traditionally associated with trade union membership. Good wages/conditions of employment, coupled with the structures to facilitate employee participation, were seen to negate the need for third party representation. Where a company meets the needs of employees in these key areas, there is little need to provide for protection in the form of trade union membership.

The view that trade unions have outlived their usefulness was supported by three central arguments. Firstly, hostility to the unions partly stems from the general rise of living standards in recent years, which has greatly reduced inequalities of wealth and status. Those which remain are mitigated by generous social welfare services (for example, supplementary benefits) and the emerging trend towards single status employment.[2] By continuing to press their sectional interests, the unions are failing to recognise both the achievements of labour to date and the changing economic environment (for example, competitive pressures from countries where employers are not similarly constrained). Secondly, the traditional union role has been superseded by changes in the conduct of the employment relationship. For example, across the range of HR practices (both substantive and procedural) reviewed in this research, the non-union companies compared favourably, and in many cases were superior, to unionised companies. In particular, non-union companies are characterised by an expansion in consultation efforts, which substitutes the traditional information role undertaken by unions. To support this, a number of the HR respondents stated that employees continually expressed satisfaction with their jobs and the employment relationship generally,[3] despite the absence of a representational structure. Finally, central to the view that the necessity for trade unions has diminished lies an assumption that the traditional industrial relations process is wasteful in terms of the energy and time devoted to conflict management. In contrast, the high commitment model of organisation is characterised by a win-win focus which overcomes the central "defect" of the traditional model, that is, its adversarial nature. Direct communication (implied in the absence of trade unions) cements the core relationship between organisations and employees, reinforcing the inherent mutuality in the employment relationship. Pete Goss, the round-the-world sailor, captured the point well in his comment to a CIPD conference in Harrowgate on the topic of teamwork when he said, "the competition is outside the boat".

Overall, those who advocated the non-union model believed it to be superior in several respects. It is more competitive in terms of adaptiveness to change, quality consciousness and productivity. The benefits to employees are that it provides more satisfying work and a more "pro-people" work environment. In short:

> . . . it does well in balancing and integrating the complementary interests of the many stakeholders of the enterprise.[4]

The view that trade unions have outlived their usefulness was challenged on several counts. Firstly, those who support the demise of the union movement either do not fully appreciate, or choose to ignore, the question of relative power in the employment relationship. Secondly, the argument that a company provides the services normally associated with trade unionism may mask a search for unilateral management control. While outwardly allowing employees an input into the decision-making process, participation may be limited to a narrow range of issues and traded off against collective bargaining influence. Thirdly, the very presence of trade unions in the wider society may well have influenced the developments noted. Each of these objections will be considered below.

OBJECTION # 1: POWER IS A CENTRAL FEATURE OF THE EMPLOYMENT RELATIONSHIP

The high commitment model of organisation exists in its most highly developed form within the non-union sector. The literature uncovered on human resource management strategies supported the view that these are most effective in the absence of trade unions. Resulting from this, a fundamental criticism was levelled at the argument that we are witnessing the emergence of an industrial relations model under which the core values of employees are elevated and the need for trade unions diminished. At the heart of the new model is the complete identification of employees with the aims and values of the business. This represents employee involvement on the company's terms, with power remaining firmly in the hands of the employer. The absence of any discussion of power in human resource management literature indicates a blindness to the role of trade unions in providing a degree of balance in the exercise of economic authority. The account of the employment relationship, outlined by the ASTMS in their submission to the Commission on Industrial Relations, supports the above:

> The worker as an individual must accept the conditions that the employer offers, that is if he wishes to work for him. Yet the individual employer represents an accumulation of material, capital and human resources, and is in effect a "collective power". In the same way, to balance this, power has got to be collective from the labour side, and this balance must be maintained. Thus there will exist the following: the individual worker is subordinated to the power of management, but the power of management is controlled and co-ordinated by and with that of organised labour.[5]

Indeed, the premise that industrial enterprises are co-operative social institutions finds little support in the general industrial relations literature. As Hill argues:

> Employees and employers are enmeshed in economic relations which by their very nature contain powerful oppositional elements.[6]

While employees may express satisfaction with their present jobs or the employment relationship generally, this does not mean that they have economic or political power. From a radical perspective it merely means that employers have been able to manipulate them into believing that they are satisfied. The satisfactions thus expressed may be nothing other than "the morale of cheerful robots".[7] The interest of capital lies in the production of greater profit while the interest of labour is to increase its share of such profits. These are contradictory objectives and can only be balanced through the establishment and maintenance of an independent representational structure which allows a degree of "power equalisation". This cannot be achieved by employees negotiating their terms and conditions of employment on an individual basis. As Crouch argues:

> While the labour contract pretends to be an even-handed relationship between two equal partners, this is purely a legal fiction. The individual employee is always precisely that, an individual man or woman; but the "individual employer" is probably a company, including among its employees those working on problems of how to control labour and keep its costs down.[8]

Trade unions developed as a direct consequence of the surge of capitalism, and the rationale for trade unionism will therefore continue as long as capitalism remains in place. Viewed in this broader context, a continuing need exists for trade unions to represent labour's interests as the employment relationship can never be completely drained of conflict.[9]

One senior union official suggested that the lessons of history had shown that the objectives of companies and employees were diverse and, in many cases, contradictory. This cannot be lessened by any amount of altruism on the part of employers. By over-emphasising the mutuality within the employment relationship, those who support the demise of the trade union movement ignore the diversity of interests which are also present. Further, the view that there is a continuing need for trade unions goes beyond a simple reworking of the capital versus labour argument. All employment relationships, regardless of their economic base, create a situation where the interests of the parties will at times be in conflict. For example, officials in what was then the ITGWU[10] had established a staff association to "fight their own case" within the union. Thus, even *within* a trade union, particular groups need to have their interests protected.[11]

OBJECTION # 2: IS THE NEW MODEL SIMPLY UNILATERAL MANAGERIAL CONTROL?

A second objection raised by several of the respondents was that many of the changes detailed reflect an anti-union rather than a pro-employee bias. The so-called "union substitution" argument may be in reality a "union suppression" tactic based on fear and coercion. In this sense the high commitment model may be understood as a more sophisticated form of its traditional predecessor. Proponents are not concerned with creating a new, equal partnership between employer and employed, but simply offering a covert form of manipulation. Capitalism has simply adjusted to the power of organised labour. This viewpoint finds some support in the literature on managerial responses to effective labour organisation. Fox captures the essence of the arguments made under this heading:

> We might say that the implication of employees giving full consent is that they "authorise" management to govern them, thereby giving a special significance to the term "authority". Management can govern without this authorisation by employing coercion, but it faces at best passive indifference and at worst militant hostility. The value to management of consent is therefore apparent.[12]

The central argument put forward is that collective bargaining is itself a collaborative process. The conditions necessary for collective bargaining to proceed (freedom of association, recognition of trade unions, a willingness to bargain in good faith and so on) imply an essentially collaborative orientation on the part of the industrial actors. While this mode of operation may increasingly be regarded as cumbersome and outdated, it does constitute a de facto celebration of collaboration between management and employees. Under the high commitment model sketched earlier the participation and joint control being extended to employees represents a trade-off against areas in which they *currently* (in unionised companies) exercise a degree of influence through collective bargaining. As one source notes:

> It is clear that in the past management has been less than enthusiastic about any form of participation. Both the philosophy of private enterprise, the high value of formal efficiency and the structure of hierarchical authority are likely to incline them in this direction. Participation is likely to be considered, therefore, only when there are threats to these and paradoxically in order to maintain them.[13]

OBJECTION # 3: THE PRESENCE OF UNIONS HAS INFLUENCED THE DEVELOPMENT OF HIGH COMMITMENT WORK SYSTEMS

The final objection to the argument that the new model of industrial relations makes trade unions superfluous is that the presence of unions in the wider society has directly influenced the developments noted. To remain non-union, companies have had to develop a range of policies and practices which are at least comparable to those in the unionised sector. Whether non-union companies would continue to innovate in the human resource area if the influence of unions in the wider society were, over time, to decline remains an unanswered question. One possibility is that as the threat of the unions diminishes we could:

> . . . expect a slowing of the rate of innovation in human
> resource management policies in non-union firms unless or
> except in those situations where the declining union threat
> is offset by significant pressure from labour market
> shortages, government regulations or top corporate
> executives committed to innovative policies.[14]

Innovative non-union policies are likely to be maintained or expand where their economic contribution is high and creates a momentum of its own. The dilemma is how the legitimate interests of employees, in firms where this is not the case, can be protected in the absence of a countervailing power. Fox, taking up this point, argues:

> However lavish the care devoted to employee needs and
> interests, such a policy remains within the strategy of
> treating labour as a means to managerial ends if its purpose
> is to evoke a more profitable or productive performance
> and it is tapered off as soon as this return is no longer
> evident.[15]

Current benefit levels in the non-union sector provide a good case in point. While non-union employees currently enjoy good employment conditions, in relative terms, the fear must remain that a second generation of non-union companies would develop where the need to continue this positive stance would diminish because of declining union power.

THE POSITIVE ELEMENTS OF THE
HIGH COMMITMENT MODEL

Notwithstanding the objections cited above, the high commitment model of industrial relations has a number of positive elements which should not be overlooked. Improved organisational methods have increased reward potential for the multiple stakeholders in an organisation. The argument that the outward changes simply camouflage traditional capitalist values offers little in its place other than a continuation of the traditional adversarial mode. The fact that the traditional model has not significantly altered the relative power position of labour provides a central dilemma to critics of the new model who fault it solely on the basis that it upholds the current order.

The objectors to the non-union model also ignore the significant quality of work life advances which can be achieved when employees are fully utilised in all their human capacity. Under the high commitment model, the view that employees are a key business resource represents a significant advance forward. The existence of unionised companies where the high commitment model elements are in place supports the argument that the methods detailed do not simply denote a union-avoidance strategy. Commitment to employees goes beyond the union/non-union debate. It flows from an emerging recognition that organisations that fully utilise their human resource potential are provided with a significant economic advantage.

It seems clear that the development of the non-union model of organisation has a number of intrinsically valuable aspects. The importance of managerial inspiration and leadership, the focus on the mutuality in the employment relationship and the reminder of individual potential are all critically important messages. While the developments noted are primarily driven by the possibility of higher productivity, without question they maximise the role of employees at the workplace. For employees, operating on a non-union basis (in the sophisticated HRM companies) is the industrial equivalent of being governed by a benevolent dictator. While the parameters of "benevolence" are unilaterally decided and there is no guarantee about its continuance, most seem to accept these "political downsides" on the basis of the substantive gains which can be made.

Karl W. Deutsch has written that in measuring changes it is important to ask whether and when a "critical mass" or "threshold" has been reached.[16] While the evidence does not support the contention that this threshold has yet been reached, the research findings suggest that there will be an increasing movement towards the non-union model of industrial relations in the coming years. Current trends seem to indicate a continued focus on organisational flexibility. In addition, we are likely to see increases in temporary employment, part-time working and homeworking. Skill distinctions will continue to be blurred by technology, which will enhance the trend towards smaller plants and business units. Buying in specialist outside services such as catering, cleaning, security and others such as software expertise will also likely expand. These developments will support the central tenets of the non-union model, the rejection of the idea of the employer as an enemy and the replacement of the class struggle with the struggle for markets. It is no longer us (the workers) against them (the management) but us (our company) against them (the competition).[17]

Industrial relations practices in a large number of companies operating in Ireland remain firmly located within the traditional model. Borrowing a concept from mathematics, large numbers change slowly. In the short term it is likely that industry will continue to display as wide a diversity in the future as it has in the past.[18] It would be misleading and somewhat premature therefore to suggest that a permanent change in the Irish industrial relations system has taken place. Current and emerging practices suggest a good deal of experimentation, innovation and some return to earlier areas of intense conflict. The contradictory and parallel attempts of employers to restore unilateral managerial control and to build lasting co-operation at the workplace reflect deep uncertainty about the most promising path towards industrial revitalisation.[19] Yet while the route is somewhat unclear, the target is less so. A less adversarial employment relationship, coupled with a continuing search for improved organisational flexibility, is underway and will hugely impact the conduct of industrial relations over the coming years.

The aim of this book has been to examine current industrial relations trends, particularly the development of the non-union sector, and attempt to locate them within a conceptual framework. Given the breadth of the topic it is almost inevitable that some issues were excluded while others have been left somewhat inconclusive. It is hoped that, if nothing else, this book will stimulate further inquiry along some of the paths identified.

Endnotes

[1] Eugene V. Debs after the Pullman strike, 1894.

[2] Personnel Manager: Company A. Points made during interview with author.

[3] The normal method of evaluating employees' level of satisfaction is through conducting climate surveys (at several organisations I had an opportunity to review their trend data which supported the arguments made).

[4] Walton, Richard E. "From Control to Commitment: Transforming Workforce Management in the United States". Paper prepared for the Harvard Business School's 75th Anniversary Colloquium on Technology and Productivity, March 27-29, 1984.

[5] Commission Report. "Report of the Commission of Enquiry on Industrial Relations". Stationary Office, Government Publications, Dublin 1981.

[6] Hill, Stephen. *Competition and Control at Work: The New Industrial Sociology*, Heinemann, London 1981: 2.

[7] Braveman, Harry. *Labour and Monopoly Capital: The Degradation of Work in the 20th Century*. Monthly Review Press, New York, 1974.

[8] Crouch, Colin. *Trade Unions: The Logic of Collective Action*. Fontana Paperbacks, UK, 1982: 45.

[9] Ibid: 119.

[10] Now amalgamated with the FWUI and re-christened SIPTU.

[11] "Trade Union Official A". Points made during interview with author.

12 Fox, Alan. *Man Mismanagement*. Hutchinson, London, 1974: 67.

13 Brennan P. et al. *The Worker Directors*. Hutchison, UK, 1976.

14 Kochan, T.A., McKersie, R.B. and Cappelli, P. "The Effects of Corporate Strategy and Workplace Innovations on Union Representation". *Industrial and Labor Relations Review*, Vol. 39, No. 4, pp 487-501. 1985.

15 Fox, Alan. *Man Mismanagement*. Hutchinson, London, 1974: 51.

16 Deutsch, K.W. "The Systems Theory Approach as a Basis for Comparative Research", *International Social Science Journal*, Vol. 103/1, 1984.

17 Bassett, Philip. *Strike Free — New Industrial Relations in Britain*, Macmillan, 1987: 171–174; Bain, George Sayers. *The Growth of White-Collar Unionism*. Oxford University Press, London, 1970. Research evidence that the personal characteristics of white collar workers make them unsympathetic to trade unionism is somewhat contradictory, with some authors giving little credence to this view.

18 Kochan .Thomas A and McKersie, Robert B. "The Industrial Relations System in Transition: Findings of a Three Year Study". From Barbara D. Dennis (ed.) Proceedings of the 37th Annual Meeting, Madison WI, IIRA 1985: 272.

19 Streeck, Wolfgang. "The Uncertainties of Management in the Management of Uncertainty: Employers, Labour Relations and Industrial Adjustment in the 1980s" *Work, Employment and Society*, Vol. 1 No. 3, 1987.

Appendix A

NON-UNION ASSESSMENT TOOL

This instrument has been developed to help companies assess their vulnerability to trade union recognition. It is normally completed by a "vertical slice" of the management team.

Factors Evaluated

a. Community Climate

b. Union Avoidance: Early warning systems

c. Employment stability/job security

d. Plant Operations/Change

e. Superior Assessment

f. Personnel Practices

g. Work Rules

h. Complaint Identification/Resolution

i. Salaries

j. Benefits

k. Employee Communications Systems

l. Management/organisation

Strength/Weakness Evaluation Codes

Based on its relative strength or weakness from a union-free point of view, each question is evaluated and awarded one of five coded responses, ranging from "Exceptional/Very Strong" at one end (Code A) to "Inadequate/Marginal/Weak" at the other (Code E), with a mid-range of "Adequate" (Code C) in the middle.

Evaluation Codes A, B, C, D or E as follows:

A. Exceptional, very strong

B. Good, better than average

C. Adequate, normal, O.K., About average

D. Below average

E. Inadequate, marginal, weak.

One way to look at Codes D or E is to ask yourself whether the factor is sufficiently negative from the employees' view that they would be tempted to look to a union for help, and whether or not a union could do anything about the problem. Inputs from supervisors and individual staff contributors are obviously important here, in addition to senior management.

Circle A, B, C, D, or E, as you feel appropriate.

A: COMMUNITY CLIMATE

A1.   Does your community view you *as a desirable employer* (high standards, steady jobs, good pay, fair treatment etc.)?

A   B   C   D   E

A2.   What is the general *community attitude towards unions?* Would such attitude tend to help or hurt a union's efforts to organise your plant? Have there been any changes in this attitude?

A   B   C   D   E

A3.   Are *neighbouring plants* unionised? Has your community been targeted by any particular union drive?

A   B   C   D   E

A4.   Is the existence of highly unionised operations *in your area* harmful/helpful? Does it *require extra efforts* in your employee relations programmes?

A   B   C   D   E

A5.   Does your *purchasing programme* positively discriminate in favour of local suppliers?

A   B   C   D   E

A6.   In the event of a *business downturn* (general downturn or lack of supplier performance) do you "ease the burden" on local suppliers?

A   B   C   D   E

A7.   Is your company highly rated with regard to *social activities* undertaken (e.g. support for local schools, old folks, etc.?)

A   B   C   D   E

A8.   Is your *management team actively involved* in external community support activities?

A   B   C   D   E

A9.   Have you targeted particularly *influential people* in the local community and made efforts to ensure their goodwill towards the plant?

A   B   C   D   E

A10. Is your *credit policy* (payment of debts) similar to/better than other buyers in the locality?

A   B   C   D   E

A11. Do you make specific efforts to *"train-up"* local suppliers where existing skills/product purchases cannot be substituted?

A   B   C   D   E

B: Union Avoidance: Early Warning Systems

B1.   Do you ask your supervisors to *make a periodic assessment* of how their work force might respond to *card-signing activity?*

A   B   C   D   E

B2   Do you have a *workable early warning system* in place so you will know when organising activity begins? (Are supervisors, other staff an integral part of this?)

A   B   C   D   E

B3. Do you *provide supervisors with training regarding the maintenance of a union-free operation,* how to communicate with employees regarding unions, contract comparison, etc.?

A   B   C   D   E

B4. *Do you keep aware and make supervisors aware of union activity* labour legislation, latest union organising techniques and other such developments? If you can predict which union is most likely to seek you out, are you familiar with their style of organising?

A   B   C   D   E

B5. Does your management know the history of *previous campaigns and issues* involved in those campaigns? (Have those issues since been resolved?)

A   B   C   D   E

B6. Have special management *efforts have been made to relate to different employee populations* such as male/female, different shifts, production, maintenance, short/long service, etc.? Are there particular groups whom you feel are vulnerable?

A   B   C   D   E

B7. In the face of an aggressive union organising campaign and a card signing petition, are your *total "in-house" resources* experienced enough and in touch with union election processes to dissuade employees to join?

A   B   C   D   E

B8. Do personnel *benefits procedures* and *actual performance* match or exceed employees' expectations? (When were these last checked in detail, e.g. premium pay, opportunities for progression as well as basics like accurate pay checks/prompt corrections, timely insurance claim processing)

A   B   C   D   E

Employee Treatment

B9. Do employees know that *they receive the same pay and benefit improvements* as unionised employees? (Do you remind them?)

A   B   C   D   E

B10. How does actual employee treatment stack up *with standard union contract provisions?* (Is this reflected in the employee handbook and supervisory manual? Are there any significant items *that fall short* of contract/union standards (e.g. treatment of service in times of layoff vs performance)?)

A   B   C   D   E

B11. What meaningful local examples can be cited to demonstrate employee treatment that is *better than standard union contract provisions?*

A   B   C   D   E

B12. Do managers/supervisors attend funerals/mark other significant occasions in employees' lives?

A   B   C   D   E

More

B13. What additional factors in this Key Element are unique or important to your employees/business and should be evaluated?

_____

_____

_____

_____

B14. Are you aware of existing and any recent changes? Have you a good information network in this area?

_____

_____

_____

_____

B15. Are there particular "irritants" which have been continuously mentioned by employees but have not yet been actioned?

_____

_____

_____

_____

C: EMPLOYMENT STABILITY/JOB SECURITY

C1. Do you utilise *temporary employees* as a "buffer" against a downturn in business? How well are the temporary employees screened, managed?

A   B   C   D   E

C2. What is the recent history of *employment stability* (rapid fluctuations in employment, either up or down)? What impact has this had on individual employees?

A   B   C   D   E

C3.   If there have been recent *layoffs,* do employees have any reason to feel that the layoff was *unnecessary or the fault of management,* or that the procedure followed was unfair? (For example, are any employees working overtime, or are new employees being hired while other are on layoff or short time?)

A   B   C   D   E

C4.   Have there been any recent *rearrangements* (employment of
temporary employees, subcontracting, etc.) which might
cause employee concern? What has been the impact of
movement of production facilities and jobs offshore, if any?

A   B   C   D   E

C5.   Has the plant experienced wide swings in *production requirements?* Is it likely to do so in the future?

A   B   C   D   E

C6.   Have there been any recent changes in the *kinds of work* employees are doing, *changes in skill requirements,* or in the *structure of jobs* which would give employees cause for concern?

A   B   C   D   E

C7.   To what extent have the above *change factors* contributed to a
feeling of *insecurity,* or led employees to feel that they *need
union protection* in the areas of employment stability or job
security?

A   B   C   D   E

C8.   How well have employees been *kept informed* on a continuing basis of *changes to come and reasons for such changes* as
head-count reductions?

A   B   C   D   E

More

C9. What additional factors in this Key Element are unique or important to your employees/business and should be evaluated?

_____

_____

_____

_____

D: PLANT OPERATIONS/CHANGE

Strategic Plan Impact

D1. What changes are coming in the *level of business?* (Do you expect a significant downturn/upturn in employment? Do employees expect layoffs or reductions in employment?) Are you preparing employees for these changes?

A　　　B　　　C　　　D　　　E

D2. Do you foresee any *major changes* occurring in *facilities, machines, processes or methods?* (How will employees be affected? Are plans in place to minimise the effect or maximise the benefits of these factors to the long-range health of the business?)

A　　　B　　　C　　　D　　　E

Availability of materials, tools, support

D3. How adequate is the *supply of materials, tools, etc.,* which employees need to do their jobs?

A　　　B　　　C　　　D　　　E

D4. How adequate and timely is the assistance provided by maintenance, materials and other service organisations in supporting production?

A　　　B　　　C　　　D　　　E

D5.   Are their *bottlenecks in your factory flow* that make it difficult
       for employees to do their job/cause frustration? (Why do
       they exist? How can they be corrected?)

       A   B   C   D   E

Production Changes

D6.   Does your plant experience *predictable seasonal fluctuations* in
       business which hurt employees through layoffs, short-
       timing, downgrading, etc.? (How could this be better ac-
       commodated?)

       A   B   C   D   E

D7.   When plans are made regarding production rate changes,
       introduction of new products, phasing out of old products,
       changes in the work place, etc., do you ensure that *impacts
       on employees* are factored into the plan?

       A   B   C   D   E

Productivity and Measurement

D8.   Have there been major changes such as *cost-reduction drives,
       head-count reductions etc.*? What was the effect on your em-
       ployees?

       A   B   C   D   E

D9.   Have there been recent *increases in workloads* or *tightening of
       standards* on individual employees? Are these seen as
       "speed-ups"?

       A   B   C   D   E

D10. Are parts of your plant being *automated*? Jobs eliminated? Jobs combined? Any possible negative impact?

A   B   C   D   E

D11. Are your *employees fully employed?* (That is, when machine downtime, material flow bottlenecks occurs, is there something for them to do?)

A   B   C   D   E

D12. Are *positive/negative trends* developing in measurements, i.e. productivity, quality, cost? (If so, what are the employee relations implications?)

A   B   C   D   E

D13. Do you have standards for *quality* on which employees can rely and are they accepted as realistic (or are they determined by individual inspectors or supervisors)?

A   B   C   D   E

D14. Do your employees know *what's expected of them* (production, quality, attendance, etc.)? Do any grievances/issues arise under this general heading?

A   B   C   D   E

Physical Working Conditions

D15. Have there been any recent changes in *working conditions* which could result in legitimate employee complaints?

A   B   C   D   E

D16. Have employees indicated major dissatisfaction with such services as *cafeteria, rest rooms, employee store, parking facilities etc.?*

A   B   C   D   E

More

D17. What additional factors in this Key Element are unique or important to your employees/business and should be evaluated?

_____

_____

_____

_____

E: SUPERVISOR ASSESSMENT

E1.   Are supervisory positions designed to include *full responsibility* for the management and leadership of employees? (If the *number* and *location* of employees reporting to each supervisor such that they have time to handle their *employee relations responsibilities* properly?)

A   B   C   D   E

Leadership Competence

E2.   In screening supervisory candidates, is sufficient emphasis placed on identifying *leadership, communication, interpersonal relationship* and *problem-solving skills* to meet union-free needs?

A   B   C   D   E

E3.   Is *employee relations assistance* and *technical support* (Mfg., Eng., Materials, QC etc.) provided to the supervisor in a way which *does not diminish* their stature *or undercut* their authority?

A   B   C   D   E

E4. Do *employees* consider their supervisor *competent?*

A   B   C   D   E

E5. Do supervisors generally know their *individual employees* (background, goals, sensitivities, problems, etc.)?

A   B   C   D   E

E6. Have there been a significant number of actions taken by supervisors which might be interpreted by employees as *favouritism, discrimination, unreasonable pressure, harsh treatment,* etc.?

A   B   C   D   E

E7. Is there *consistency* throughout the supervisor group in the treatment of employees, or do employees feel that some supervisors are *"tough"* and others *"soft"?*

A   B   C   D   E

E8. In the past couple of years, has it been necessary to replace supervisor/managers for *inability to handle the "people-leadership"* part of their responsibilities? Are there some supervisor/managers who remain potential liabilities?

A   B   C   D   E

Company Relationship with Supervisors

E9. Have profit/cost pressures required a *reduction* in number of supervisors, *cutbacks* in support personnel, *elimination* of off-shift medical/ER coverage, etc.? Has this affected the quality of the overall supervisory relationships from a union avoidance point of view?

A   B   C   D   E

E10. *How do supervisors see their own treatment,* e.g., dignity of their work place, number of employees supervised, salary increases, overtime pay, development opportunities, advance information on the business, opportunities to input on plans and decisions, being "in the loop"?

A   B   C   D   E

Performance–Relationships

E11. In addition to your regular supervisor development and training activities, do you provide them with *encouragement* and specific *know-how* to lead a union-free work group?

A   B   C   D   E

E12. How well are supervisor handling their *informal day-to-day contacts* and *communication* responsibilities? (How much upward communication are supervisors receiving from employees on matters of current concern? Do supervisors report such upward communication?)

A   B   C   D   E

E13. What *formal communication channels* do supervisors make use of (e.g. monthly departmental meetings etc.? How effective are these channels? (Do the supervisors get help in planning such meetings and do they provide feedback reports on them?)

A   B   C   D   E

E14. Do most supervisors use the *HR function as a helping-hand* in their relationship with employees, or do they look upon the function as an *obstacle*?

A   B   C   D   E

E15. How *visible* is your supervision, i.e., shift start-up, end, breaks, lunch or are they in meetings, doing paper-work, chasing parts, etc.?

A   B   C   D   E

More

E16. What additional factors in this Key Element are unique or important to your employees/business and should be evaluated?

_____

_____

_____

_____

F: PERSONNEL PRACTICES

Employee Perceptions

F1. If employees receive periodic formal *performance reviews* from their supervisors, do they consider these *helpful*?

A   B   C   D   E

F2. Is *training considered adequate* by employees? (Consider learning time allowed opportunities to acquire new skills.)

A   B   C   D   E

F3. Are there negative indications in your current *Labour turnover* (voluntary quit) rates?

A   B   C   D   E

F4. Are employees concerned over a *lack of opportunity* in advancement to higher-rated jobs? If so, what are the reasons for such concern? How has such concern manifested itself?

A   B   C   D   E

F5.   How are your job posting/Internal recruitment procedures perceived by employees?

A   B   C   D   E

F6.   Are your practices on *lateral transfers, and shift changes* perceived by employees as overly flexible?

A   B   C   D   E

F7.   Do employees generally accept *internal transfer procedures* as fair and equitable?

A   B   C   D   E

F8.   To what extent do employees feel they have timely *opportunities to participate, be involved, or offer alternatives* in decisions which affect them?

A   B   C   D   E

Hiring/Induction Practises

F9.   Are your *employee selection techniques* giving you people who make excellent employees?

A   B   C   D   E

F10. Does your *orientation programme* cover the subject of unions adequately?

A   B   C   D   E

More

F11. What additional factors in this Key Element are unique or important to your employees/business and should be evaluated?

_____

_____

_____

_____

G: WORK RULES

Overtime–Absenteeism

G1. What procedure is in place to *monitor overtime work*? How is the amount of overtime measured (plant, component and individual?). Do employees generally accept overtime practices as equitable?

A   B   C   D   E

G2. *What kind of problems* do employees experience with overtime? Do they get *too much of it over too long a time span*, or perhaps *too little* after getting used to living on the higher take-home pay? How do your overtime practices compare with those in *unionised plants*? Any problem with *forced versus voluntary overtime*? How much *advance notice* is given to employees?

A   B   C   D   E

G3. What safeguards are in place to *avoid overkill in absenteeism* and *tardiness* control programmes? Do employees feel that Management expectations and actions are fair and consistent?

A   B   C   D   E

Discipline–Discrimination

G4.   Is the frequency of *disciplinary action* trending up or down? Have there been any recent disciplinary actions which employees might feel were unfair — *too severe/lenient/inconsistent?*

         A   B   C   D   E

G5.   Is a warning notice or other standard procedure of *progressive discipline* used so that an employee has adequate *opportunity to correct misconduct before suspension or discharge* is imposed? (How are employees made aware of the procedure and your use of it?)

         A   B   C   D   E

G6.   Is discipline *uniformly applied* — equitable in comparison with the treatment being given other groups, and appropriate to the severity of the misconduct. Are employees *informed as to the matters which will result in discipline?*

         A   B   C   D   E

G7.   Do *female employees* feel discriminated against? Have any employees entered discrimination charges (e.g. equal pay/sexual harassment) with government agencies?

         A   B   C   D   E

Safety

G8.   Have employees contacted *any governmental safety agencies* to complain about allegedly unsafe conditions? Have employees been educated on hazardous materials and their proper use as required by Legal regulations?)

         A   B   C   D   E

G9. *How good* is the *plant safety record*? Do employees consider the plan *a safe place to work*? (Recent serious accidents? Medical facilities satisfactory? Do employees consider 2nd, 3rd shift medical coverage adequate? How about adequacy of professional Doctor coverage?)

    A   B   C   D   E

G10. When changes are contemplated in work *practices, procedures and rules which may impact safety,* to what extent do employees and supervisors have an opportunity to make inputs via "Sounding Boards" or other *participative means*?

    A   B   C   D   E

Administration Consistency

G11. Are there particular conditions or practices in *some area* of the plant which employees *elsewhere* hold against management for not improving? (For example, unusually bad working conditions in part of the plant or an unreasonably strict supervisor/manager).

    A   B   C   D   E

G12. How well do employees understand *key work/rules/practices*? Is the documentation in employee handbooks and management procedure manuals *understandable and up-to-date with current applications*?

    A   B   C   D   E

G13. Have employees indicated dissatisfaction with *work practices* such as lunch/rest periods, relief arrangements, wash-up time, etc.?

    A   B   C   D   E

G14. Do you provide adequate *recognition and positive incentives for good work performance* by individuals and groups? What formal and informal systems are in place to accomplish this?

A   B   C   D   E

More

G15. What additional factors in this Key Element are unique or important to your employees/business and should be evaluated?

_____

_____

_____

_____

H: COMPLAINT IDENTIFICATION/RESOLUTION

Formal–Informal Avenues

H1. Is a multi-step *problem-solving/grievance* procedure *currently available* to employees? (How well is it communicated and understood?)

A   B   C   D   E

H2. How satisfied are employees with the grievance procedure? *How much is it used? How have employees fared in using it?*

A   B   C   D   E

H3. Is there any *reluctance* on the part of employees *to raise problems* with supervisors or higher management? (How do employees bring complaints to attention of management?)

A   B   C   D   E

H4. How well are *corrective actions communicated,* if appropriate?

A   B   C   D   E

H5. Do you have an ongoing effort to convince employees that *you want to hear their grievances* and act promptly on them?

A   B   C   D   E

H6. How is the procedure *monitored and measured* to ensure uniform, *consistent,* fair treatment? (Do employees have access to counsellors/ombudsmen?)

A   B   C   D   E

H7. *What other informal avenues are available* to employees for the venting of problems or concerns? (Question Box, M.B.W.A., Open Door, Round Tables etc.)

A   B   C   D   E

H8. Do you conduct periodic *attitude/opinion surveys* among employees? Are results communicated to employees? Do employees feel that such surveys help them *to surface and solve problems?*

A   B   C   D   E

More

H9. What additional factors in this Key Element are unique or important to your employees/business and should be evaluated?

_____

_____

_____

_____

I: SALARIES

Community Concept—Standing

I1.   Do your employees and supervisors understand and accept the *market positioning wage concept as a fair way* to compensate employees?

A   B   C   D   E

I2.   How do your rates *stack up with other prominent companies in the area*? How reliable and up-to-date are your job comparisons and data?

A   B   C   D   E

I3.   Are employees' pay levels *significantly lower than some other plants* (sister/headquarters)? (Is this a significant irritation or do they accept it as realistic? Could unions make an issue out of this comparison?)

A   B   C   D   E

Administration–Structure–Classifications

I4.   Have there been any recent changes in pay levels or procedure — *tightening up of standards, productivity or effectiveness drives*? What is anticipated? Will employees accept or resist?

A   B   C   D   E

I5.   Are employees *dissatisfied* with such matters as starting rates, progression schedules, job rates, measurements, time-study procedures, call-in pay, shift bonus, etc.?

A   B   C   D   E

I6.   A comparison of the *compensation practices* covering this
      group and the corresponding provisions of a *typical union
      contract* reveals what *differences?* (On each point of differ-
      ence, would employees consider your practice superior to or
      not as good as the union contract and why?)

      A   B   C   D   E

Assurance of Equity

I7   Do your employees fully understand *that they always receive at
      least the same pay improvements that union plants receive?* (Does
      this meet their sense of equity or do they have a feeling that
      they should be getting more than unionised plants receive?)

      A   B   C   D   E

More

I8.   What additional factors in this Key Element are unique or im-
      portant to your employees/business and should be evaluated?

      _____

      _____

      _____

      _____

J: BENEFITS

Competitive Aspects

J1.   Do employees regard the *benefit package* generally *as good as
      or better* than what other community employers offer?

      A   B   C   D   E

J2.   Do you suffer *by comparison with other community employers* on any specific aspects of benefits? (Which ones and what if anything can be done about it? Do employees consider this significant?)

A   B   C   D   E

J3.   Do your employees fully understand that they now have the *same benefit package* as unionised employees have? (Is there pressure for doing better?)

A   B   C   D   E

J4.   Have actions been taken which employees perceive as being *arbitrary* — such as changes in vacation shutdown dates, divided vacation period, etc.?

A   B   C   D   E

J5.   Is there an *active* employee *recreation association or sports and social programme*? To what extent do production employees and management *jointly* participate?

A   B   C   D   E

More

J6.   What additional factors in this Key Element are unique or important to your employees/business and should be evaluated?

_____

_____

_____

_____

K: EMPLOYEE COMMUNICATIONS SYSTEMS

K1.   Do you have a *formal communication plan* which is followed to assure that employees receive a *balance of information* about the business, the advantages of non-union status, employee benefits etc.? (Does the plant provide recognition for employee performance records, gains, etc.?)

    A   B   C   D   E

K2.   How *responsive is communication planning* to current/anticipated business problems and employee concerns?

    A   B   C   D   E

K3.   How promptly is *supervision* kept informed and *"in the loop"*?

    A   B   C   D   E

K4.   How well are employees kept informed about the Plant's business condition, problems and opportunities?

    A   B   C   D   E

K5.   Do employees feel that they are kept up-to-date, particularly about future *changes* affecting them?

    A   B   C   D   E

K6.   Do employees understand *the connection* between *their efforts* and the *success of the business,* and do you express *appreciation* for special efforts?

    A   B   C   D   E

K7. How do you rate your *plant newsletter*? How do employees rate it? What is the quality of the other written media?

A   B   C   D   E

Management Participation

K8. Does the plant or general manager meet periodically with employees to discuss the *state of the business*? *How do employees rate such meetings?*

A   B   C   D   E

K9. Do your supervisors hold *periodic informative conferences* with employees? *Do employees consider them effective* in obtaining information they want? Do the meetings encourage employee questions and inputs?

A   B   C   D   E

K10. How effective is the *employee handbook* as a working tool? (How current is it?)

A   B   C   D   E

K11. Does any of your plant communication media (newsletters, meetings, communications systems, etc.) need upgrading?

A   B   C   D   E

Feedback Function

K12. Does management take advantage of *informal* lines of communication to build its *credibility* with employees? Have you targeted specific individuals who would be helpful in steering the "grapevine" pro-company? What political connections would be useful?

A   B   C   D   E

K13. How adequate are *feedback channels* and the *measurements* used to evaluate them?

A   B   C   D   E

K14. How effective is the *"early warning"* system for identifying employee issues and concerns?

A   B   C   D   E

More

K15. What additional factors in this Key Element are unique or important to your employees/business and should be evaluated?

_____

_____

_____

_____

L: MANAGEMENT/ORGANISATION

Management Credibility, Exposure

L1. Do employees feel that *the business is "in good hands"*? (Have there been or do you expect changes in top jobs that would leave employees *unsure* that the business is "in good hands"?)

A   B   C   D   E

L2. Is the resident manager the *top man* in the eyes of employees, or do they have reason to feel that important decisions affecting them are being made *elsewhere*? (Are you a "satellite"?)

A   B   C   D   E

L3.   How adequate is the *visibility* of the Plant/manufacturing manager on the *floor? On-off shifts?*

     A   B   C   D   E

L4.   How well does the Plant/manufacturing manager do in getting to know *individual employees* (first name basis, family situation, interests, aspirations, etc.?)

     A   B   C   D   E

L5.   How adequate is the visibility of the Employee Relations professionals on the floor?

     A   B   C   D   E

L6.   To what extent do employees feel *higher management cares* about them and their problems?

     A   B   C   D   E

L7.   To what extent is management's interest in employees' problems demonstrated through promptness of remedial action?

     A   B   C   D   E

L8.   How effectively are *remedial actions communicated* where appropriate?

     A   B   C   D   E

Organisational Effectiveness

L9. Are you experiencing situations where *effective intra- or inter-functional integration is blocked* by something or somebody, and impacts negatively on employees? Is there a poor working relationship/scapegoating between shifts/departments etc?

A   B   C   D   E

L10. Does local management have an organisational relationship with headquarters which generally allows *local latitude to adjust* the specific ways and means for reaching required budgets, targets and objectives (thus supporting local management credibility and accommodating local union organising objectives)?

A   B   C   D   E

L11. How effective and responsive are *headquarters personnel* located elsewhere in providing needed business data, notice of schedule changes, and other vital information?)

A   B   C   D   E

L12. How effective are visits from Headquarters Personnel in helping to maintain the union-free status. Any downsides to such visits?

A   B   C   D   E

More

L13. What additional factors in this Key Element are unique or important to your employees/business and should be evaluated?

_____

_____

_____

_____

Appendix B

EXPLAINING YOUR NON-UNION PHILOSOPHY TO EMPLOYEES
(Example for illustration purposes)

KEY QUESTIONS AND ANSWERS

Q. **Will Company X allow staff to join a union?**

A. We acknowledge the right of any individual to join any association, including a trade union. However, there is no obligation in Ireland for any company to recognise a trade union in the running of their business.

Since the formation of the company in (location) we have operated with a model which emphasises the direct relationship with staff and has not involved a union or any external third party. To date we have been very successful with that model. It has helped us through both good times and tough times and we have no intention of changing it. It is no accident that this is also the model for many of the most successful companies in our industry.

We want to work with employees to ensure that we have a work environment where there is no need for any union involvement and where we can continue to be successful and all share in that success. In [X] years of operation, our people have never had a need for third party representation.

We intend to continue to manage the business in a way that ensures our people do not feel a need for a third party to represent their interests. While it is difficult for all staff to be 100% content all the same time, there is nothing to stop us taking this as our goal.

Q.   Would a trade union help to improve pay and conditions of employment?

A.   Company X has a culture that promotes fairness. A key ingredient in this revolves around the way we handle pay. Our pay and conditions are competitive versus other companies. We are fortunate in being involved in a modern, clean working environment, which is very safe. Specifically in relation to pay and conditions, we conduct an annual salary and benefits survey. This is completed in [date] of each year. In addition to this we subscribe to three surveys which are conducted by outside consultants (name these surveys). In this way we ensure that we maintain our pay position relative to competitor companies.

Our benefits programme is deliberately designed to communicate this caring philosophy. Issues like vacation time, flexitime, the cafeteria, health screening every two years, internal promotions, continuous learning and stock purchases are all in place to underpin a central point. If we wish to deliver world-class customer service, externally we need to build a world-class internal organisation. Managing our people well is the cornerstone in this.

Q.   In the event of a significant union recruitment campaign, Company X would have to recognise a trade union as it wouldn't pull out of Ireland with all the money invested.

A.   Company X sees Ireland as an extremely attractive location and has invested heavily in (location). We are now one of the largest operations within our division — larger than [named location] or [named location]. However, none of us can be complacent that this, on its own, assures us a long-term future. If Ireland was to become either too costly, or if employees wanted to change the model for successfully doing business, then this would very likely have negative consequences on current investments and any potential future investments.

Our past success has relied heavily on Company X's culture of direct communication with employees. We believe that union encroachment would negatively impact the continued success of Company X. The need for a union has not existed historically in (location) and we would be desperately disappointed if staff felt the need to seek help from some outside third party. If an individual employee or a group of employees feels the need to address any issue, then lets use the open door policy to work together to resolve this.

Q. **Would Company X hold it against any person who seeks to have a union recognised?**

A. If an employee perceived the need for a union, our first concern would be to understand why he/she felt the need to be represented by a union. Any employee who has a grievance or complaint (and let's face it, with over X people on site there *will* be issues) should use the established channels of the problem solving procedure, open door policy etc. to raise the issue. We are fully committed to working with any individual to help them resolve issues that arise.

But ... there is an important responsibility here.

It is important to note that we have a guideline on the distribution of non-Company X information that does not allow the marketing or promoting of services at our workplace. If someone was using the work environment to promote union membership, then this would be in breach of our policy. Employees may not distribute non-Company X material on the premises unless we decide to support a particular cause or issue (e.g. collections for a local charity). Information relating to products or services of third party organisations is not suitable for distribution on site.

Q.   **How come Company X does not have a problem with suppliers/contractors on the site who are unionised (e.g. security, cleaning, cafeteria)?**

A.   These people are not Company X employees. Some companies in Ireland have as a condition of employment the requirement that people become a member of a particular trade union We are not in a position to dictate to external companies how they should run their business. Company X's success in Ireland has been built on a culture which has not included any role for a union. Other companies, for historical and other reasons, choose to involve a union in the running of their business and this is their prerogative.

We judge and evaluate suppliers/contractors on a number of criteria (competitive pricing, quality of service, compatibility with working on a Company X site and reliability). Once they meet these criteria we are happy to do business with them.

Q.   **Communications can be one way and staff are not always involved or consulted. This might not be the case if we had a union.**

A.   We are trying to build an environment where we can all work together to ensure the continued success of Company X. Over the past [X] years we have grown from [X number] to [Y number] staff and it is a continual challenge to keep everyone in the loop. The reality is that we do have areas we can improve upon. However, there are a number of ways that all of us keep in touch with the business and raise issues that concern us: employee lunches, 1:1's, staff meetings, business update meetings and the open door allows anyone to involve any level of management in the problem resolution process.

Q. Does that mean we will be more individual in the future?

A. It would be unrealistic and dishonest if we tried to give the impression that staff can expect to be involved in all decisions that may affect them. With the rate and speed of change in our business, some decisions do not give us the opportunity for involvement and some strategic decisions need to be taken by the senior team on site etc. However, it is our intention to involve people wherever possible in decisions that affect them. We believe our track-record to date demonstrates this. However, we do need to do more under this heading to redouble our efforts.

Q. If the market downturns, we feel vulnerable. Wouldn't a union help to secure our jobs?

A. Firstly, let's remember that we all share the same interests, i.e. to make Company X a successful company, providing all of us with job security and good pay and conditions. In reality unions do not protect jobs. If you look at the history of redundancies in Ireland, most of them occur in the unionised sector. Excellent customer service protects jobs. Our current model of working is the best guarantee for employment security because it provides a customer focused responsive organisation.

This is not just "talk". Company X has a [Y] year history, which proves this to be the case. Since we commenced operations we have never experienced redundancies or any form of layoffs or short-time working. While there have been some peaks and valleys in demand for our products, every effort has been made to minimise the impact of this to avoid employment instability. This is a key, ongoing priority for Company X. While, in reality, no company can absolutely guarantee job security (as market forces are not totally within our control), this is a pivotal part of our philosophy. In the event of a severe business downturn, headcount reductions would be a last rather than a first option for us. We will do everything within our power to avoid this. If head-count reductions did occur, we would endeavour to recognise the staff's commitment to the company and to help them find suitable alternative employment. But to stress this central point again, job security is a foundation stone for us. If would be seen as a failure of the management team if we had to have even a single, involuntary redundancy.

Q.   What would happen if I fundamentally disagreed with something my manager wanted me to do?

A.   Company X is strongly committed to its open door policy which allows any employees to raise an issue or appeal any decision which you feel is unfair. You may appeal to any level of manager up to and including the general manager. In addition, the human resources manager is also available to you to assist you in using the problem resolution process or to appeal a decision. In the past employees have used this process and we have had some decisions overturned as a result. Managers are not always right; neither are employees. This is a workable system which can overcome any potential difficulties in this area.

Q.   Why are Company X staff content to operate on a non-union basis?

A.   Because the company (in its stated philosophy, in its actions, in the design of workplace processes) communicates that:

(a) Company X respects the rights of each individual employee. The company was established on a pioneering spirit by our first general manager (Mr. X) to build a world-class operation in (location). This spirit has remained within the company to this day.

(b) Makes every effort to build a strong successful and healthy business which is focused on the needs of our customers and provides for security for our staff.

(c) Ensures that terms and conditions in comparable employments are matched or beaten.

(d) In the event of a problem arising, acts speedily and fairly to overcome this.

Q.   How does Company X make a difference?

A.   We also like to think that staff can easily identify with the organisation goal of (X). In the very near future we intend to broaden our sponsorship of community support with scholarships, sponsoring local community games and running environmental and educational programmes with local schools. We want Company X to continue to be a company that everyone can be proud to work for. Not by the resting on our laurels — on what's been achieved over the past decade — but by continuing to push the boundaries outwards.

Q.   What is the role of the Human Resources Group in Company X?

A.   Any company that wishes to manage its people effectively has to be prepared to invest sufficient resources (both time and money). In this regard, we know that the sophisticated companies in Ireland have a direct relationship with staff and make a heavy investment into the HRM function. It is reflected in both the headcount and the quality of the people leading the function. The benefits of doing this far outweigh the costs. To be more specific, the HR function ensures that the "voice" of staff is continually factored into decision making. In the event of a problem moving beyond immediate line manager the HR team can give full support to the individual.

Q.   Are "junior" staff in Company X vulnerable?

A.   In Company X we try to avoid "badges of authority". Infor-
mality is stressed at the plant in a number of ways. Everyone
eats in the same cafeteria, uses the same toilets and car park,
participates equally in sports and social activities. Everyone is
on first name terms and a casual, open environment is encouraged including a casual dress code. Rules that apply to
one person apply across the board. Our philosophy is one of
internal equity. No one in Company X, provided that they are
making an honest effort to complete their job, is "vulnerable".
And we would like to believe that the word "junior" simply
does not exist in the management vocabulary.

Q.   Why would Company X be a target for a trade union?

A.   The trade union membership is in decline throughout Ireland. The vast majority of multinationals establish a direct
relationship with employees. Given the fall-off in union
numbers, the trade union movement is keen to sell its services. In our particular case, the IDA site in Blanchardstown
would be a good bridgehead for the unions (e.g. as most of
our neighbouring companies are non-union).

**Q.   What, in the Company's view, is the downside of estab-
lishing a link with a trade union?**

A.   Some of the issues have been covered above vis a vis establishing a direct relationship with staff. On the business front,
a key success factor for our site is an ability to move with
pace to meet changing customer requirements. Speed needs
to be part of our DNA at the plant and the way to maintain
this is to have a direct, robust relationship with our own
staff. Our partnership is an internal one. It also allows us to
manage our affairs (including addressing some specific staff
needs) flexibility and proactively.

Appendix C

NON-UNION TRAINING MATERIALS

Do Non-Union Companies Do Anything Extra?

The argument throughout the book is that managing people well makes a difference in keeping people "pro-company". However, the better managed non-unions go beyond this and target a range of issues which specifically address their non-union status.

Getting Ready: Non Union Training Materials

Example: Working with one non-union company, I devised the following training materials for their extended management team.

Maintaining a Direct Relationship with Our People: Executive Team Training Programme		
Scenarios	*Role Plays*	*Presentations*
Series of dilemmas presented to the management team.	Scenarios developed onto "Stage 2" where some face-to-face meetings take place.	Range of presentation topics detailed on "cards". Participants select one card.
Open discussion around "what to do" and "what not to do".	Managers role play these issues.	Three minutes "preparation time" to provide a response.
	Followed by full group analysis and discussion.	Discussion around the presentation content (not the delivery style).

SCENARIO # 1: LEAFLETING CAMPAIGN

You have just received an emergency letter from Tony, the Security Guard supervisor from Chubb. A man who identifies himself as Michael Ball from ("Union X") is currently in the car park, putting leaflets under the window wipers on the cars. When Tony asked him to stop doing this, he replied that this was a legitimate campaign under the 1990 Industrial Relations Act. What should you do?

SCENARIO # 2: TRADE UNION PICKET

Coming into work, you are amazed to see five people carrying placards at the entrance to the plant. The plant has been working away as normal over the past couple of months and you did not have any indication that anything was wrong. The placards state that this is an "official" dispute. When you stop to ask one of the protesters what they are doing, you are told that Company X is "denying workers their constitutional rights to belong to a trade union". What should you do?

SCENARIO # 3: LETTER FROM "UNION X"

When you arrive back from holidays, your desk looks like the "EU paper mountain". You have a quick scan at the envelopes to see which are the important ones. One looks formal, unusual. It contains the following:

Dear Ms. Butler,

I would like to meet you to discuss the negotiation of terms and conditions of our members in Company X. We now have a significant number of members on site and we need to meet as soon as possible to formalise our bargaining relationship. I know that we can work together to achieve our mutual aims of developing a highly successful business and an excel-

lent place to work for staff which is socially just. I look forward to hearing from you"

Yours Sincerely, Michael Ball

SCENARIO # 4: CONVERSATION WITH AGITATED STAFF

Therese Brogan, Night Shift Manager, has just called to inform you that three employees are on their way to see you. Before you can find out any more details there is a loud knock at the door and three operators come into your office. Paddy Black, one of the operators spills out a war story about being bullied by Therese and the other two staff members nod their agreement. "It's been going on now for over three months, ever since she joined the company. It is really stressful. We hope that you can work with us to get this issue resolved." How should you respond?

SCENARIO # 5: THE "SOLICITOR" E-MAIL

Later today you are due to have a formal appraisal with Terry Leyden. He is a very middle of the road employee and you are not sure if he has any long-term future with Company X. He looked good at the interview and checked out well but there have been a litany of work errors which should not have been made by someone with his experience. When you log onto your email, Terry has sent you the following note:

Hi Michael, we are due to meet at 14:30 which still works well for me. I was hoping to bring along a friend of mine, Ann O'Brien who is a solicitor. She is very easy to deal with and should be able to help us resolve any issues which need to be addressed. See you later, Terry."

How would you react to this note?

ROLE PLAYS

Scenario# 1: Leafleting Campaign: Conversation with Trade Union Official Michael Ball

Key Arguments

Scenario# 2: Trade Union Picket: Discussion with Protestor

Key Arguments

Scenario# 3: Letter from Union Official

Key Arguments

Scenario# 4: Conversation with agitated staff

Key Arguments

Scenario# 5: Discussion with Terry Leyden about Solicitor's E-mail

Key Arguments

PRESENTATION EXERCISES

Choose from any of the following topics . . . (and have fun!)

1. Unions did provide a good service at one point in history, but they are effectively a "product which has gone past its "sell by" date.

2. Company X, has a different policy towards unions than (Y Company) because . . .

3. If a trade union got into Company X it would have a number of negative implications including . . .

4. The benefits of having a direct relationship with our people includes . . .

5. I know that some of the contractors on site have very good pay and conditions and that they are unionised but . . .

6. There is a slowdown in business. Wouldn't a trade union protect our jobs?

7. Our products are worth a lot of money. If you made a mistake here, the company could come down on you like a "ton of bricks". We need some form of insurance "just in case" something goes wrong in the future.

8. The last place I worked in was unionised and there was never any hassle. What's the big deal anyway?

9. If I was a trade union official, I would use the following arguments to persuade Company X people to join . . .

10. It makes sense to join a union and "see what happens". If it doesn't work out, we can always leave.

AND THE ANSWER IS . . .

Scenario One

This is not a legitimate trade dispute under the Industrial Relations Act 1990. In essence a union official is canvassing on private property. He should be advised that he is trespassing and asked to vacate the property and should he fail to, the gardai may have to be called.

Scenario Two

The company has not been approached by the union and no notification appears to have been received by the company from the union. Thus the actions of these protestors is in blatant breach of the Industrial Relations Act 1990 and specifically sections 14 and 19, which set out the procedure for carrying out a secret ballot, and also the requirement for seven days' notice to be given before engaging in a strike or other industrial action. There is nothing to suggest that the company is denying people their constitutional rights so the company is not legally obliged to recognise any union negotiation purposes. These employees should be told that their conduct constitutes unofficial action and they should return to work immediately. The company may also consider taking disciplinary action. As their actions are in breach of the Industrial Relations Act the company could seek an injunction through the civil courts.

Scenario Three

The company has a number of options open to it.

- Firstly, they can ignore this letter and hope that they don't hear any more.

- They could send a letter advising the union that they deal directly with their staff on all issues and therefore decline the invitation to a meeting.

- They can agree to a meeting but declare at the outset what level of involvement they are prepared to have with the union. If the union force the issue, both parties may agree to use the LRC advisory service under the voluntary code of practice to discuss terms and conditions of employment only. As this is essentially the union "looking for recognition" they may decide to pursue their claim to the Labour Court under a section 20.

Scenario Four

The staff members need to be advised that if they have a grievance it needs to be processed through the grievance procedure. In the absence of a company procedure they should follow S.I. 146, the Code of Practice on Grievance and Discipline. Also, the company should have a bullying and harassment policy. Once the company has been aware of all the details relating to the grievance a decision can be made as to the appropriate route (informal or formal scenario).

Scenario Five

This is a formal appraisal which should be conducted directly between the company and the employee alone. It is not appropriate or necessary that they should bring along a solicitor. This is not a disciplinary meeting. It is an appraisal to discuss performance.

If in the future the company wish to hold a disciplinary meeting, the employee might be offered "representation" (company policies differ in this regard).

ABOUT THE AUTHOR

 Paul Mooney is one of the best known organisation development consultants in Ireland. He began his working life as a butcher in Dublin. He moved into production management, working for several years with Initial Services, a British multi-national. He subsequently joined General Electric and, over a six year period, held a number of Human Resource positions in manufacturing.

After G.E., he worked with Sterling Drug as Personnel Manager for the start-up of their highly successful Irish Plant. Subsequently, as Human Resource Director for the Pacific-Rim, he had responsibility for all personnel activity in the dynamic economies of South-East Asia.

On his return to Ireland, Paul established PMA Consulting (1991). Since then, he has specialised in providing clients with customised Organisation and Management Development programmes. He has worked on a range of improvement projects for blue-chip companies including Intel, CRH, Motorola, Oracle, Bank of Ireland, Pepsi, Glaxo SmithKline, Statoil, Bulmers, The World Bank, An Garda Siochana and Wyeth. Paul has run consulting assignments in more than 20 countries across five continents.

Paul is the author of seven books: *Amie: The True Story of Adoption in Asia*, (1990), *Developing the High Performance Organisation*, (1996), *The Effective Consultant*, (1999), *Keeping Your Best Staff*, (1999), *Turbo Charging the HR Function*, (2001) and *The Badger Ruse* (2004), a thriller set in Dublin.

Paul's academic qualifications include a Ph.D. (Doctorate in Industrial Sociology), G.D.I.R. (Grad. Dip. Industrial Relations), N.D.I.R. (National Dip. Industrial Relations) and F.C.I.P.D. (Fellow of the Chartered Institute of Personnel & Development).

He can be contacted at PMA Consulting, 205 Mount Prospect Avenue, Clontarf, Dublin 3. Telephone: +353-1-8330897. Email: pmaconsult@eircom.net.

INDEX